The lot is cast into the lap,
but the decision is wholly from the Lord.

(Proverbs 16:33)

Table of Contents

DANIEL E. LOEB

HEBREW CASTING LOTS

Practical Kabbalah Talismans

REDFeather™
MIND | BODY | SPIRIT

Other REDFeather Titles by the Author:

Rota Mundi Tarot: The Rosicrucian Arcanum, ISBN 978-0-7643-6150-0

The AlcheMystic Woodcut Tarot: Secret Wisdom of the Ages, ISBN 978-0-7643-5467-0

Library of Congress Control Number: 2024942489

Designed by BMac
Type set in Baldessare/Minion

ISBN: 978-0-7643-6934-6
ePub: 978-1-5073-0573-7
Printed in China

Published by REDFeather Mind, Body, Spirit
An imprint of Schiffer Publishing, Ltd.
4880 Lower Valley Road
Atglen, PA 19310
Phone: (610) 593-1777; Fax: (610) 593-2002
Email: Info@redfeathermbs.com
Web: www.redfeathermbs.com

Lots, Charms, and Talismans

גּוֹרָלוֹת סְגֻלוֹת וּקְמֵיעוֹת

Goralot, Segulot, V'Kameot / Fates / Casting Lots, Charms/Remedies, and Bindings/Talismans

Have you ever wondered about the mysterious and ancient practice of casting lots that was used throughout the Bible, or how such a technique might be incorporated into your own life to unlock deeper insights? Divination was viewed as more than simply flipping a coin or rolling dice to randomly select among different options; it involved obtaining divine guidance, or extracting intuitive impressions from one's subconscious. It was practiced by the wisest of Sages, and many times, interpreting the omens was as important as the selection. Casting lots was used throughout the Bible; Aaron, as the High Priest, would cast lots to select one goat as a sacrifice to *HaShem* (YHVH) and the other lot to identify the scapegoat (Leviticus 16:8). The Promised Land was divided among the Twelve Tribes of Israel by lot (Joshua 18:10). Both the Urim and Thummim and the casting of lots were used to identify Jonathan as the one to had eaten honey against the king's orders (1 Samuel 14:42), and the sailors on the ship used lots to correctly identify Jonah as the cause of the storm (Jonah 1:7). Lots were used to assign duties to people (1 Chronicles 25:8) and to delegate responsibilities (Nehemiah 10:34), and following the death of Judas, the disciples of Jesus cast lots to select Matthias as a replacement for Judas (Acts 1:26).

ך,כ	י	ט	ח	ז	ו	ה	ד	ג	ב	א
K, CH	Y (i)	T	CH	Z	V (o)	H (e)	D	G	B, V	A
Kaf	Yod	Tet	Chet	Zayin	Vav	Hei	Dalet	Gimel	Bet	Alef
20	10	9	8	7	6	5	4	3	2	1
ת	ש	ר	ק	ץ,צ	ף,פ	ע	ס	ן,נ	ם,מ	ל
T (th)	SH, S	R	K (q)	TZ	P, F	A	S	N	M	L
Tav	Shin	Resh	Qof	Tzadi	Pei	Ayin	Samech	Nun	Mem	Lamed
400	300	200	100	90	80	70	60	50	40	30

Table 1: Gematria table

The Hebrew word used for lot in most passages is Goral (Gimel, Vav, Resh, Lamed), which describes a lot used for casting, but it also means *allotted portion, fate, destiny, fortune,* or *share*. Lots were used to produce impartial judgments (Chronicles 24:5), as a subjective means of describing a person's destiny/lot in life (Jeremiah 13:25, Ecclesiastes 5:18–19, Psalm 16:5, Zephaniah 2:10), or one's final destination (Sirach 20:25, Revelation 21:8). Lots were also used by gentiles; soldiers who cast lots for Jesus/Yehshua's garments (Matthew 27:35, Psalm 22:18), and when Haman cast the *Pur* (Esther 3:7) to select a day for the destruction of the Jews. The Hebrew word *Pur* (*Pei, Vav, Resh*), also means *lot, fate*, or *luck* and is thought to be derived from the Akkadian word *Puru* (stone).

In Hebrew, each letter also has a numerical value associated with it, and in the mysticism of the Kabbalah, the value of the Hebrew letters is calculated with a technique called *Gematria* to find hidden mystical significance and connections among words, concepts, or verses (*parashah*). Kabbalah refers to the mystical aspects of Judaism, and those who engage in this practice study the significance of Hebrews letters and their associated gematria values, which are overlooked by mainstream religious sects. In doing so, they gain profound insights and venture into the orchard to seek a deeper enlightenment. Words or Bible verses that have the same gematria value are somehow related to each other, and kabbalistic mystics contemplate such relationships as a means of gaining a deeper understanding of the scripture. The word *pur* (*Pei 80, Vav 6, Resh 200*) has a gematria value of 286, which can be kabbalistically reduced using Gematria to seven (286 = 2 + 8 + 6 = 16, and 1 + 6 = 7).

The number seven has a great deal of meaning within Judaism. God created the world in seven days, and there are seven spirits associated with the seven-branched menorah. Additionally, the seventh *Sefirah* (emanation) of the Kabbalah represents Victory (*Netzach*). Haman cast the *Pur* to select the day for the destruction of the Jews, but through *fate*, God granted the Jews *victory*, and Haman and his sons were ultimately destroyed. The plural form of *Pur* is *Purim*, which is a Jewish Festival of Lots commemorating the events in the book of Esther (Esther 9:21).

In the practice of Gematria, anagrams are also used to gain a deeper understanding of Hebrew words and to uncover connections with other words of the same numerical value. Since anagrams use the exact same letters rearranged, the gematrical value of the Hebrew words remains identical. The same letters *PUR* (*Pei, Vav, Resh*) can also be used to spell *PeRU* (*Pei, Resh, Vav*), meaning to *grow*, *be fruitful*, or *reproduce*. Haman believed he was deciding the *fate* of the Jews, but God turned it into a *victory* for them and a joyful celebration for their descendants.

Adding the plural ending of *Yod Mem* to form *Purim* adds a value of 50 to the root word, giving it a gematrical value of 336. This value reduces to 12 (3 + 3 + 6 = 12, and 1 + 2 = 3), reminding us of the Twelve Tribes being assigned their portions of the land by lot, and the third *Sefirah* of the Kabbalah, which connects all these concepts to an *Understanding* (*Binah*) of *HaShem*'s eternal plan—predestining everyone's *fate* (Lot in Life) from the beginning of creation (Matthew 13:35, John 17:24, Romans 8:29, 1 Peter 1:20, Revelation 17:8).

The holiday of *Purim* (the Festival of Lots) is the result of an enemy using *Pur* (lots) against the Jews. However, when the Hebrews cast lots, they use the Hebrew word *Goral* (Fate) to describe this means of divination. The gematrical value of *Goral* (*Gimel 3, Vav 6, Resh 200, Lamed 30*) is 239, which reduces both to 14 and five (2 + 3 + 9 = 14, and 1 + 4 = 5). The fifth *Sefirah* of the Kabbalah is *Geburah*, which pertains to the *power* and the *judgment* of God (Proverbs 16:33)—so that the *lot* represents God's *judgment*. Some significant Hebrew words that share the same gematrical value as the word *goral* are *zahab* (gold), *david* (David), and *yad* (hand).

Gold is used throughout the Bible, starting with the River *Pishon* flowing out of Eden (Genesis 2:11, Sirach 24:25) and concluding with the description of the New Jerusalem (Revelation 18.16). The Ark of the Covenant and altar of incense within the Tabernacle were made of refined gold (1 Chronicles 28:18), and God also refines/purifies his people like gold (Malachi 3:3, Sirach 2:5, Wisdom 3:5–6). The reference to David is significant, because the first king of Israel (Saul) was selected by using lots (1 Samuel 10:21). Scripture does not specifically state that Samuel used lots in order to select David, but Samuel was led by God to select David from among his brothers by some means, and it was by casting lots that he previously selected Saul.

The most significant corresponding gematrical value to *Goral* is probably the word *Yad*, which means *hand* and is often used to refer to the *Hand of God* (since Yod is the first letter in the name of God). It is as if the chosen *Lot* (*goral*) was selected by the *Hand of God*, which is why the casting of lots can be considered a method of divination. The word *Yad* (hand) is constructed of the letters *Yod* and *Dalet*, which together also spell the Hebrew letter *Yod*. The Hebrew letter *Yod* is sometimes used as a stand-alone symbol of God. *Yod* is an abbreviation of the four-letter name of God (Tetragrammaton), which is spelled *Yod, Hei, Vav, Hei*.

The gematrical value of 14 (Y = 10 + D = 4) can also be reduced to five (14 = 1 + 4 = 5). The Hebrew letter *Hei* has a value of five, which also has a great deal of significance in kabbalistic mysticism. The letter *Hei* is spelled with the letters *Hei* and *Alef*, and the letter *Hei* also serves as an abbreviation for God (as a shortened form of *HaShem*—the name). *Hei* also serves as the definite article in Hebrew, which provides specificity and clarity to a word/concept/noun. The Hebrew letters *Alef* and *Yod* are also letters in the Hebrew *Alef-bet* that can serve as a symbol of God, which will be discussed in the section on those letters.

Yod + Dalet = Hei

In the mysticism of Kabbalah, it is said that the letter *Hei* is constructed by the Hebrew letter *Yod* holding up the letter *Dalet* (with the *Yod* preventing the *Dalet* from falling over). The letters *Yod* and *Dalet* spell the letter *Yod*, which is an abbreviation of the Tetragrammaton, and since the letter *Hei* contains both a *Yod* and *Dalet*, it can do the same (Wisdom 7:26). When the Hebrew letters *Yod* and *Hei* are together, they spell *YaH*, which is a name of God and another abbreviated form of the Tetragrammaton. *Yod* means *hand*; *Hei* is also associated with the hand, because a hand has five fingers—which is the Gematria value of the letter *Hei*. The talisman used to ward off the Evil-Eye (*Ayin HaRa*) is known as a *Hamsa*, which is the Arabic spelling of the number five (*HaMeSh* in Hebrew). The *Hei* provides another reference to the *Hand of God*, providing guidance through the *Goral*.

The Hebrew letter *Hei* is also used to represent *breath* (*Ruach*), because the letter makes the sound of a strong exhalation (it is the *breath* that gives *life* to the spoken word). God's first exclamation in Genesis (*B'reishit*) was "*Let there be light*," and the word *light* is used *five* times on the first day of creation (Genesis 1:3–5); therefore, the letter *Hei* is associated with the enlightening presence of the Holy Spirit (*Ruach Ha-Kodesh*). The letter *Hei* being added to the names of AbraHam and SaraH (Genesis 17:5, 15) represents God's Spirit (*Ruach Elohim*) being united/joined with them. When the letter *Hei* is used as a suffix to a noun, it denotes the feminine gender in Hebrew, such as in the words *ShekinaH* (Indwelling Presence), *ChokmaH* (Wisdom), or *AdamaH* (Earth/Ground/Land).

God formed Adam out of the dust of the *ground* (*Adamah*) and then breathed the *Breath of Life* into Adam's nostrils in order to make him into a living soul (Genesis 2:7). Mystically, this verse could be explained as God taking the final Hebrew letter from the feminine word for *ground* (*AdamaH*) and then breathing it (the Spirit) into Adam's nostrils in order to make him a unique (definite article) soul (*nefesh*). This description corresponds to the use of the Hebrew letter *Hei* as a prefix. When used as a prefix, it denotes the definite article (equivalent of the English word *the*) and transforms the noun from being *a* person into *the* person; similar to how the Breath of Life (Spirit/*Hei*) being added to Adam made him into a *unique* individual and a *specific* person.

The letter *Hei* is also said to be shaped like a window, symbolizing that when someone is indwelt (1 Corinthians 3:16) by the *Shekinah* (*Ruach Elohim / Ha-Kodesh*), they become enlightened (Ephesians 1:8). This enlightenment enables them to look into the cloud (Sirach 24:4) and behind the veil (1 Corinthians 2:14), so they do not see into the glass darkly (1 Corinthians 13:12), nor are they blind or deaf to the message (Matthew 13:11–16). Instead, they are empowered by the Spirit with discernment (1 Corinthians 2:14; Romans 8:6) and are given a window to see into the mysteries of God.

Both the *Yod* and the Hebrew letter *Hei*, either together (*YaH*) or separately, serve as a symbol/abbreviation of the name of God. The *Yod* represents the Tetragrammaton (four-letter name of God), and the *Hei* represents an abbreviation of the word *HaShem*, which is used in place of, or to refer to, the Tetragrammaton, as a means of showing respect to God (Exodus 20:7). During prayers, the Hebrew word *Adonai* (Lord/Master) is substituted for the Tetragrammaton, but in casual speech the word *HaShem* (the Name) is used as a substitute. When reading an English Bible, anytime the word LORD appears in all capital letters, it is being used in place of the Tetragrammaton (Holy Name). *HaShem* means *The Name*, with the *Hei* serving as a prefix and the definite article of the word *SheM* (name).

The *Sefer Yetzirah* (Book of Formation) is one of the most important books in Jewish mysticism and Kabbalah, but it was written in a time before Kabbalah, when Merkabah mysticism focused on the Work of the Chariot and contemplated the chariot of God, such as in the vision of Ezekiel. The concepts within the *Sefer Yetzirah* equated Ezekiel's Wheel to the Hebrew *Alef-bet*, and this small work of mysticism went on to inspire the Kabbalah and both Jewish and Hermetic mystics and magicians of modern times.

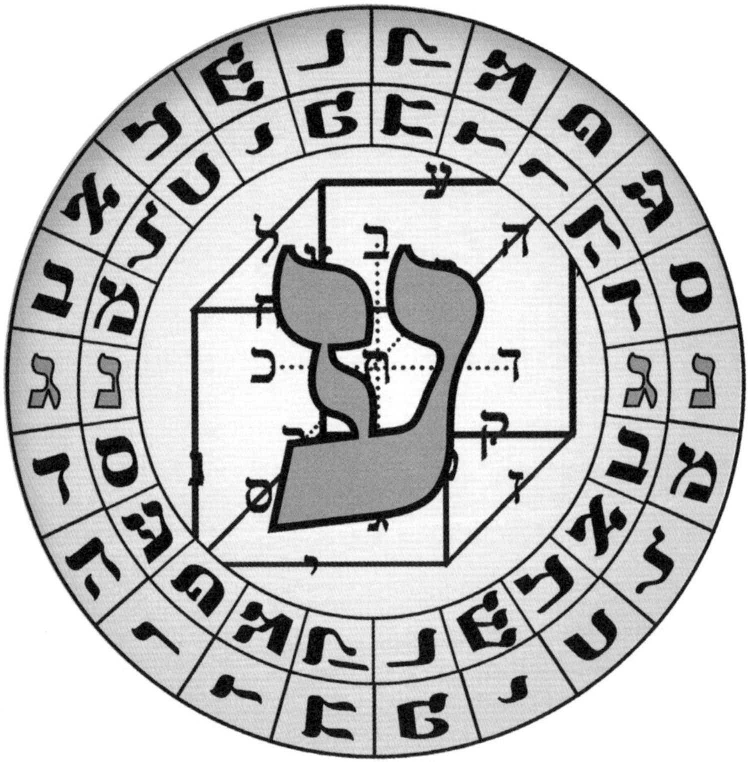

The wheel within a wheel described in the Sefer Yetzirah speaking his own name

The Sefer Yetzirah says the universe and everything in it was created by HaShem speaking his own name. When *HaShem* appeared to Moses in/at the Burning Bush (Exodus 3:14), he identified himself as *EHeYeH ASheR EHeYeH* (*Alef, Hei, Yod, Heh*), which is a conjugation of the verb *to be* or *to exist*. The *Alef* added to the three-letter root word makes it a first-person future tense (I will be/exist), because he is both the One God who *exists* and he will continue to exist for all of eternity (I exist, therefore I will always exist). *HaShem* told Moses to tell the Hebrews that his name is *YeHoVaH* (*Yod, Hei, Vav, Hei*). The *Yod* used as a prefix to the verb stem conjugates it as the third-person masculine future tense of the verb *to be*, meaning that *He is / will be*, the ever existing one (Exodus 3:16).

In the Mishnah (Oral Tradition), *Pirkei Avot* 5.1 states that "*with ten utterances the world was created.*" This refers to the 10 times in the first chapter of Genesis/B'reishit that the words "*God said*" appear as a part of the creation process (Genesis 1:3, 6, 9, 11, 14, 20, 24, 26, 28, and 29). The Sefer Yetzirah provides a mystical interpretation of the events of Genesis/*B'reishit* (In the Beginning) and says that *HaShem* sealed the universe in six directions by speaking different combinations of his own name. The Isidor Kalisch translation of the Sefer Yetzirah (1877) states, "*He selected three consonants from the simple ones which are in the hidden secret of three mothers* [*Alef, Mem, Shin*] *or first elements: air, water, and ether or fire. He sealed them with spirit and fastened them to His great name and sealed with it six dimensions.*" (Note: *Alef, Mem, Shin* means *yesterday / last night*, and *Hei, Yod, Vav* spells *there were*; both words refer to the past tense. The gematrical value of *Alef, Mem, Shin* (1 + 40 + 300 = 341, and 3 + 4 + 1 = 8) reduces to the same value as the Tetragrammaton).

He looked above and pronounced the three letters, looked down and pronounced the same three letters in a different order, and did the same thing looking forward (east), behind (west), to his right (south), and to his left (north). In addition to creating an ever-expanding cube of six directions, *HaShem* created beginning and ending, pleasure and plague (Hebrew anagrams that imply the need for perspective, balance, and moderation of the opposites), and language and mathematics, thereby creating both time and space and everything humanity understands as science and wisdom. In addition to the six directions, the creation of the *Ruach Ha-Kodesh* (Holy Spirit) and the three primordial elements provides a mystical version of the Ten Utterances and the foundations of existence (N + S + E + W + Up + Down + Spirit + Water + Fire + Air = 10).

The root of the holy name means *to be*, so the Sefer Yetzirah is implying that *HaShem* commanded the universe into existence by ordering it *to exist*. The three unique letters within the Tetragrammaton (*Yod, Hei, Vav*) were arranged in different orders, and not all the different combinations were conjugations of the word *to be*, but since the same Hebrew letters were used, the Gematria *value* of each of the expressions was equal (they contain a similar meaning), and in Gematria, it is the value/*intent* (*Kavanah*) that is important.

The Ten Utterances in Genesis include statements such as "*There will be light*," which provides a literal description of the event, whereas the mystical interpretation in the *Sefer Yetzirah* focuses only on the *value* of *HaShem* commanding whatever his intentions were *to exist*. Both interpretations complement each other, but they express slightly *different concepts*. The gematrical value of the letters *(Yod, Hei, Vav*) is 21 (21 = 2 + 1 = 3), which points the kabbalist to the third *Sefirah* of the Kabbalah. *Binah* (Understanding) is the third *Sefirah* and is associated with the act of creation.

Contemplating such connections assists the mystic in understanding the process of creation on a subjective level. This aids in comprehension, because symbolism is the language of the subconscious, and contemplation is a subjective/spiritual process. Mysticism does not neglect the literal interpretation, but it also includes a subjective understanding of the concepts. The mystical interpretation does not replace or supersede the literal concepts within scripture but provides a deeper level of understanding to the events.

THE ORCHARD

Recognizing the significance of each level of interpretation, an acronym was developed to describe four key ways of interpreting scripture. The Hebrew acronym PaRDeS (*Pei, Resh, Dalet, Samech*) is used to describe different levels of interpretation (Chagigiah 14b:8–10). The first letter in PaRDeS stands for PeShaT (*Pei, Shin, Tet*), which means *simple* and refers to the literal meaning of the text. The message is clearly stated and should be understood from the author's perspective/intent. The next level of interpretation is ReMeZ (*Resh, Mem, Zayin*), which means *hint* and implies that the literal meaning provides a clue, allusion, or analogy that allows the reader to comprehend a deeper meaning.

DRaSh (*Dalet, Resh, Shin*) means to *seek* and implies the need for the seeker to expand on the principles and to compare it with other verses, teachings, or scriptures in order to fully understand the concept. It expands on ideas and uses metaphors, analogies, and parables to aid in comprehension. The final level of interpretation is SoD (*Samech, Vav, Dalet*), which means *secret* and refers to mysteries that can be revealed only through one's connection with the Spirit (Luke 8:10, 1 Corinthians 2:14), who provides a glimpse through the window (*Hei*) to reveal the secret meaning.

PaRDeS means *orchard*; it has a Gematria value of 344 (3 + 4 + 4 = 11 = 1 + 1 = 2) and would point the kabbalist to the *Sefirah* of *Chokmah* (Wisdom). This implies that comprehending the different levels of interpretation involves or results in the application or acquisition of Wisdom (Wisdom 9:17, 1 John 2:20). The gematrical values of Hebrew words or letters can always be reduced to a number between one and ten, which links the concepts to a specific *Sefirot* on the *Kabbalistic Tree of Life*.

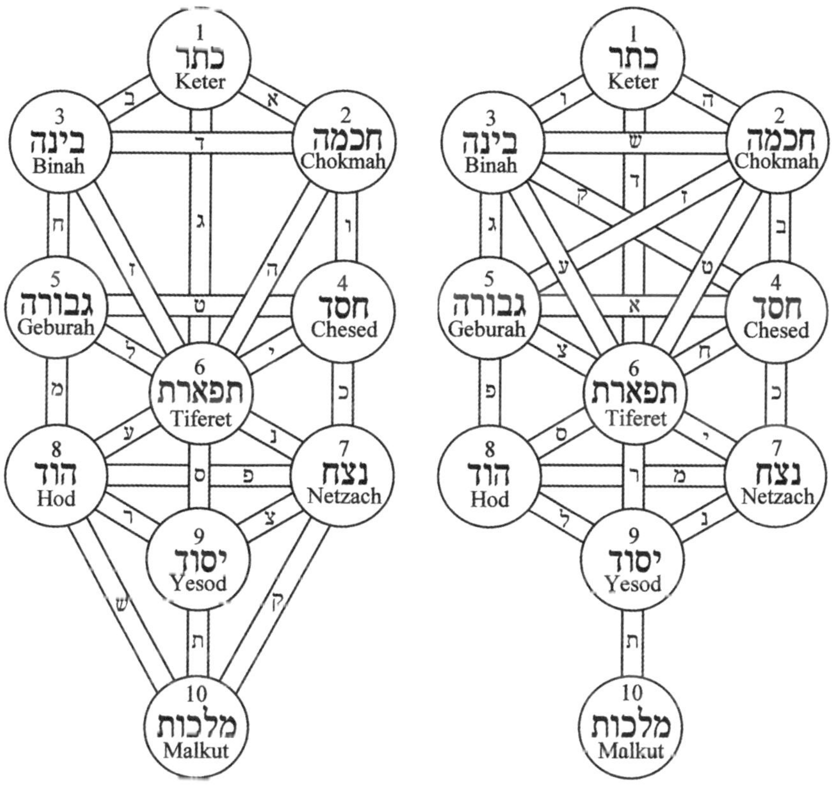

Hermetic Tree of Life *(left)* Lurianic Etz Hayim *(right)*

The word *Sefirot* means *emanations* or *enumerations*, and in the *Tree of the Sefirot* (*Kabbalistic Tree of Life*), it represents 10 different attributes of *HaShem*, as well as different stages of creation/manifestation and other mysteries. The Tree of the *Sefirot* serves as a graphical aid to assist the mystic in organizing and understanding concepts. Ten is a key number in mathematics and establishes a repeating pattern. We count from zero to nine, and when we reach the number ten, we start a new cycle from 10 to 19, and so on. We then count by 10s, 100s, 1,000s, etc. The Hebrew language does not have a separate numerical system; each Hebrew letter also represents a number. The Gematria assigned to the Hebrew letters in the *Alef-bet* count from one to ten and then count in 10s to 100, and in 100s for the final letters.

The *Sefer Yetzirah* stresses that each Hebrew letter contains a Symbol (the shape of the letter), a Sound (its vocalization), and a Value (number/intent). There are four different worlds of the Kabbalah that refer to different stages of creation, which are related to a verse from the book of Isaiah that reads, "*Every one that is called by my name, and whom I have created for my glory, I have formed him, yea, I have made him*" (Isaiah 43:7). The first world/stage is *Atziluth* (emanation/conception), which refers to the concept within *HaShem's* plan or will, and the point where He decides to call the thing into existence ("*called by my name*"; i.e., told to exist).

The next stage is *Briah* (Creation), where the intent/value is created ("*created for my glory*"). The next stage/world is *Yetzirah* (formation) and, when viewed from top to bottom, would refer to one being formed in the womb (Isaiah 44:24), but when viewed from bottom to top (the Mystic's Ascent), it represents the Great Work of balancing the opposites and the moral concepts of justice and mercy as part of one's spiritual development. The final stage/world is *Assiah* (Action), which refers to the physical world where the original intent is finally manifested, the person is *made* (Isaiah 43:7), or the word/idea/concept/logos becomes flesh (John 1:14).

The 10 *Sefirot* (emanations) are associated both with the process of creation as well as attributes of God. The top three *Sefirot* (*Keter*, *Chokmah*, and *Binah*) represent primordial/heavenly attributes, and the lower seven *Sefirot* are mentioned in a single verse from 1 Chronicles as a description of God. It reads, "*Yours, Adonai, is the greatness* [*Chesed/Gedulah*], *the power* [*Geburah*] *and the splendor* [*Tiferet*], *and the victory* [*Netzach*] *and the majesty* [*Hod*], *indeed everything in heaven and earth. Yours is the kingdom* [*Malkut*], *Adonai, and you are exalted above all* (1 Chronicles 29:11)." *Yesod* (Foundation) is not mentioned in the verse by name, but it is implied as God laid the foundation of the heavens and the earth (Job 38:4, Proverbs 8:29, Isaiah 48:13), and the principle of *God being exalted above all* establishes the *foundation* of the entire universe.

THE PROCESS OF CREATION

The *Process of Creation* in Judaism is based on 10 utterances of God; in early Jewish mysticism the 10 utterances were described in the *Sefer Yetzirah* to form the Cube of Space, and later kabbalists placed the *Sefirot* into the shape of trees (Lurianic/Hermetic Trees of Life), which can be used to explain the process of creation, as well as attributes of God, and aspect of the human soul/psyche. In relation to the *Process of Creation*, the first *Sefirah* of *Keter* (Crown) on the Trees of Life represents the *Mind of God* or his intensions prior to creation (Revelation 4:11, 1 Corinthians 2:7, 11–12). *HaShem* is represented by a *Crown,* because he is the *Ruler of the Universe (Melech Ha-Olam).* As part of the *Mystical Ascent* (the initiates return from the world [*Malkut*] back to Heaven [*Keter*]*),* the *Crown* represents the reward for completion of the *Great Work (2 Timothy 4:8, Revelation 2:10).* In the *Process of Creation, Keter* represents the point of conception, at the very beginning (2 Esdras 6:6). As the first verse in Genesis states, *"In the beginning, God created the heaven and the earth (Genesis 1:1)." In the beginning there was only God, and He alone is responsible for stretching out the heavens and the earth (Isaiah 44:24).*

God's first creation was the Woman Wisdom, which is represented on the Kabbalistic Tree of Life as the second *Sefirah* of *Chokmah* (Wisdom). In the book of Proverbs, Wisdom states, "*LORD created me first of all, the first of his works, long ago. I was made in the very beginning, before the world began* (Proverbs 8:22–23)." This concept is repeated in Sirach 1:4, where it states, "*Wisdom was created before all other things,*" and later in that same book, Wisdom says of herself, "*Before the ages, in the beginning, he created me, and for all eternity I shall not cease to exist. In the holy tent I ministered before him, and then made my home on Mount Tziyon*" (Sirach 24:9–10). Scripture also teaches that "*by the word of HaShem the heavens were made, and by the breath of His mouth all their hosts*" (Psalm 33:6).

The *Sefer Yetzirah* supports this assertion when it says that the first creation was the Holy Spirit. It reads, "*The Spirit of the living God. . . . The articulate word of creative power, the spirit and the word are what we call the Holy Spirit.*" After the creation of the *Ruach Elohim* (Spirit of God), the Primordial Elements of Air, Water, and Fire (the 3 Mother Letters) were created, followed by the events discussed previously of *HaShem*, using different combinations of the three unique letters in his own name to seal the universe in six directions (by calling it into existence through the Ten Utterances).

This same concept was referred to by the Apostle John at the beginning of his Gospel, when he summarized creation by stating, "*In the beginning was the word and the word was with God and the word was God*" (John 1:1, KJV). This verse has been so badly misunderstood over the ages, and its interpretation has been intentionally distorted in order to produce false doctrines claiming that Jesus preexisted his own birth or was actually God (or both). This error stems from the Roman Church not understanding the Jewish concepts that the Apostle John (who was a Jew) would have been engrossed in since his birth.

Since the New Testament was written in Greek, it does not use any personal pronouns that refer to *HaShem*, so whenever the English word *God* appears in the New Testament, it is a translation of the Greek word *Theos*, which can refer to gods, goddesses, magistrates, judges, or any number of divine, angelic, or human beings. When the word *Theos* is used, it may or may not be referring to *HaShem* (the Creator God). The other important word to consider in the first verse of John is *Logos*, which means *Logic* but can also be used to refer to a word, speech, saying, or utterance.

The Jewish apostle John is most likely using the word *logos* to refer to the divine plan that *HaShem* has had in place since the beginning (Matthew 13:35, 25:34; Ephesians 1:4; 1 Peter 1:20; Revelation 13:8), but he could also be using it to refer to the initial utterance by which *HaShem* spoke the world into existence (Psalm 33:6, 9). The verse could be paraphrased/translated as "*In the beginning was God's plan/logic/intent, God's plan has been in place since the very beginning, and the plan expressed God's will/intent/purpose*," or "*In the beginning was the utterance; the utterance expressed HaShem's will/thoughts/logic, and the utterance was the name of God (the letters and value of the Tetragrammaton)*." One of the most confusing aspects of the English translation is the capitalization of the *Word* (logos), which leads people to think that a name is being used instead of a concept. There is no reason to assume that *Yehshua* (Jesus) is being referred to as *logos* (logic), because multiple Jewish and scriptural sources clearly state that *HaShem*'s first creation was the female Spirit of Wisdom and that *HaShem spoke* heaven and the earth into existence (2 Esdras 6:38–40).

When *HaShem* spoke the Ten Utterances, before the sound of each letter was atoned, his Breath/Spirit/Ruach was released from his mouth (related to the Hebrew letter *Hei*, discussed previously). Wisdom (*Chokmah/Ruach Elohim*) states in the book of Sirach that "*I came forth from the mouth of the Most High and covered the earth like a mist*" (Sirach 24:3). The book of Genesis agrees with this statement, when it states that "*the earth was without form, and void; and darkness was upon the face of the deep, and the Ruach Elohim was hovering over the surface of the waters*" (Genesis 1:2). *HaShem*'s first creation was Wisdom (*Chokmah*), and from there, the two (*HaShem* and the Shekinah / Ruach Elohim / Holy Spirit / Woman Wisdom) created the world (Proverbs 8:29–30), which on the Kabbalistic Tree of Life is represented by the *Sefirah* of *Binah* (Understanding).

HaShem gives Wisdom, and out of his mouth comes Understanding (Proverbs 2:6). Both Wisdom (*Chokmah*) and *Binah* (Understanding) are references to the Woman Wisdom (*Ruach Elohim*) and are linked to the Hebrew letters *Shin* and *Mem*. Scripture states, "*By Wisdom, HaShem founded the earth. By Understanding He established the Heavens*" (Proverbs 3:19). First there was *Ein* (*Alef Yod Nun*) *Sof* (*Samech Vav Pei*), whose first Creation was Wisdom, followed by creation of the heavens and the earth. After the Spirit was hovering over the waters like a mist, God said, "*Let there be light!*" and there was light (Genesis 1:3, 2 Esdras 6:38). The connection between the Hebrew letter *Hei*, the *Breath*, and the five times *Light* is mentioned on the first day of creation all point to Wisdom being a partner in creation (Baruch 3:32–33, Proverbs 8:30).

The *Zohar* (Book of Splendor, 1305 CE) refers to woman (*Ishah*) as the *fire* (*Alef, Shin*) of *Hei* and points out that "*when the wife is joined with the husband, she is called by the name of the husband; thus the correlatives ish (man) and ishah (woman). . . . So, too, with the words asher (which) and asherah. . . . The truth is that the Hei is called Asherah, after the name of its spouse, Asher.*" At the Burning Bush, *HaShem* identified himself as *Eheieh Asher Eheieh*, and *Asher* is used in many blessings to refer to the one *Who* (*Asher*) is providing the blessing.

The *Sefer HaBahir* (Book of Illumination, 1298 CE) asks, "*Why does the Torah begin with the letter Bet?*" and then explains, "*In order that it begin with a Berachah (blessing).*" It goes on to say that "*wherever we find the letter Bet it indicates a blessing. It is thus written 'Bereshit (In the beginning); the word reshit (beginning) is nothing other than Wisdom. It is thus written (Psalm 111:10), 'The beginning of Wisdom is the fear of the LORD,' Wisdom is a blessing. It is thus written that the LORD blessed Solomon; it is furthermore written (I Kings 5:26), 'The LORD had given Solomon Wisdom.*" The letters *Kaf* and *Chet* make a similar sound; *Bet Resh Kaf* means *blessing* and *Bet Resh Chet* means *In the Spirit*, which links the *Ruach Chokmah* (Spirit of Wisdom) with the means of delivering the blessings of *Ein Sof* (unending/eternal).

Rabbeinu Bachya Ben Asher said, "*Let us now turn to the mystical aspects of the Torah, Kabbalah, revealed in our verses thus far. The words 'B'reishit Bara*

Elohim Et Hashamayim v'Et HaAretz' (In the Beginning Created God the Heavens and the Earth) contain within them an allusion to the ten Sefirot, 'emanations.' The 'Heaven and Earth' referred to here are the celestial counterparts of our terrestrial universe." The celestial refers to the creation of angels and the heavenly realms, and the terrestrial refers to the material aspects of creation—such as humans.

Rabbeinu Bachya ben Asher says that the word *B'reishit* is an allusion to Wisdom, and that "*the letter Bet in B'reishit refers to the 'second' of the emanations, i.e. Chokmah, counting from Ein (nothing / Alef Yod Nun), the highest emanation downwards. You will observe therefore that both the word RAShYTh and its first letter, Bet, are testimony to the Supreme Wisdom which was at work when the universe was created. Seeing that everything is derived from this wisdom, the letter Bet is written in larger script to alert the reader to this thought.*" The letter *Alef* and the *Ein Sof* are associated with the *Infinite/Unending* of the first emanation *Keter*. The letter *Bet* is the second letter in the *Alef-bet* and is associated with second *Sefireh Chokmah* (Wisdom), and as the first creation, it is the first word/ letter of the Bible. Similarly, in the Sefer Yetzirah, the Spirit (*Ruach*) proceeds from God (as *Chokmah* comes from *Keter*) and after the creation of the Spirit, the Heavenly Realms (along with angels) are made, followed by the physical manifestation of the universe (along with humans).

These shared concepts regarding creation are found in the Tanakh, the New Testament, the Mishnah of the Talmud, and the Kabbalah. The concepts are presented both literally and figuratively and can be understood both at face value and mystically. The Apostle Paul says, "*The universe was created through a spoken word of God*" (Hebrews 11:3), and Peter also confirms that "*by God's command, the heavens came into being, and the earth was formed out of water and by water*" (2 Peter 3:5), which agrees with the account given by Moses (Genesis 1:6, 9).

The connection between Hebrew words, their associated Gematria values, and the tradition that holds that God commanded the universe to exist by speaking Ten Utterances makes Hebrew a Holy Tongue / Sacred Language (*Leshon HaKodesh*) for adherents to the Judeo-Christian tradition and students of the Kabbalah. In practical Kabbalah, Hebrew words and letters are used to create *Kame'ah* (**Talismans**/Talismans/Bindings), and the divine names of God are used to produce cures, to protect homes, and to ward off demons. Handwritten scripture is placed inside a *Mezuzah* (which is affixed to a door post) in fulfillment of *Mitzvah* (precepts/commandments/instructions), and as a means of being considered a special treasure (*Segulah*) and earning God's favor (Leviticus 26:3–13).

Gematrical values are studied and verses are calculated in order to connect mystical significance to concepts, and Hebrew incantations are used in blessings and curses (Joshua 8:34), recognizing the power of the spoken word as an emulation of *HaShem*'s actions during the process of creation. The connections among the Hebrew letters, numbers, and the Torah (Baruch 4:1) as the Word of God make the casting of Hebrew lots a unique source of inspiration that can be used for meditative and mystical purposes, or as a means of divination; "*The lot is cast into the lap, but its very decision comes for the LORD*" (Psalm 16:32).

In Jewish folklore there is a tale that claims that the Kabbalah or a book of secrets was given to Adam by the angel Raziel (the angel responsible for the Secrets of God) as a means of returning to paradise following Adam and Eve's expulsion from the Garden of Eden. Other theories claim that Moses received it on Mount Sinai, and that it has been passed down through the Oral Tradition ever since then. The *Sefer Yetzirah* claims to have been the book of Abraham, which was passed down via the Oral Tradition until finally being preserved in written format sometime around 200 BCE to 200 CE.

Since the Kabbalah primarily consists of commentaries on the Torah, Adam, Abraham, and Moses all are key figures in it. The covenant between *HaShem* and Israel started with Abraham, who by faith believed God and left everything he knew in order to follow him. In that covenant, *HaShem* told Abraham, "*I will bless those who bless you, and curse those who curse you, and all nations on Earth shall be blessed because of you*" (Genesis 12:3). This blessing was passed down from father to son as the *Blessing of the Firstborn*. However, it wasn't until the Law of Moses that it was mandated that the firstborn receive a double portion of the inheritance (Deuteronomy 21:17).

In the first part of the blessing covenant with Abraham, God promised to bless those who bless him, and this blessing can be easily observed in the lives of Jacob and Joseph. Laban recognized that he was being blessed for Jacob's sake (Genesis 30:27), and this phenomenon was also recognized by Joseph's slave master (Genesis 39:1–5), his prison keeper (Genesis 39:21–23), and finally by Pharaoh (Genesis 41:38). It should be noted that although God was with them and blessed those around them, neither Jacob nor Joseph had easy lives. Through Moses, God established the covenant of the Ten Commandments (Deuteronomy 4:13) and the Blessings (Leviticus 26:4–12, Deuteronomy 11:14), and Curses (Leviticus 26:14–39) were then applied directly to the children of Israel and were directly related to them obeying the Commandments (Deuteronomy 11:26–28, Leviticus 26:2–3).

Obeying *Mitzvah* (precepts/commandments) is a means of ensuring the blessings of *HaShem*; failing to follow such instructions will cause God to turn his face away from the sinner. The need for *HaShem* to look favorably upon the children of Israel (and keep them in view) was of such importance that it is mentioned twice in the Priestly Blessing (Numbers 6:25–26). When *HaShem* would turn his face away from Israel, they would be devastated (Deuteronomy 31:17–18), but when he smiled down upon them, they would be restored (Psalm 27:8–9, 31:16, and 80:3). The same is true of the Holy Spirit; Wisdom will not remain with anyone who is deceitful or who is a slave of sin (Book of Wisdom 1:4, Ephesians 4:30).

In the kabbalistic text *Gates of Light* (*Sha'are Orah*), written by Rabbi Joseph Gikatilla (1293 CE), the concept was expressed that *HaShem*'s blessings flowed through the 32 Paths of Wisdom of the Kabbalah, and that the blessings collected attributes of each *Sefirah* and path as it moved down from *Keter* to *Malkut*, where it would be distributed to the rest of the world through Israel. Gikatilla connected this process to the Nation of Israel serving as *HaShem*'s priests on the earth (Exodus 19:6), which was related to the second aspect of the blessing given to Abraham, which stated, "*All nations on Earth shall be blessed because of you*" (Genesis 12:3). In this concept, the blessings of the entire world were directly tied to the actions of Israel, who served as priests to the world.

The concept of Israel being a chosen people has led to jealousy and anti-Semitism among many non-Jews. Naturally, everyone would like to believe that they are loved by God equally and without favoritism—which is how the world was created to be. However, scripture clearly states that *HaShem* has since made special covenants between himself and certain peoples, while having fewer or no interactions with other nations. This separation started at the Tower of Babel, where the nations were divided over their unwillingness to follow *HaShem*'s first instruction/mitzvah (Genesis 1:28, 11:4). Since the majority of people defied *HaShem*'s instruction, he made a covenant with Abraham, the one man who was willing to follow him.

The other nations were given free will and were left to their own devices. Their level of righteousness is considered in relation to the Noahide Laws or that of a *Ger Toshav* (faithful gentiles), which are the different standards that the Apostle Paul tried explaining to his Gentile converts (Romans 2:25–29). A major point of contention among religions is the concept that only one religion or denomination is the "*right one*" and that everyone else will be sent to hell or will not be saved; that is not what it means for the Jews to be in a covenant with God. Jethro was a Midianite priest who worshiped *HaShem*, and Baalam was also a gentile prophet who had direct knowledge and interactions with God. One's relationship with God is a personal one, and God judges a person's level of righteousness by the intentions of their hearts and the individual's actions/deeds (Jeremiah 17:10, Proverbs 21:2). It is not a matter of attending the right church, synagogue, or mosque, nor is it a matter of choosing the right religion.

God causes the sun to shine and gives rain to the righteous and the unrighteous alike (Matthew 5:45), but those in a special covenant with him can benefit from the promises (blessings and curses) he specified to them. Just as *HaShem* was willing to spare Sodom and Gomorrah if 10 righteous persons could be found within them (Genesis 18:32), it is said that the world is sustained by the presence of 36 (*Lamed-Vav*) *Tzadikim* (righteous persons) in each generation (Sanhedrin 97b:11).

The concept expressed in the *Gates of Light* was that the actions of the Nation of Israel (who served as priests for the entire world) would influence the amount of blessings and specific attributes that the entire world (Israel and the other nations) received from *HaShem*. If there was an imbalance in the priesthood, such as a lack of justice, there would be a lack of that attribute within the entire world. In accordance with that concept, kabbalists devote considerable effort into their actions, because their efforts affected not only them, but they also believe they affect the rest of the world. By the priest/kabbalist expressing charity or some other positive trait, good blessings and positive vibrations are sent throughout the entire world.

A cursory study of the Tanakh (the Jewish canon of books in addition to the Torah) reveals that the Nation of Israel had constant struggles with keeping the commandments and following the instructions of God. The very name *Israel* means *struggles/contends with God*. The Nation of Israel was rarely pleasing to *HaShem*, and the world, in general, has been filled with strife. The possibility of the entire priesthood behaving well is extremely unlikely, so there will always be imbalances in the world. Eventually, Israel failed to remain faithful to their covenant with *HaShem*, and since they served foreign gods in their land, they were told they would serve strangers in a foreign land (Jeremiah 5:19). The Jews were conquered by Nebuchadnezzar and taken into captivity in Babylon. *HaShem* promised to restore the children of Israel to the earlier covenant (Jeremiah 30:20), and he promised to make a New Covenant with those who are freed from captivity (Jeremiah 31:31–32).

The New Covenant involved *HaShem* writing his commandments within the hearts of individuals (Jeremiah 31:33), and the covenant was made with those who love him and keep his commandments (Daniel 9:4). This did not nullify the previous covenants (Galatians 3:16–18) but expanded upon them and clarified them. The New Covenant was available to everyone who was willing to follow the commandments (Romans 3:29, Galatians 3:28, 1 Corinthians 12:13), and those who did would then be considered part of the chosen people, the holy nation, and would be a royal priesthood (1 Peter 2:5,9, Revelation 1:6, 5:10). Jesus and his Disciples were Jews, and the Jews remained in the covenant with *HaShem* (Romans 1:16, 2:9; Colossians 3:11); however, faithful gentiles (*Ger Toshav*) could also be adopted (*Ger Tzadik*) into it (Ephesians 1:5, Galatians 4:4–6, Romans 11:17). The New Covenant is not based on genetic heritage but relies on a commitment to love *HaShem* and to follow his commandments (Matthew 22:37). Anyone who is called by God is welcomed, while awaiting the final covenant of peace in the *Olam HaBa* (Ezekiel 34:25, 37:26; Isaiah 11:6).

CHARMS, BINDINGS, AND SUPERSTITIONS

Observing *Mitzvah* within Judaism is a means of earning or maintaining *HaShem*'s favor. In practical Kabbalah, *segulah* (treasure/charm/remedy/protection) refers to a similar notion. The concept of *segulah* is related to the Children of Israel being proclaimed as a Chosen People (Deuteronomy 7:6) in the Torah (Exodus 19:5–6), which states, "*If you obey my voice and keep my covenant, then you shall be a special treasure (segulah) to me above all people. And you shall be a kingdom of priests, and a holy nation.*" In Judaism, *segulah* has come to represent superstitious behaviors that are meant to bring about good luck/fortune, and includes actions such as wearing a red string for protection or wearing a bride's jewelry while she stands under the wedding canopy (as a means to improve one's chances of finding love, similar to the practice of catching the bouquet at a secular wedding). *Segulah* is based on the principle that by doing things pleasing to *HaShem*, the person will be viewed as a *special treasure* to him and will receive additional blessings as a result.

Observing mitzvah keeps one in *HaShem*'s favor, and performing *segulah* serves as an attempt to be recognized as a special treasure in order to gain additional blessings. Segulah involves going beyond what is expected and has been associated with good-luck charms and talismans. *Kame'ah* (binding) refers to a talisman that is made for a specific purpose, such as a protection against evil, to ensure a healthy pregnancy, or good fortune. Talismans and **talismans** were often engraved with divine names of God, or the purpose of the item might be written on it in Hebrew letters, in their corresponding numerical values, within magic squares, or in magical sigils (**חֹתָם**).

Since the Hebrew *Alef-bet* is considered holy and because such a great deal of mystic thought has been put into each word and letter, *segulot* and *kame'ot* containing Hebrew letters were considered powerful and binding remedies (Matthew 18:18). As these practices continued to evolve, medieval Solomonic Grimoires were developed, which reinforced the belief that lower spirits and demons were required to be obedient to higher entities in the spiritual hierarchy (Acts 19:15). Since *HaShem* is the Most High God, divine names referring to him were used in ceremonial magick as a means of controlling lesser spiritual beings.

In Jewish folklore, Rabbi Judah Loew (Liwa, Loeb) Ben Bezalel used a special formula taken from the Sefer Yetzirah to bring a Golem to life, by writing the name of *HaShem* on either its forehead or on a scroll placed into its mouth. Other theories as to how talismans work are related to synchronicity, or the belief that the item can be charged with certain energy. A magical ritual/ceremony might include *binding* (*Kame'ah*) specific attributes to the charm, or the associated attributes might be the result of synchronicity that developed over time.

Recognizing a connection between two objects or events that are not directly related but seem to somehow be linked to each other describes synchronicity. One might notice that every time he/she wears a certain item of clothing or does a specific activity that a desired phenomenon happens to occur, and the person might then start considering the object or activity a good-luck charm, necessary ritual, or psychological compulsion to bring about the desired effect.

Many superstitions, such as knocking on wood or throwing salt over one's shoulder, are done similar to the practice of segulah, and either concept may have been developed by recognizing synchronistic events. Comparing the phases of the moon or the months of the year with certain occurrences may lead someone to recognize meaningful coincidences. The relationship between the events may not be understood rationally, but a connection does seem to exist between the two otherwise unrelated activities/events.

This differs from recognizing signs or using discernment that is based on a rational explanation or understood phenomena. Comparing the appearance of the sky to a similar appearance observed in the past may allow one to predict the weather (Matthew 16:2–3, Luke 12:56), or understanding the behaviors of birds (Matthew 24:28) might enable someone to locate a corpse by observing circling vultures. Recognizing such signs is a matter of comprehending natural events, and although the uninformed may be mystified by such predictions, they are not supernatural occurrences, and the Talmud recognizes these omens as acceptable forms of divination (Akeidat Yitzchak 22:1:7, Chullin 95b:7–8).

Interpreting signs such as a black cat crossing one's path or a black crow being a messenger of death most likely began solely on the basis of superstition; however, if one starts connecting such superstitious beliefs with coincidental events, a synchronistic association may be accepted on a subconscious level, which might cause it to become a self-fulfilling prophecy within that person's psyche. Similarly, if someone believes that a synchronistic event, superstition, astrological activity, talisman, or other lucky charm will cause a specific result, then this psychological belief may produce a placebo effect, and the results may seem like magic or divine providence (or both); it will be up to the concerned individual to decide if it was the result of a psychological phenomenon or if something supernatural has occurred.

When casting lots, any or all the above could be true, and it might vary by situation, as well as other factors. As the same Hebrew lot is cast on different occasions, the observed relationship it has to the coincidental events may create synchronistic connections or meanings for the diviner that are not found in this book, but they may also be true. The connection might be the result of linking unrelated coincidences, or the connection might be a valid one that is just not understood at the time.

The Hebrew lot may have been cast in accordance with God's divine plan under the direction of the Spirit of God, or one's own intuition might influence the interpretation of a randomly selected lot. The interpretation could also be based solely on one's creativity and imagination. The truth of what is occurring can be understood only by the individual diviner; making such decisions and improving one's discernment are the very skills that the diviner is seeking to develop by casting lots either for divination or mystical contemplation.

The Hebrew Alef-Bet

> *God and the seventy angels that surround His throne cast lots concerning the various nations. Each angel received a nation, and Israel fell to the lot of God. To every nation a peculiar language was assigned, Hebrew being reserved for Israel—the language made use of by God at the creation of the world.* (Ginzberg, *Legends of the Jews*, 1:4:103)

The Talmud states that God and seventy angels cast lots over the nations and that the "*lot of the Holy One, blessed be He, fell upon Abraham and upon his seed, as it is said, 'For the Lord's portion is his people; Jacob is the lot of his inheritance'*" (Pirkei DeRabbi Eliezer 24:9–10). The Zohar expands on this concept and refers to the "*great chiefs in heaven appointed over the gentiles.*" Since angels are also referred to as *elohim* (judges/gods), the other angels assigned to the gentile nations by lot would represent the multiple gods found in the various religions of the world.

In the Zohar, the other nations are governed by specific angels, all of which are subordinate to the hierarchy of the four archangels (Michael, Gabriel, Uriel, Raphael), of which the Zohar states, "*There are four rulers on high who, by the will of God, rule over all the other nations; and for all that, not one of these has the power to do the smallest thing except as He commands them.*" Through the process of casting lots, *HaShem* received the descendants of Abraham, Isaac, and Jacob as his portion (Deuteronomy 32:8), and the Hebrews received their language from their God: "*To every nation a peculiar language was assigned, Hebrew being reserved for Israel—the language made use of by God at the creation of the world*" (Ginzberg, *Legends of the Jews*, 1:4:103).

The Hebrew *Alef-bet* is part of a *Lashon HaKodesh* (Holy Language), and its letters are said to be the very symbols and sounds that *HaShem* used to seal the universe. The letters represent language, mathematics, sound, and the embodiment of concepts and values within a symbol. The sacredness of the Hebrew language is the reason that prayers and blessings are still said in Hebrew today; from the *Shema* to the Priestly Blessing to the lighting of the *Shabbat* candles, or the blessings recited over the bread (*HaMotzi*) and wine during *Kiddush*. Songs/Psalms of praise and worship services are done in Hebrew, and the handwritten letters on a Torah scroll or within a *Mezuzah* are esteemed as the word of God (Deuteronomy 6:9, John 17:17) and are considered holy, sacred, and powerful; they are the instruments of manifestation.

Table 1 provides an example of the different types of Hebrew Letters and their Gematria Values, meanings, and associated attributes listed in the Sefer Yetzirah, according to the translation of Isodor Kalish (1877). The shapes of the Hebrew letters developed over time, and specific types of lettering are used for different purposes. For talismans, Hebrew block lettering is used in grimoires such as the "*Keys of Solomon,*" the "*Sefer Raziel HaMalakh,*" and the "*Sixth and Seventh Books of Moses,*" and in the talismans created to accompany this book.

TABLE 2: LETTERS TABLE

Hebrew Letter Name	Hebrew Letter Meaning	Gematria Value	Hebrew Block Letter	Hebrew Script Letter	Hebrew STaM Letter	Sefer Yetzirah Planetary Attribute	Sefer Yetzirah Direction/ Body
Alef	Ox / Man Above / Below	1	א	א	א	Air	Atmospheric Air, Body
Bet	House, Beginning	2	ב	ב	ב	Moon	1 Height, Right Eye
Gimel	Camel, Benefactor	3	ג	ג	ג	Mars	2 Depth, Right Ear
Dalet	Door	4	ד	ד	ד	Sun	3 East, Right Nostril
Hei	Breath / Spirit Window	5	ה	ה	ה	Aries, Nisan	East Height, Right Foot
Vav	Nail, Hook, Tent Peg, Connection	6	ו	ו	ו	Taurus, Iyar	North East, Right Kidney
Zayin	Sword, Arrow	7	ז	ז	ז	Gemini, Sivan	East Depth, Left Foot
Chet	Fence, Field, Life Chet / Yod	8	ח	ח	ח	Cancer, Tamus	South Height, Right Hand
Tet	Container, Serpent	9	ט	ט	ט	Leo, Ab	South East, Left Kidney
Yod	Hand, Finger	10	י	י	י	Virgo, Elul	South Depth, Left Hand

Kaf	Palm, Hand	20	כך	כ	כ	Venus	4 West, Left Eye
Lamed	Arm, Ox, Learn, Teach	30	ל	ל	ל	Libra	West Height, Gall
Mem	Water, Woman, Blood	40	מם	מ	מ	Water	Water, Breast/Heart
Nun	Fish Gaff, Fruit, Continuation	50	נן	נ	נ	Scorpio, Marchehvan	South West, Small IntesIntines
Samech	Support, Trust, Ouroboros	60	ס	ס	ס	Sagittarius, Kislev	West Depth, Stomach
Ayin	Good/Evil-Eye, Perception	70	ע	ע	ע	Capricorn, Teves	North Height Liver
Pei/Fei	Mouth, Blow, Scatter	80	פ	פ	פ	Mercury	5 North, Left Ear
Tzadi	Fishhook, Hunt, Righteousness	90	צ	צ	צ	Aquarius, Schwat	North West, Esophagus
Qof	Revolution, Growth, Cycles, Monkey	100	ק	ק	ק	Pieces, Adar	North Depth, Milt
Resh	Head, Beginning	200	ר	ר	ר	Saturn	6 South, Left Nostril
Shin /Sin	Tooth, Pillars, Transformation	300	ש	ש	ש	Fire	Heavens, Head
Tav	Sign, Omen, Completion	400	ת	ת	ת	Jupiter	7 Temple, Mouth

Hebrew script is handwritten and may be compared to cursive writing in English. A special type of Hebrew lettering (*Ksav Ashuris*) is used for ST"M/ STaM, which is an acronym for *Sefer Torah*, *Tefillin*, and *Mezuzot*. STaM is written by Scribes (*Sofrim*) on *Klaf* (parchment made by the skin of a kosher animal), using a feather quill and a specially mixed ink. For a *Torah Scroll* to be considered kosher, it must be handwritten using this lettering, and since *Tefillin* and *Mezuzah* are holy objects that contain verses from the *Torah* within them, they too use this lettering.

The need for each individual Jew to write a *Sefer Torah* is one of the *613 Mitzvot* specified by Maimonides in the 12th century CE. Torah Scrolls are written in STaM and contain *Taggin*, which are decorative *Crowns* (*Keterim*) that have the appearance of small *Zayin* at the top of certain letters. The letters that have a *Gag* (roof shape) usually have one *Tag* (the letters *Bet*, *Dalet*, *Hei*), and letters that share a similar top as the *Zayin* will often have three *Taggin/ Keterim*. Sometimes letters have extra *Taggin*, and the meaning of these additional *Taggin* is not always understood, but *Sofrim* (scribes) copy/duplicate the scrolls exactly in order for them to be considered kosher. The single *Tag/Keter* can be thought of as the Middle Pillar, and the three *Taggin* can be thought of as the Three Pillars of the Kabbalah, which adds significance and meaning to the letters and the words and verses containing them.

The Hebrew language relies on the Oral Tradition in order for someone to truly understand the significance of Hebrew writings. The values and secrets contained within each letter make the language a continual source of revelation and allows for new and ever-evolving mystical discoveries. When someone reads an English Bible, the punctuation helps them understand the text. Torah scrolls do not have any punctuation marks or vowels in them and are written only in capital letters. The meanings of the words can be drastically different on the basis of the vowels used with the capital letters, and these vowels and punctuation marks are not included on a Torah scroll.

The punctuation and vowel sounds that give meaning to the words designate where a comma should be, and when a verse begins or ends is obtained through the cantillation of the verse(s), which is a ritual chanting that has been passed down through the Oral Tradition, which includes different trope and musical melodies for reading/chanting Torah and Haftarah (Tanukh) to provide the punctuation and give meaning to the text. The *T'amim* (sounds) contain specific notes and melodies that are memorized and handed down through the Oral Tradition. It is these notes, melodies, and sounds that allow us to know which words are being used and where the punctuation should be. In order to help the reader understand these concepts, I have provided the first verse (the Shema) written in the *Mezuzah* (Deuteronomy 6:4) in Hebrew script (1), in STaM (2), and in block letters with the *Niqqud* (vowel points) and *T'amim* (trope/cantillation marks) added (3).

שמע ישראל יהוה אלהינו יהוה אחד

Shema Israel Adonai Eloheinu Adonai Echad
Hear O' Israel, the Lord is our God, the Lord is One.

שמע ישראל יהוה אלהינו יהוה אחד

STaM—as the text would appear on a Torah scroll

שְׁמַ֖ע יִשְׂרָאֵ֑ל יְהוָ֥ה אֱלֹהֵ֖ינוּ יְהוָ֥ה אֶחָֽד׃

Tikkun Korim—in block letters with Niqqud (vowels)
and T'amim (trope/cantillation marks)

You might notice that the last letter of the word ShMA (*Ayin*) and the last letter of EChD (*Dalet*) in the first and last words of the *Passuk* (verse) are larger than the rest of the letters. This is because when those letters are combined, they spell the Hebrew word for *Witness* (*Ayin Dalet*), implying that the person reciting the *Shema* is bearing witness to their belief in the truth of the statement. There are different cantillations for Torah (five books of Moses) and Haftorah (the other books in the Tanukh), and there are different melodies for the *Megillot* (Song of Songs, Ruth, Lamentations, Ecclesiastes, and Esther) and high holidays. Providing a summary of all that content is well outside the scope of this book.

Table 2, which is located on pages 28–29, contains a listing of the *Niqqud* (the vowel sounds added to the consonant letters to clarify their meanings) and the *T'amim* (the trope symbols that let the reader know which melody to chant when reading the words, and also provide the punctuation). The absence of *Niqqud* in the Torah has allowed kabbalists to find deeper meaning in the text. For example, the Zohar says, "*The word BeReSHiTH . . . can be analyzed into BaRa-ShiTH (He created six),*" linking the concept of God sealing the universe in six directions to the first word in the Bible. Rabbi Yomtov Lippman Heller compared these different characteristics of the Hebrew letters to the different aspects of the soul:

> *The Rabbis teach us that the letters of the Torah have four dimensions, which are known as* **אתנט**. **אתנט** *is an acronym for the Hebrew words taamim* (**טעמים**)*, "the cantillation notes"; nekudos* (**נקודות**)*, "the vocalization signs"; taggin* (**תגין**)*, "the crowns" . . . and osios* (**אותיות**)*, "the letters." According to the Kabbalah, the osios, the letters, represent the body and the other three dimensions represent the three levels of the soul—nefesh, ruach, and neshamah. The nekudos, vocalization signs, are associated with nefesh, the lowest level of the soul, while the taamim are associated with neshamah, the highest level of the soul.* (Derush Chidushei HaLevana 3:2:1)

In addition to providing mystical meanings, the T'amim helps us comprehend the meaning of the text. While discussing the word B'reishit, Rabbeinu Bachya Ben Asher notes that "*the tone-sign tipcha on the word . . . separates it from the word which follows it.*" The trope symbols are broken up into *Mafsik* (Disjunctive/Separators/Pauses) and *M'Chaber* (Conjunctive/Connectors). The *Mafsik* denotes different length pauses and would be comparable to periods, commas, and semicolons, which separate words or concepts to add context to a verse. In addition to the symbols that are used for punctuation, different sounds are associated with the symbols on the basis of Trope Families (phrases, clauses), which are collections of melodies that cause the words to flow together and relate to each other.

בְּרֵאשִׁ֖ית בָּרָ֣א אֱלֹהִ֑ים אֵ֥ת הַשָּׁמַ֖יִם וְאֵ֥ת הָאָֽרֶץ׃

Genesis 1:1: with cantillation marks and Niqqud

Etnachta and Sof-Pasuk phrases

Genesis 1:1: Hebrew transliteration with related Etnachta and Sof-Pasuk phrase notes

The first verse of the Bible includes two trope families, the *Etnachta phrase* and the *Sof-Pasuk phrase.* As Rabbeinu Bachya Ben Asher noted, the word *B'reishit* has a *Tipcha* under it, which separates it from the word *Bara* (he created) following it. It is interesting to note that the first trope family in the Bible is missing the *Merkha* in the phrase (the beginning of it), as if the trope is starting midsentence and not mentioning what occurred immediately prior to the "*Beginning*." The missing aspects of creation could be understood as creation beginning with the letter *Bet*, and Wisdom/*Chokmah* being the first aspect of creation to emanate (*Chokmah* coming out of *Keter*) from the Ein Sof (unending / without end).

The *Munach* under *Bara* connects it with the word *Elohim* following it, linking the words "*He created Judges/Elohim*" together. *Elohim* is the noun and *Bara* is the verb (third-person past-tense masculine singular); the word *Et* with a *Merkha* under it denotes the definite article and the direct object, and as a *M'Chaber* it *connects* the word to *HaShamayim* (the Heavens), and the next two words act similarly for "*The Earth*." The Hebrew letters provide the body, the vowel points give the letters their lower soul, and the cantillation marks provide the spiritual aspects or higher soul. The first verse of the Bible can be understood on multiple levels (PaRDeS), and the beauty of any scriptural text is that each of these levels and understandings is simultaneously correct. There is more than one level of meaning to each aspect of it (to each chapter, verse, and letter).

Hebrew Niqqud Name	Hebrew Niqqud Symbol	Hebrew Niqqud Sound	Hebrew T'amim Name	Hebrew T'amim Symbol	Hebrew T'amim Name	Hebrew T'amim Symbol
Patach	◌ַ	"ah" Father	Merkha (M'Chaber)	◌֥	Mapach (M'Chaber)	◌֤
Qubuts	◌ֻ	"oo" Moon	Tipcha (Mafsik)	◌֖	Zarka (Mafsik)	◌֮
Chirik	◌ִ	"ee" Tree	Munach (M'Chaber)	◌֣	T'vir (Mafsik)	◌֛
Segol	◌ֶ	"eh"	Etnachta (Mafsik)	◌֑	Gershayim (Mafsik)	◌֞
Kamatz	◌ָ	"ah" Father	Segol (Mafsik)	◌֒	Pazer (Mafsik)	◌֡
Tzerei	◌ֵ	"ay/ei" Stay	Katon (Mafsik)	◌֔	T'lishag'dolah (M'Chaber)	◌֠
Cholam	וֹ	"oh" Boat	Zakef Gadol (Mafsik)	◌֕	T'lishaK'tanah (M'Chaber)	◌֩
Shuruk	וּ	"oo" Moon	R'vi-i (Mafsik)	◌֗	Darga (M'Chaber)	◌֧
Sheva	◌ְ	Silent "e/i" Bet/Bit Syllable Stop	Geresh or Azla (Mafsik)	◌֜	Kadma (M'Chaber)	◌֨
Dagesh	◌ּ	Double Letter Modifier	Pashta (M'Chaber)	◌֙	Sof pasuk (Mafsik)	׃

TABLE 3 shows the names and sounds of each Hebrew vowel and cantillation mark.

VOWELS/CANTILLATION

In preparation for an *Aliyah* (ascent)—which refers to a congregation member being called to the *Bimah* (elevated platform that holds the Torah)—a congregant will usually use a *Tikkun Korim* (Corrected Reader), which contains two columns of identical text, with the scripture written in STaM on one side/page (so they can see what it will look like on the scroll) and with duplicate verses across from it that includes the *Niqqud* and *T'amim*. This allows the congregant to practice the sounds and melodies in order to prepare for the *Aliyah*, when they will be expected to read the *Sefer* (scroll) without the additional *Niqqud* and *T'amim* present. Since reading scripture in this manner is still practiced today, there are many resources, apps, books (Portnoy and Wolff 2001), and videos on the internet available if the reader wishes to explore those concepts further. The information contained in this section is meant to provide only a basic summary, which provides the reader with a deeper understanding to the Hebrew *Alef-bet*.

The Hebrew *Alef-bet* is a complex and holy alphabetical system, with layers upon layers of meaning that can be derived from it, which is why it has been used in religion, magick, and mystical practices for thousands of years. The Hebrew *Alef-bet* has been a key aspect of the Kabbalah since the writing of the Sefer Yetzirah (200 BCE–200 CE), and each letter is associated with a path connecting the *Sefirot* on the Kabbalistic Tree of Life. In addition to assigning different combinations of the divine name to the six directions, the Sefer Yetzirah assigns each Hebrew letter (as listed in table 1) to the different aspects of an every expanding cube of the universe, as in the following image.

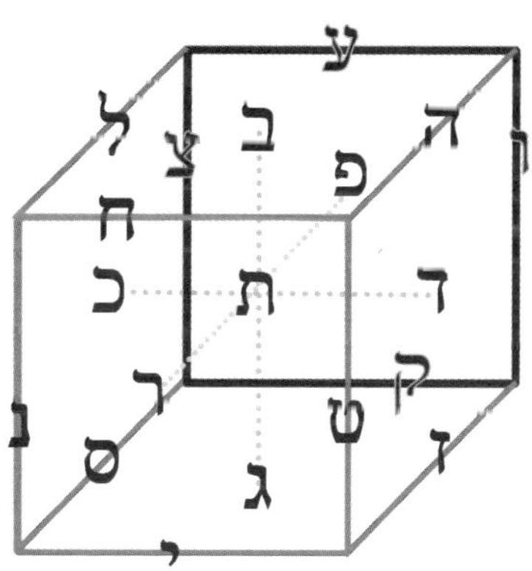

Kabbalah Cube of Space

The Kabbalah Cube of Space could also be contemplated spherically, and visualized as three rings (one horizontal and two vertical) that can be combined together, resembling Ezekiel's Wheel or an armillary sphere. The Temple (foundation stone) is at the center, as in the following images.

Cube of Space constructed out of rings

The Sefer Yetzirah arranges the 10 Emanations of God, the 22 Hebrew Letters, and concept of God sealing the universe in six directions as a cube with the Temple or the Throne of God at its center. The description of God facing eastward and creating this cube is imitated on *Sukkot* with the *Etrog* and *Lulav*, or by ceremonial magicians when performing the Lesser Banishing Ritual of the Pentagram (LBRP). The Zohar relates these six directions with the word B'reishit and Wisdom/*Chokmah*.

> *What is the meaning of B'reishit? It means "with Wisdom," the Wisdom on which the world is based, and through this it introduces us to deep and recondite mysteries. In it, too, is the inscription of six chief supernal directions, out of*

> *which there issues the totality of existence. For the same there go forth six sources of rivers which flow into the Great Sea. This is implied in the word BeReSHiTH, which can be analyzed into BaRa-ShiTH (He created six).* (Sefer HaZohar)

Later graphical representations of the Kabbalah were arranged into the Tree of the *Sefirot*, but originally the emanations and letters were associated with a cube of six directions. In the following images, the Height, Depth, North, South, East, and West are presented with 22 Hebrew letters associated with the different aspects of the cube according to their placement in the Sefer Yetzirah, with the 10 *Sefirot* numbered from 1 to 10 using the Gematrical values of the letters, and the combination of the father letters (the letters used in the Tetragrammaton) used to seal the six directions are also in their places/directions.

These six sides of the cube are presented in a cut-and-paste graphic in the appendix of this book, if the reader desires to make a Kabbalah Cube for contemplation. The Kabbalah Cube provides a three-dimensional representation of the *Sefirot*, with the *Sefirot* of *Geburah* and *Chesed* superimposed on each other, representing that the balance between good (*Yetzer HaTov*) and evil (*Yetzer HaRa*), justice and mercy, or plague and pleasure is a central aspect of our reality.

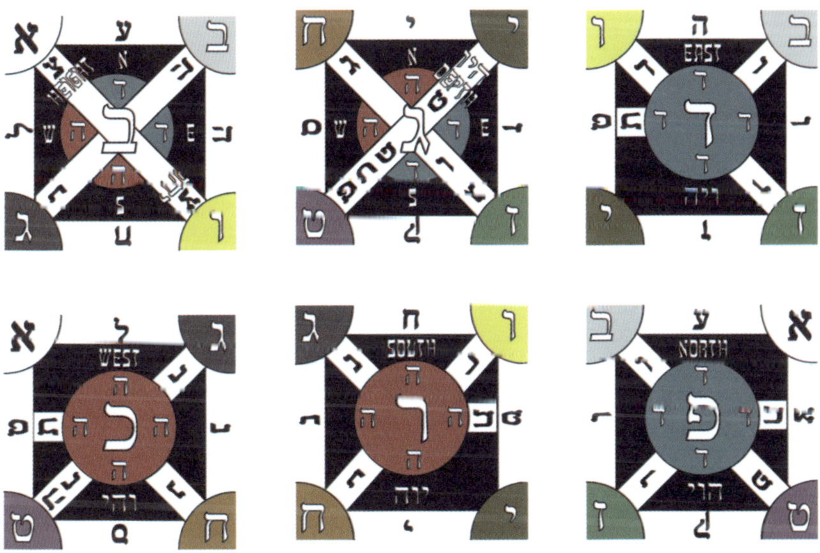

If one were to view the Kabbalah Cube from a specific angle, with the *Sefirah* of *Tiferet* closest to the viewer and with *Keter* at the top and *Malkut* at bottom, then the placement of the *Sefirot* on the later Trees of the *Sefirot* can start to be understood. If the three-dimensional shape were to be flattened when being viewed from that angle, the *Sefirot* would be roughly in the positions they are displayed on the modern Kabbalah Trees. The viewer may notice that by changing the cube's angle and rotating it either forward or backward, it would cause the *Sefirot* of *Tiferet* and *Yesod* to switch places interchangeably (*Tiferet* higher or lower on the flattened tree). Looking directly at *Tiferet* would superimpose *Tiferet*, *Yesod*, *Chesed*, and *Geburah* onto each other at the center of the cube, with other connecting paths moving right through them.

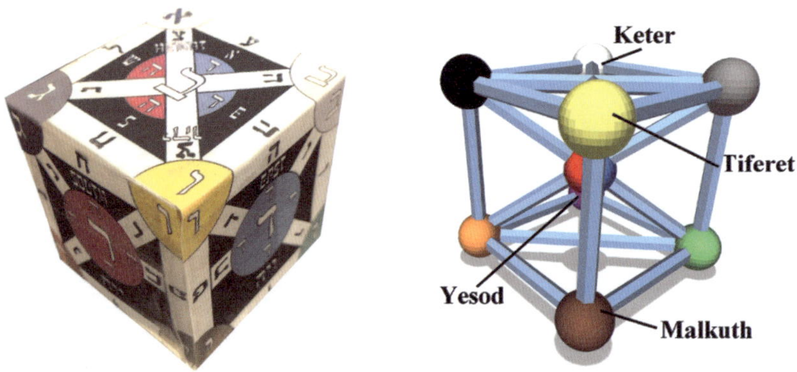

If the cube were tilted downward, *Tiferet* would move below *Geburah/Chesed* (*in the center*) and *Yesod* would appear higher.

Depending on the perspective and the angle the cube is being viewed at the time that the image is flattened will alternate whether *Tiferet* or *Yesod* is higher on the tree, and one of those *Sefirot* would fill the void where some modern trees place the additional *Sefirah* of *Daat* (Knowledge). In the following flattened representation of the Kabbalah Cube, *Tiferet* is shown above *Yesod*, and the paths are labeled on the basis of the paths that connect the *Sefirot* in its cube shape, based on the positions listed in the Sefer Yetzirah. Some of the paths have the same or multiple letters on them, which is because paths such as the Middle Pillar are three-dimensional on the cube, and the depicted path may be running behind the visible aspects of the three dimensional cube.

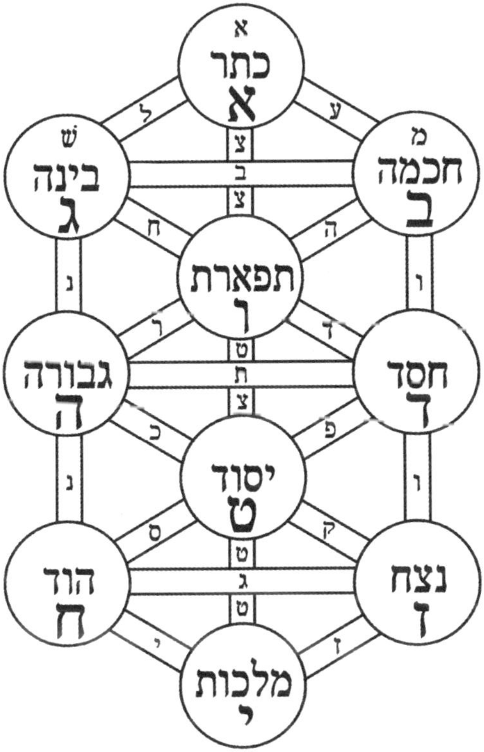

Flattened Tree where *Tiferet* and *Yesod* are interchangeable depending on the angle of the cube when it is flattened

Examining the Kabbalah as a three-dimensional shape adds several new dimensions to one's mystical contemplations. By rotating the cube in different positions, connections can be understood in a manner that is not discernible on flattened Trees of the *Sefirot*. The different Trees of the *Sefirot* were developed approximately one thousand years after the Sefer Yetzirah presented it as a cube, and the graphical depictions we use today developed over time. The arrangements of the connecting paths used today are organized according the angles of the paths in the Lurianic Tree (3 horizontal, 7 vertical, and 12 angled, to match the categorization of the letters in the Sefer Yetzirah) or numerically in the Hermetic/Kircher Tree. If the Lurianic Tree were to be viewed as a cube, it would appear as follows, and if the *Sefirot* of *Keter* and *Malkuth* were pulled in opposite directions, it would flatten into the Lurianic Tree many are familiar with.

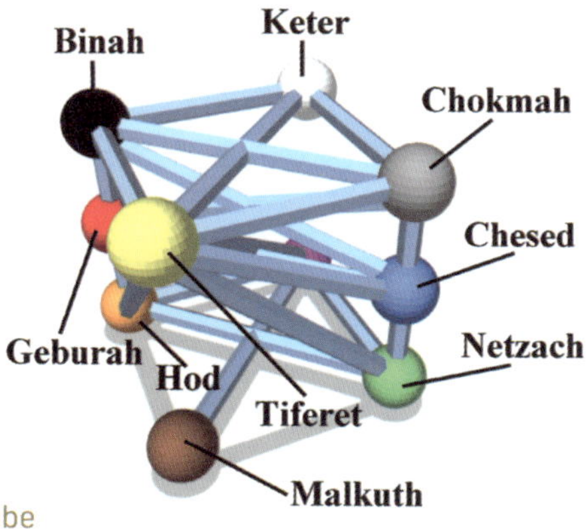

Lurianic Tree as a cube

So, with all these different options, how do we know which one is the correct one? All of them are correct and none of them are correct. Like the PaRDeS, there are different levels of understanding, and each realization is valid within its own unique perspective. At the same time, it is important to realize that both the Kabbalah Trees and the Kabbalah Cube are symbolic representations of the 10 Utterances described in Genesis/B'reishit. Kabbalah is a system of mysticism, and there is a level of subjectivity to it. The Kabbalah is not dogma to be memorized but is a system of mysticism; contemplation enables individuals to *receive* their own revelations and realizations about God, the universe, and their individual roles within it.

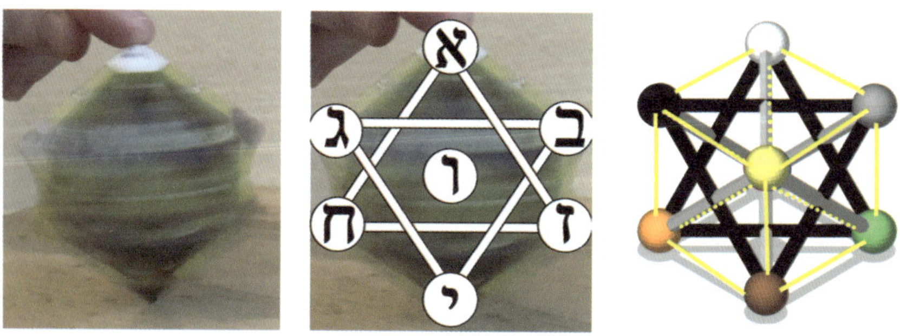

Spinning Cube forms a Star of David.

In addition to contemplating the Kabbalah Cube from different angles, if it were to be spun or rotated (as the world rotates), then we can find the shape of the Star of David in a flattened depiction of the spinning cube. Each of the shapes and arrangements used in the different depictions of the Kabbalah can benefit the mystic in their contemplations, but Kabbalah is much more than any shape or depiction. Kabbalah is the reception of revelation, which can occur in many forms. We can learn through life events and mundane experiences just as much as we can through mystical contemplation. Action and thought (the Pillars of Severity and Mercy) are equally important to our spiritual growth. Kabbalah is language, mathematics, numbers, and letters and consists of our understanding of God and all aspects of Wisdom, intellect, and psychology. The Kabbalah contains meaning related to concepts as broad as the universe, or as specific as to how a *Niqqud* (Vowel Points) influences the soul of the letter.

CASTING HEBREW LOTS

Throughout history, various methods of casting lots have been used to randomly and impartially select between multiple options. Biblical examples include selecting lots with the names of tribes written on them (1 Chronicles 6:65), or the lots designating the goats for either *HaShem* or Azazel (Leviticus 16:8). A modern example might be drawing straws or having people write their names on pieces of paper to be drawn out of a hat. There are also forms of divination that employ the use of magical alphabets, such as the Runes of the Norse/Proto-Germanic alphabets, which also have key words/attributes associated with each letter.

For adherents of Judeo-Christian mystical traditions and other Western esoteric paths, the letters of the Hebrew *Alef-bet* have much more profound significance and have thousands of years of mystical thought attributed to them. In addition the usage of Hebrew letters on the connecting paths on a Tree of the *Sefirot*, 18th-century (CE) French occultist Eliphas Levi suggested a connection between the 22 Hebrew letters and the 22 Major Arcana of the Tarot. Later Rosicrucians expanded on Levi's concept, and the Hebrew letters (and their associations with the Kabbalah) have now been used as a method of divination and mystical contemplation for several centuries in association with the Tarot. In Levi's study of the Tarot, he located a manuscript on the *Little Keys of Solomon*, which included the Tarot in the form of talismans, which he suggested was the Tarot prior to the existence of paper cards. Levi later produced a short book based on that information titled *Clefs Majeures et Clavicules de Salomon* (1860), which includes Hebrew talismans linked to the Tarot.

A. E. Waite was a Rosicrucian and Christian mystic who studied Levi's work and produced the Rider-Waite Tarot deck, which remains one of the most utilized and popular Tarot decks in the world today. Due to its associations with Judeo-Christian symbolism and Kabbalah, the runic alphabet was adopted by some in the 20th century as a means of divination by people who were looking for a pagan alternative to the Tarot.

The Proto-Germanic Runes are based on an alphabet that was used from the second century CE, until it was replaced with the Latin alphabet during Roman domination. Since the Germanic Runes are based on Norse mythology (which is not a shared belief among all pagans), some 21st-century wiccans/pagans have begun using 13 unique symbols they refer to as *Witches Runes*, which provides them with meaningful symbols that are not associated with any specific religion. Although Tarot cards and the different types of runes and lots are based on different theologies and symbols, their usage in divination are almost identical. Since the Tarot has 78 different cards, larger and more-elaborate Tarot spreads can be employed while keeping a sense of randomness to the reading. When selecting from a smaller set of criteria, less elaborate spreads should be utilized.

A spread or layout describes the meaning of the different positions that the selected lot/rune/Tarot card is meant to represent. For example, three position layouts might be selected to signify Past, Present, Future, or they could represent the Situation, Outlook, Advice, or the Situation, Greatest Challenge/Obstacle, or Greatest Attribute. The possibilities and meanings of spreads/layouts are limited only by the practitioner's imagination, and it is all a matter of personal preference. Depending on the question/situation the reading is considering, the criteria, number of lots, and meaning of the positions in the layout all can be adjusted according to what seems the most reasonable to the practitioner.

This book will not cover different spreads/layouts, because they are a matter of personal preference. Instead, it will focus on drawing a single Hebrew lot as a means of either answering a question or selecting an attribute for mystical contemplation. The instructions for drawing lots are easy: ask a question and then draw a single lot out of the container/bag. The question can be as vague as "*What attribute/concept should I focus on today?*," or as specific as "*How should I handle this situation?*" Using Hebrew lots, the reader/practitioner selects a lot at random, and the selection of the chosen letter is governed by chance.

Depending on the reader's intuition (gut feelings/instincts), the selection of the lot may be an aspect of divination, or the divine guidance might not come into play until the interpretation of the lot. Logic would suggest that the lot was chosen impartially, at random, on the basis of statistics and the laws of probability, but for those who believe in fate, providence, and predestination, who is to say that you did not select that particular lot at that particular moment in time in accordance with the divine plan and in fulfillment of destiny? The validity of that concept is subjective, and it will be up to the diviner to decide on the basis of their feelings at the time as to whether or not the selected lot was the work of chance or providence. Alternatively, divine guidance might take place during the interpretation phase of the reading, when the Spirit influences one's thought processes.

The secret to divination is that there are no "*correct*" answers or "*set meanings*." Although this book lists a series of attributes associated with each letter, which concepts, if any, seem most related to the question/situation is solely based on the intuitive feelings of the reader. The same Hebrew letter can be read in many different ways, and its interpretation will change on the basis of the context of the question and the reader's understanding of the situation.

At its most basic level, divination is a psychological process that utilizes symbolism to extract intuitive information out of one's subconscious mind, and makes that information available to the conscious, analytical mind, to be used while brainstorming a solution to a certain dilemma. It involves the use of one's full psyche (soul/mind), and the application of both the objective and subjective aspects of one's mental processes to a given situation. The *psychic reading* is a psychological endeavor that utilizes a combination of a medium/instrument (lots) and one's whole psyche (mental processes) to formulate a creative solution to a specific situation.

On a deeper level, divination is a process that uses symbolism and intuitive impressions to communicate with the divine spirit within you (Joel 2:28, Acts 2:17). Symbolism is the language of the subconscious, which is also how the Spirit of Wisdom communicates with those who are indwelt by her (Wisdom 9:11). Jesus and the Prophets (*Nevi'im*) in the Tanakh directly heard the voice of the Spirit and spoke in the name of *HaShem* (John 14:10, 24, 17:8; Exodus 4:22, 9:1); however, for most of us, the guidance we receive from the Ruach Elohim will be subtle and filtered through symbolism (Numbers 12:6).

We are led by the Spirit through the interpretation of signs and by recognizing the whispers (1 Kings 19:12, John 3:34, Matthew 10:20). The Spirit of Wisdom speaks to our Souls; she knows the lessons of history, can anticipate the future, and can help us solve our problems (Wisdom 8:8). Intuitive ideas and feelings are given to us to consider, and our consciences guide and convict us (John 16:13, Romans 9:1, 2 Corinthians 5:11), but we are allotted discretion and free will to decide how we choose to act upon those instinctual feelings (Sirach 15:14–15).

This is because all our actions are recorded (Revelation 20:12; Luke 12:3; Book of Wisdom 1:9), and we will be judged according to the choices we make (Deuteronomy 30:19; Matthew 25:21, 38; Romans 2:6). Our spiritual development depends on us learning discernment and applying wisdom to the situations we encounter. We are given opportunities to decide between good and evil (Genesis 3:22) and to demonstrate sound judgment in order to prepare us for our future roles (Book of Wisdom 6:20; 1 Corinthians 6:3; Revelation 5:10, 20:4).

Receiving guidance from the Spirit is an instinctual and subjective process, but those who build a relationship with the Most High God will come to understand the truth and will recognize his ways (Wisdom 3:9). The acquisition of Wisdom is a lifelong progression; it requires the initiate to be tested and to learn and grow through both experience and contemplation (Sirach 4:17, Wisdom 3:5–6). Devotion to the Most High is a multifaceted task. It requires academic study to gain a solid Understanding (*Binah*) of scripture, but it also requires subjective contemplation in order to utilize Wisdom (*Chokmah*) and apply it within one's life. Finally, there must be practical application, because faith without works is dead (James 2:20, 26). It is through the trials and challenges we face in life that we learn judgment and demonstrate good stewardship (Matthew 25:21). The Great Work (purification of our souls) incorporates Mind, Body, and Spirit. The *Mind* is trained through academic study and scholarly research, the *Body* represents the physical application of the principles within one's daily life, and the *Spirit* teaches us through symbolism, contemplation, and intuitive intelligence.

Kabbalah and the use of Hebrew lots as a divinatory tool or contemplative aid, as done in this book, focuses on the mystical aspects of the Great Work. It utilizes symbolism and analogies to understand God on an intuitive level. Mysticism unveils the deeper mysteries and the secret wisdom of God. It allows concepts to be understood in a subconscious manner, by speaking the language of the spirit/intuition. Subjective contemplation allows the objective information to be realized at a core aspect of our beings. Rationally, we know that the letters within the Tetragrammaton serve the literal purpose of representing the name of God, but when mystical interpretations are applied to the letters, they take on much-deeper symbolic expressions. Through analogy, they help us comprehend the mind of God and understand his plan and mysteries.

Using Hebrew lots in order to select random topics of contemplation is fairly straightforward. A lot is drawn at random, and the concepts and attributes associated with it are considered immediately and throughout the day. For example, if the Hebrew letter *Qof* was selected, it has a gematria value of 100, which reduces to 1 and would therefore be related to the letters *Alef* and *Yod*, both of which are used as the first letters in the names of God (YHVH/he will be, and AHYH/I will be). The Hebrew letter *Qof* is also the first letter in the words *Kodesh* (Holy/Sacred) and *Kabbalah* (Reception), both of which are related to *HaShem*, because his name is *sacred*, and it is through the Kabbalah that we might *receive* an understanding of him.

The Shema states that *HaShem* is One (Deuteronomy 6:4), and the *Sefirot* of the Kabbalah reminds us that although 10 attributes are examined, they refer to a single God (10 = 1 + 0 = 1). The Hebrew letter *Qof* is spelled *Qof, Vav, Fei* and has the appearance of the *Vav* serving as a mirror between the other two letters, so that the *Qof* and *Fei* appear as reflections of each other, just as humanity was created in the image of God (Genesis 1:27). The mystic might consider these or other associations at the beginning of the day, throughout the day, and at its conclusion, with the hope of understanding the spiritual application of those concepts within the material world.

When casting lots for the purpose of seeking advice/guidance, in addition to the attributes and associations of the randomly selected lot, one's entire psyche should be utilized during the interpretation phase, to produce the most-useful guidance or to decide the best way forward. The interpretation should consist of a balance between one's intuitive impressions, and an analytical appraisal of the connections, rationalizations, and synchronicities between the presented attributes and the question/situation being considered. Chance does not replace reason, so after deciding on a question, deductive reasoning should be utilized throughout the process.

Begin the reading by selecting a question. If you are casting lots to answer questions for others, you are likely to be asked about relationships, careers, and other topics that are of major concern to a person's mundane life. Questions such as "*Does this person want to be in a relationship with me?*," "*Will I get a promotion?*," or "*Should I do such and such thing?*" can be most effectively answered by initially applying deductive reasoning to narrow down a conclusion, which can then be considered intuitively. The other person also has intuition and likely already knows the answer to the question they want you to cast lots about.

You can begin the divination process by asking *the person* the exact question they just asked you in order to get some background information and to gain a better understanding of the situation. As the person responds to your question, you may pick up subconscious clues or impressions that will influence your intuition during the interpretative aspects of the reading. When the person describes their intuitive feelings about the situation (e.g., "*Yes, I do think the person is interested in beginning a relationship with me*"), you can follow up by asking, "*Why do you feel that way?*" The person will likely provide you with both objective reasons for their belief and intuitive feelings. You can then deduce, on the basis of the person's feelings, whether the belief is reasonable before even *Casting a Lot* or beginning the reading.

When considering a subjective question involving facts that are not known, intuitive feelings are used to estimate the unknown variables in order to reach a reasonable conclusion. As with all forms of divination, the diviner does not *see into the future* but utilizes their mental faculties (psyche) to contemplate the situation; on the basis of their wisdom, discernment, and life experience, they produce a prediction as to what seems most probable, and then offer suggestions and advice to aid the questioner in selecting the best way moving forward.

Intuition refers to instinctive feelings or natural/inherent insights that are already perceived or understood. These impressions are expressed on a subconscious level and may seem like truth, even though rational evidence for such feelings is not consciously understood. The *Sefirah* of *Binah* refers both to Understanding (gaining mastery over a concept/topic) and Intuitive Intelligence. The Intuitive Intelligence describes the innate and instinctual understanding of morals and principles that people are born with, which account for different cultures that have never had contact with each other developing similar concepts, such as a belief in a God, the use of language, or the formation of a society.

The Intuitive Intelligence associated with the *Sefirah* of *Binah* could be described as the means to which the Spirit of Wisdom communicates with one's soul. However, not everything in a person's subconscious mind is the product of divine revelation. Through contemplation and during times of intense emotions, people can program their subconscious minds with incorrect beliefs or maladaptive behaviors (or both). The word *intuition* comes from the Latin word *intueri*, which means to *look at*, *consider*, or *contemplate*. Our understandings (subconscious beliefs) and intuition are the result of the things we have considered in the past and have accepted as the truth. This process can aid us in acquiring wisdom, or it could affect our self-esteem or confidence or cause us to develop phobias.

Understanding and Wisdom (*Binah* and *Chokmah*) is at the top of the Kabbalistic Tree of Life, because mastery of these traits is critical to our interactions within the world and our general happiness. Psychological development begins with the introduction of *knowledge* (*Daat*), which represents basic information, facts, or trivia. In the Garden of Eden, Adam and Eve ate from the Tree of Knowledge of Good and Evil; this simply made them *aware* of those concepts (facts/knowledge), but they did not have mastery over them.

By contemplating (comprehending) facts/knowledge/information, humans can gain an intuitive understanding of the principles being considered. The person ingrains the information into his/her long-term memory, or programs the belief into his/her subconscious mind; once this information is *understood* (accepted as truth on a subconscious level), it will intuitively/instinctually be acted upon. The proper application of one's understanding is what describes *wisdom*. Because this process occurs naturally and continually, purposeful development through mystical contemplation is an excellent method for obtaining both mental and spiritual growth.

Since human intuition could either represent guidance from the divine or be the product of one's own ingrained belief system, distinguishing whether the intuitive impressions are coming from the Spirit or one's own subconscious may be challenging. However, even if the Spirit subtly suggests a concept to you, we are not placed in the world to be told what to do. We are given free will and are expected to make our own decisions, so that we can learn discernment, obtain wisdom, and develop sound judgment. It does not matter if your feelings are prompted by the Spirit or your own intuition; the feelings should be interpreted and put to the most positive use, regardless of their origin.

After deciding on a question, cast/draw a lot from the container and then contemplate its attributes by looking at the side facing you. The remainder of this book will list several attributes and associations with the different Hebrew letters. These qualities/concepts will give you a place to begin and will help you formulate interpretations. The more you practice mystical contemplation or divination using Hebrew lots (*Goralot*), the more familiar with the lots/letters you will become. With time and practice, you will develop your own meanings, associations, and synchronicities, and the process will flow instinctually/intuitively. At the end of this chapter there is a Characteristics Key, which explains the different categories of attributes and the information associated with the different Hebrew letters that will be then be explore individually.

There are many mystical connections and associations with each Hebrew letter that you can draw from while formulating an interpretation of a lot. Which attribute should you look at first, and which information is the most correct? There is no right answer. The skill or art form you are developing is not a matter of memorizing answers or outcomes; it is about learning to use your psyche and making rational use of your intuitive feelings. Whatever the lot causes you to think about, or what you feel is most applicable to the question, is the concept that you should explore and consider.

After evaluating the situation, deciding on a question, *Casting a Lot*, and formulating an initial intuitive response, those different aspects must be organized into a rational solution that can be applied to the situation. For example, if someone is worried that their efforts are going unnoticed at work, they might ask for advice about how to get their actions recognized. You could begin by gathering more information about the situation, such as why the person thinks they are being overlooked and what the environment at work is like. What does the person *think* about the situation, and how do they *feel* about it? You can then *Cast a Lot*, which will provide you with several different randomly selected attributes that you can apply to the question.

For example, if the *Tet* Lot was selected, you might consider attributes such as *Womb/Container*, *Serpent/False Witness,* and *Yesod/Foundation*. Select an attribute and then try to creatively relate it to the question or situation. Maybe the person is not being noticed at work because they are symbolically in a *container*, which might mean they are keeping things bottled up inside (not expressing themselves enough), or maybe they are isolated at work (stuck in a cubicle away from the other employees). Perhaps a baby metaphor could be used to describe the person developing ideas in the womb that they are about to give birth to (manifest) at work. Comparing such symbolic interpretations to your understanding and the background information provided should help your intuition *feel* if these concepts and interpretations are plausible.

Maybe there is a *serpent* (a competing employee) who is bearing *false witness* (sabotaging, spreading rumors, bad-mouthing) about the person's work. When developing a solution, you might focus on the person's work ethic as a solid *foundation* to build upon. Advise them to be confident in the skills they have *contained* within them and encourage them to get out from behind the cubicle and interact with the other employees—so that they will witness the person's work for themselves, and the *serpent* will not be able to say anything bad against the person (1 Peter 2:12). *Yesod* is the location of the Chymical Wedding (Mystical Union), and the ninth Hebrew Letter, meaning womb, could imply transformation and rebirth, or alchemical analogies could be used to discuss burning off the dross (experiencing unpleasantness) in the process of purifying gold and producing the Philosopher's Stone (goal).

Perhaps one of the attributes in this book will seem more related to the situation than the others, or you may come up with your own completely unique solution, such as ignoring all the information in this book and thinking of an English word or concept that starts with the same letter as the lot that was drawn. The objective of the divinatory process is to stimulate your creativity in order to brainstorm outside-the-box solutions to the question or situation. You want to make rational use of your subjective feelings in order to gain insights that may have otherwise gone unnoticed or been overlooked. Regardless of the selected lot, always remain positive. Even if your intuition gives you a feeling of dread, you must turn that feeling into something optimistic. There are no bad lots. If something seems negative or as if it expresses bad news, figure out how to make positive use of that information. Give the person (or yourself) hope and encouragement and develop a plan for success.

If a reading seems to convey bad or unwanted news, remember, it is not showing you the future—it is showing you only possibilities to consider. If something appears to be negative, consider it as a warning and devise a plan to avoid the negative outcome. Incorporate that information into your reading, figure out how to avoid the negative outcome, select a goal, and decide on the best way to move forward. Develop a concept / goal / desired outcome, outline the necessary steps (create a plan) for its achievement, begin working toward the goal (so that the plan begins to take shape), and cause your dreams to become a reality (manifest your intensions / cause the word/idea to become flesh). This approach follows the four stages/worlds of the Kabbalah: Conception (idea/goal), Creation (develop a plan), Formation (implement the plan / work toward the goal), Action (manifest your intent / bring it to fruition / harvest the results).

Divination is not about seeing into the future by supernatural means; it is about receiving guidance from the divine (or your own intuition) and gaining insight to help you understand and comprehend a situation, so that you can apply wisdom and pursue the best possible outcome. Life is about continued growth; you should always be setting and working toward goals, growing in wisdom, and using your gifts (Lot/Fate/Destiny) to serve God and aid your neighbor (Matthew 12:30–31).

After drawing a lot and contemplating its attributes, you might choose to carry that lot with you as a good luck charm (*Segulah*) or wear it as a Talisman (*Kame'ah*)—then you will have it with you all day to reflect upon its meanings. By noting the synchronicities and coincidental occurrences that happen while you are carrying a certain lot/Talisman, you may develop your own unique meanings, superstitions, or associations that you can use in future readings and contemplations.

CHARACTERISTICS KEY

- **Letter:** Shows the spelling of the Hebrew letter.
- **Transliteration:** Shows the English equivalent of the spelling.
- **English Letter:** Shows the equivalent English letter.
- **Sound:** The sound or sounds of the letter.
- **Gematria value:** The numerical value of the Hebrew letter.
- **Reduced value:** The Gematrical value of the letter reduced to a number between 1 and 10.
- **Etz Chayim Sefirot:** The related *Sefirah* (Emanation) on the Kabbalistic Tree of Life
- **10 Commandments:** The Commandment associated with the reduced Gematrical value.
- **Name value:** The Gematrical value of the spelling of the letter.
- **Name meaning:** The meaning or mystical interpretation of the letter.
- **Sequential number:** The number of the letter of the alef-bet placed in numerical order (1–22).
- **Sefer Yetzirah classification:** The category of the letter according to the Book of Formation.
- **Sefer Yetzirah attribute:** The attribute associated with the letter in the Book of Formation.
- **Hermetic Tree Path:** The connecting path on the Hermetic version of the Tree of Life.
- **Hermetic Tarot:** The associated Tarot card in the Hermetic System.
- **Lurianic Tree Path:** The connecting path on the Lurianic version of the Tree of Life.
- **Kabbalah Cube of Space:** The connecting path/location of the cube in the Sefer Yetzirah.
- **Numerical Tarot:** The Tarot card based on the value of the card matching the Hebrew letter.
- **Constructed Gematria:** The mystical construction of the Hebrew letter and its associated values.

- **Prefix/suffix:** How the letter is used in the Hebrew language.
- **Mystical associations:** Provides attributes and associations to the letter, to understand its symbolism in order to use the information during divinatory interpretations or mystical contemplations/meditations.
- **Talisman symbolism:** Provides a summary of the symbolism on each lot/Talisman (Goralot, Segulot, Kame'ot).

THE LETTER *Alef*

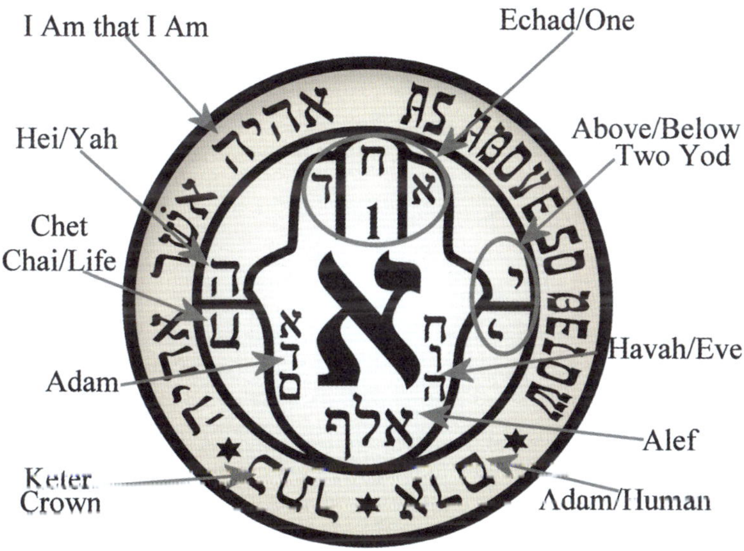

Letter: Alef, Lamed, Fei

Transliteration: Alef

English Letter: A

Sound: Silent letter (takes on the sound of the vowel marks)

Gematria Value: 1

Reduced Value: 1

Etz Chayim Sefirot: Keter

Ten Commandments: I am the LORD your God; you shall have no other gods besides me

Name Value: Alef 1 + Lamed 30 + Fei 80 = 12 = 3

Name Meaning: Ox (pictograph) / man / worker (Adam)

Sequential Number: 1

Sefer Yetzirah Classification: 3 Mothers

Sefer Yetzirah Attribute: Equilibrium

Hermetic Tree Path: Keter-Binah

Hermetic Tarot: Fool

Lurianic Tree Path: Geburah-Chesed

Kabbalah Cube of Space: Atmospheric air

Numerical Tarot: Magician

Constructed Gematria: Yod, Vav, Yod = 26 = 8

Prefix/Suffix: First-person singular masculine future tense (I will)

Mystical Associations: *Alef* is the first letter in the Hebrew *Alef-bet* and is also the first letter in the name of God *(Alef, Hei, Yod, Hei)* revealed to Moses at the *Burning Bush* (Exodus 3:14). It represents *HaShem* on a personal level, since AHVH is the first-person future conjugation of the verb "to be" (he will continue to exist / the eternal one) and reminds us the YHVH is our *Elohim,* and YHVH is *One* (Deuteronomy 6:4). The Hebrew letter *Yod* is related to *Alef,* because *Yod* has a value of 10 and reduces to 1, but *Yod* is also used to symbolize the Tetragrammaton—since it is the first letter of YHVH, just as *Alef* is the first letter of the first-person future conjugation of it.

Another divine name, known as the *Secret Name of God*, is obtained by taking the first letters of the Hebrew words describing *Heaven and Earth* in the first sentence of the first book of the Bible (Genesis 1:1). It is used in the word *Et* (*Alef, Tav*), which is an untranslated word used to indicate the *definite direct object* of *the* heavens *and the* (*Vav, Alef, Tav*) earth. The letters AHVH (*Alef, Hei, Vav, Hei*) means *I will constitute* and contains the same letters used in God's two most holy names (YHVH and AHYH). The *definite direct object* identifier *Et* (*Alef, Tav*) is the first and the last letters of the *Alef-bet*, so it implies that the *Elohim* who *constituted* heaven and the earth was the First and the Last, the Beginning and the End, and everything in between. When the Hebrew letter *Mem* is added to *et* (*Alef, Tav*), it spells the word *Emet* (*Alef, Mem, Tav*), which means *truth* (John 17:17, 2 Timothy 2:15).

Alef is a silent letter, which takes its sound from the vowel symbols around it. This is metaphoric of God, who is mostly silent in his communication with people but is described or given sound/voice by the smaller seemingly insignificant dots (*niqqud*) next to him—human prophets who deliver his message. Although the *Alef* does not make a sound, there is a great deal of mystical significance contained within it. The numerical value of One is significant, not just because the LORD our God is One and the first commandment states not to have any other Gods besides him, but because One is the first number and is the very start (both mathematically and alphabetically). It is linked to the first *Sefirah* (*Keter*/Crown) and represents the Eternal One (AHYH) prior to creation—before he *Constituted* (AHVH) the heaven and the earth and demonstrated his *Love* (AHBH) by creating paradise.

The first letter of the Bible is *Bet*, which is used in the word *B'reishit* (In the beginning) and describes *creation*, but the *Alef* existed prior to that event (A comes before B in the alphabet). In the *Great Arcanum* (Levi 2000), Eliphas Levi determined that the Great Mysteries are summed up by Jesus's prayer to God, which states that all their followers become One just as they are One (John 17:11). The objective of life is to comprehend God, be conformed to his image (Genesis 1:26, Romans 8:28), and be united with him (Revelation 19:7).

The letter *Alef* shows this union and connection between *Heaven and Earth* (AHVH) in its construction. The Hebrew letter *Alef* is mystically said to be constructed of two *Yod* and a *Vav*, with the *Yod* above representing heaven, and a *Yod* below representing the earth. The *Vav*, which in Hebrew serves to connect concepts (English word *and*) and connects the above with the below—just as *Tiferet* (which is the 6th *Sefirot* and is related to the *Vav* [sixth letter]) connects *Keter* (Heaven) and *Malkut* (Earth/Kingdom).

The Gematrical value of *Yod, Vav, Yod* (the letters used to form the symbol of *Alef*) is 26 (*Yod* 10 + *Vav* 6 + *Yod* 10 = 26), which is the same *value* as the Tetragrammaton (*Yod* 10 + *Hei* 5 + *Vav* 6 + *Hei* 5 = 26). This symbol shows the connection between God and humanity, since humans were made in the Image of God (Genesis 1:26). This can be seen in the shape of the *Alef*; if the *Vav* is viewed to serve as a mirror, with the higher *Yod* representing God in Heaven, and the lower *Yod* symbolizing humans on Earth having been made in the image of God.

The *Alef* is also used as the first letter in the divine names *Elohim* (God/Judges), El (God), and *Adonai* (Master/Lord). When *Alef* is combined with *shin* it spells *fire* (*Alef, shin*/ash), which represents God as a *consuming fire* (Deuteronomy 4:24, Hebrews 12:29). This *fire* (*Alef, Shin*), when combined with alternative letters from the sacred name *Yah* (*Yod, Hei*: a shortened form of the Tetragrammaton), produces *man* (*Alef, Yod, Shin*) and *woman* (*Alef, Shin, Hei*). The Hebrew letter *Yod* is used as a symbol of the masculine Tetragrammaton, so it being added to *fire* (*Alef, Shin*) produces *man* (*Alef, Yod, Shin*). The Hebrew letter *Hei* is associated with the feminine Spirit/Breath of God, so when it is added to *fire* (*Alef, Shin*), it produces *woman* (*Alef, Shin, Hei*). Since *HaShem* created the Woman Wisdom as the first of his works, there was both a divine male and female (*Yod, Hei*) present at the time of creation (Proverbs 8:22); when God said, "*Let us make humanity in our image*," "*male and female he created them*" (Genesis 1:26–27).

The word *Adam* (*Alef, Dalet, Mem*) also begins with an *Alef*, just as Adam's creation started with *Elohim* (*Alef, Vav, Lamed, Hei, Yod, Mem*). Prior to modern Hebrew, the letter *Alef* was a pictograph of an ox. The ox is a beast of burden and is symbolic of Adam having been created for the purpose of tending to the garden (Genesis 2:15). The letter *Alef* is spelled *Alef, Lamed, Fei* and can be mystically interpreted to represent the need to contemplate the concepts contained within the letter *Alef*, in order to *learn* (*Lamed*) about *HaShem* and serve as his *arm* (*Lamed*) worker (ox/man) on Earth. One can contemplate/hear the words of the silent God's *mouth* (*Pei*) or be blown and *scattered* (*Pei*) as those who are disobedient (Genesis 11:8). The value of the spelling of *Alef* (*Alef* 1 + *Lamed* 30 + *Fei* 80 = 12, and 1 + 2 = 3) reduces to 3, implying that those who explore the mystical/secret aspects of *Alef* can be carried by *HaShem* along their journey, just as the *camel* (*Gimel*, 3) carries its rider safely across the desert.

When used as a prefix to a verb, *Alef* denotes the first-person future tense *I will*. At the Burning Bush, *HaShem* identified himself to Moses as *Eheyeh Asher Eheyeh* (I will be / will exist, therefore/whom, I will be / will exist). Since he was speaking with Moses at the time, it is understood that *HaShem* existed at that time, so the sentiment was that he was the God who actually exists (in contrast to idols) and will continue to exist for eternity (the *Alef Tav*, First and Last, Beginning and End).

In the Sefer Yetzirah, *Alef* is listed as one of the three Mother Letters and is associated with the Primordial Element of Air, which serves as an equilibrium/ balance between *fire* (*Shin*) and *water* (*Mem*). On the *Kabbalistic Tree of Life* (*Etz Chayim*), *Alef* is associated with the *Sefirah* of *Keter* at the top of the Middle Pillar of the Kabbalah. *Fire* (*Shin*) is associated with the *Pillar of Severity*, and learning through experience (trial by fire), and *water* (*Mem*) is associated with the *Pillar of Mercy*, which is related to learning through contemplation (the sea of the subconscious / water baptism). The Middle Pillar represents the perfect balance between fire and water, justice and mercy, action and contemplation.

Since Hebrew letters contain multiple associations and values, the Kabbalah uses the *Alef* in more than one manner. *Alef* represents the number One (*Echad/ Alef, Chet, Dalet*) and the first emanation, which associates it with the first of the *Sefirot*. Beyond its use as a number, it is also linked to one of the 22 connecting paths of the Tree of Life, which are each associated with a specific letter of the Hebrew *Alef-bet*. The Kabbalistic Tree of Life consists of 10 emanations (numbers) and 22 paths that connect them (letters). The connecting path assigned to the letter *Alef* is different both in the Hermetic Qabbalah (used by occultists) and the Lurianic Kabbalah (used by Jewish mystics). On the Lurianic Kabbalah, the *Alef* is associated with the Path connecting *Geburah* (Strength, Power, Justice) and *Chesed* (Mercy, Covenant, Loving kindness) and serves as a balance between the two opposites, in the same way that *Alef* serves as an equilibrium within the three Mother Letters (Air/*Alef* as the balance and ingredient both in Fire/*Shin* and Water/*Mem*).

On the Hermetic Qabbalah, the *Alef* is associated with the Path connecting *Keter* (Crown) and *Chokmah* (Wisdom) and is associated with the Fool Tarot card (the Major Arcana of the Tarot counts from 0 to 21 instead of 1 to 22). This path can be interpreted as Adam at the beginning of his journey, when he was given the possibility to understand God and his relationship to him (having been created in his image), but in a stage of innocence and naivety—as Adam Kadmon steps out of *Keter*/Heaven (Eden) into the physical world. This could also represent the *fire* (*Alef, shin*) of the *Yah* (*Yod, Hei*), *HaShem* and the Spirit of Wisdom (*Chokmah*) working together to create humans in their image. The Tarot card with the same gematria value as *Alef* is the Magician card, which depicts a human serving as a conduit of *HaShem* (his arm / worker / ox / representation on Earth), representing God giving dominion over the earth to humans and making them partners in creation.

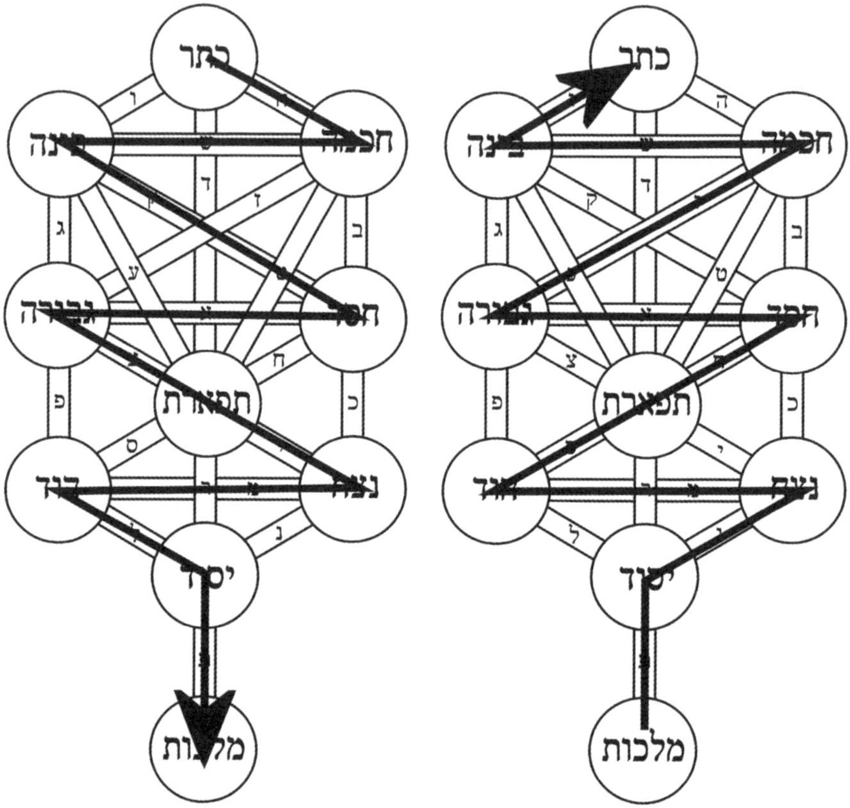

When using the Kabbalah for pathworking, the Path of the Flaming Sword (Lightning Path) is used to demonstrate the process of creation (from *Keter* to *Malkut*), and the Mystical Ascent shows the spiritual growth and progress of the mystic leaving *Malkut* (the earth) to return to *Keter* (Heaven).

The Lightning Path (Path of the Flaming Sword) and the Mystic's Ascent can be viewed together in association with the Tarot. The Fool card represents the person at the beginning of their journey, prior to gaining Wisdom and Understanding, and returning to *Keter* (Heaven / receiving the Crown) through the Magician card. In the Hermetic Qabbalah, the Magician card represents someone who has gained mastery over all the principles in the Kabbalah. The Hermetic Qabbalah places the Magician card on the Path connecting *Binah*

(Understanding) and *Keter* (Crown), which is the final position on the Path of Mystical Ascent.

Talisman Symbolism: The talisman associated with the letter *Alef* has *Alef* with a value of 1 on front and a *Yod* with the value of 10 on the back. The *Alef* represents *Keter*, and the *Yod* represents *Malkut*; it represents Heaven and Earth, Spirit and Manifestation, the starting point and finish line. The talisman contains the divine name *Eheiah Asher Eheiah* (I am that I am) and includes the words *Keter*/Crown, Adam, *Havah*/Eve, *Alef*. It expresses the concept of "*as above, so below*," humans having been created in the image of God (*B'tzelem Elohim*), and includes the complementary opposites of male/Adam and female/Eve, who together make one whole.

On the right side there is a *Yod* above and a *Yod* below, which is suggestive of the construction of the letter *Alef*, and on the opposite side there is a *Hei* above and a *Chet* below. Reading the *Yod Hei* above the line spells *Yah*, which is a name of God and mystically expresses the connection between the divine masculine and feminine (as a contrast to the worldly versions of Adam and Eve). The heavenly couple is above, and the worldly couple is below. The *Chet Yod* on the lower half of the Talisman spells the Hebrew world *Chai*, which means *life* and is related to *Havah*/Eve, whose name means mother of all the living. *Chai* has a *Gematria* value of 18, which reduces to 9, which connects it to the *Sefirah* of *Yesod*, the location of the Chymical Wedding (union of the Red King and White Queen), and is the place where the male and female come together to create life. Adam (*Alef, Dalet, Mem*) also has a value of 9 (1 + 4 + 40 = 45 = 4 + 6 = 9), and Eve (*Chet, Vav, Hei*) has a value of 6 (8 + 6 + 5 = 19 = 10 = 1 + 0 = 1); joined together, they are both 10 and 1 (both sides of this *Kame'ah*).

THE LETTER *Bet*

Letter: Bet, Yod, Tav

Transliteration: Bet

English Letter: B, V

Sounds: Beginning, veil

Gematria Value: 2

Etz Chayim Sefirot: Chokmah

Ten Commandments: Do not make idols or provoke God to jealousy

Name Value: 2 + 10 + 400 = 7

Name Meaning: House/home/family

Sequential Number: 2

Sefer Yetzirah Classification: 7 Double

Sefer Yetzirah Attribute: Wisdom/folly

Hermetic Tree Path: Keter-Binah

Hermetic Tarot: Magician

Lurianic Tree Path: Chokmah-Chesed

Kabbalah Cube: Height

Numerical Tarot: High Priestess

Constructed Gematria: N/A

Grammar: Prefix/preposition (in, with, by)

Mystical Associations: The first letter of the first word of the Bible begins with the letter *Bet*. In the word *B'reishit* (in the beginning), the Hebrew letter *Bet* is used as a prefix to the word *Reshit* (beginning/head/RAShYT) and is used as a preposition to denote the word *in*. The letter *Alef* represents the primordial cause or *Eheieh* (AHYH / I am), existing prior to creation (or both). The letter *Bet* represents the *beginning* (first act) of creation. *HaShem*'s first creation was the Woman Wisdom (Proverbs 8:22). She is the *Ruach Ha-Kodesh* (Holy Spirit), *Ruach Elohim* (Spirit of God), and the *Shekinah* (Indwelling Presence), who was told to make her dwelling among the tents of Israel. She dwelled within the tent of the Tabernacle (Sirach 24:10). She is also referred to as the *Spirit of Truth* (John 16:13, 1 Esdras 4:37, Proverbs 23:23), and the *Spirit of Wisdom* (Isaiah 11:2; Ephesians 1:17; Wisdom 1:6, 7:7). She is the spirit who inspired scripture (2 Peter 1:21) and is even referred to as the scripture/Torah itself (Baruch 4:1). *Bet* is the second letter of the Hebrew *Alef-bet*, its gematria value is two, and it refers to the second *Sefirah* of *Chokmah* (Wisdom).

The word *Bet* means *House* or *Tent* and refers to the *Indwelling Spirit* uniting with the souls of individuals (Proverbs 24:3, 2 Timothy 1:14, 1 Corinthians 6:19, Wisdom 7:27). The *Spirit* (*Ruach*) is feminine, and the concept of a woman representing the house/home of her spouse applies both to those spiritually united (Isaiah 54:5, Revelation 22:17) and to human marriages (Genesis 18:9, Titus 2:5, Proverbs 14:1, Wisdom 8:16). Human women, such as Sarah, were associated with their spouse's home/tent; the man was expected to go out and work in the field and to bring back substance for his household/tent, which was ruled by his spouse/helpmate (1 Esdras 4:22). Adam worked by the sweat of his face to provide for his wife/household (Genesis 3:19), and he listened to her (Genesis 3:6, 17). Abraham also listened to Sarah (Genesis 21:10, 21:12), as all humans should listen to the Spirit dwelling within them.

The Sefer Yetzirah categorizes the letter *Bet* as one of the seven double letters. The letters are considered double because the letters can make two different sounds (*Bet* can be pronounced as either a *B* or a *V*). *The Sefer Yetzirah* expands on this concept of duality by assigning attributes with opposite meanings to each of the letters. It associates the letter *Bet* with the concepts of wisdom and folly. Those two concepts are also contrasted against each other in the book of Proverbs, where Wisdom sets up her house on seven pillars (Proverbs 9:1), and the Woman Folly sits at the door of her house calling to the simpleminded by telling them that "*stolen waters is sweet, and bread eaten in secret is delicious*" (Proverbs 9:14–18).

The letter *Alef* represents a perfect union of the above and the below, and *Bet* represents a similar concept; only the opposites are within creation, and they need to be balanced appropriately. Humans, as a part of creation, are expected to differentiate between opposites, such as good and evil (Genesis 3:22, Deuteronomy 30:15), wisdom and folly (Proverbs 9), and kabbalists seek to rectify such traits within themselves, so they can walk before God and be perfect (Genesis 17:1).

The value of *Bet* is 2 and relates to the second commandment; it tells the Israelites not to create or worship idols, which would provoke God to jealousy. As a means of understanding the covenant between God and humanity, a parallel is made and an analogy to the institution of marriage is used. The Ten Commandments warn against committing adultery against one's human spouse; worshiping idols is the equivalent of committing adultery against one's spiritual spouse. Those who worship idols stray from their homes/spouse/households, and the house of the strange woman (idol) leads them to death/hell/sheol (Proverbs 2:18, 7:27, 9:18).

As a numerical value, *Bet* is associated with the second *Sefirah* and second commandment, but as a Letter, in the Lurianic Tree of Life, it is associated with the path that connects the *Sefirah* of *Chokmah* (Wisdom) and *Chesed* (Loving kindness / Covenant). This reaffirms *Bet*'s connection to the attributes of Wisdom and the covenant of marriage. The equivalent numerical value in the Major Arcana of the Tarot is the High Priestess card, which in the Rider-Waite deck shows the *Shekinah* sitting behind the veil within Solomon's Temple (Sirach 24:10, 1 Corinthians 3:16).

On the Hermetic version of the Tree, *Bet* is assigned to the path connecting *Keter* (Crown) and *Binah* (Understanding). After *HaShem* created Wisdom, the two worked together to create the material world (Proverbs 8:30; Sirach 1:4, 24:3) and humanity (Genesis 1:26). The *Sefirah* of *Binah* is associated with the physical creation of the universe, so the path connecting *Binah* and *Keter* would represent the blueprints of the architect being used in creation (the creation aspect of the concept), just as the Magician/humans are partners in creation. The Hermetic Qabbalah associates the Magician Tarot card with this path. The Magician card represents an ideal conduit/servant/apostles/disciple/adept that manifest *HaShem*'s will on Earth through human actions. In the Path of the Flaming Sword and Mystical Ascent, the Magician card would represent the perfected human or final Adam (1 Corinthians 15:45) that all humans should strive to become (Romans 12:2).

Talisman Symbolism: The name *Yah*, which is associated with the *Sefirah* of *Chokmah*, also represents the mystical union between the divine male and female (the *Yod* and the *Hei*, or the *Alef* and the *Bet*). Simeon was the second Son of Israel and is known for rescuing his sister Dinah from her rapist/kidnapper. Judith, who is the heroine of the Jewish people during the Second Temple period, was a descendant of Simeon. The word *Ishah* (Wife) in written near the *Bet*, as a reminder that the wife is the center of the family and is the home.

THE LETTER *Gimel*

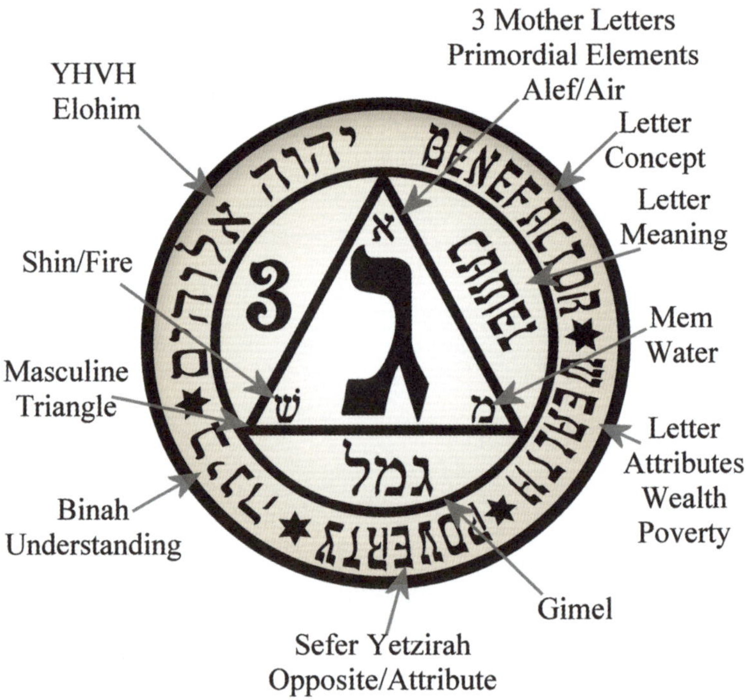

Letter: Gimel, Mem, Lamed

Transliteration: Gimel

English Letter: G

Sounds: Great, journey

Gematria Value: 3

Etz Chayim Sefirot: Binah

Ten Commandments: Do not misuse/profane (treat with emptiness) the Holy Name

Name Value: 3 + 30 + 40 = 10 = 1

Name Meaning: Camel/recompense/benefactor

Sequential Number: 3

Sefer Yetzirah Classification: 7 Double

Sefer Yetzirah Attribute: Wealth/poverty

Hermetic Tree Path: High Priestess

Hermetic Tarot: Keter-Tiferet

Lurianic Tree Path: Binah-Geburah

Kabbalah Cube: Depth

Numerical Tarot: The Empress

Constructed Gematria: Vav, Yod

Prefix/Suffix: N/A

Mystical Associations: The third letter in the Hebrew *Alef-bet* is *Gimel*, which means *camel*, *benefactor*, or *recompense*. Recompense can refer to either a punishment or a reward for one's actions. When Adam and Eve sinned, they were recompensed by being forced to walk away from the garden, but recompense can also refer to the reward/benefit/blessing received following the deliverance from danger (making amends/restoring/rectifying). *Gimel* deals with consequences of behavior (punishments and rewards / blessings and curses) but also symbolizes God's willingness to carry us through our difficult times. Through the Holy Spirit, one is sealed for the day of redemption (Ephesians 4:30), and according to God's will, she will carry you along your journey, as the camel carries its rider safely across the desert. Jesus said it was easier for a camel to go through the eye of a needle than it was for a rich man to enter the Kingdom of Heaven (Mark 10:25–27)—his point being, what is too difficult for humans can be accomplished with the assistance of God (Mark 10:27)

The Gematrical value of *Gimel* is 3. According to the account of Creation expressed in scripture and Kabbalah, the Woman Wisdom came forth from God (Sirach 24:3), just as *Chavah* (Eve) was taken directly out of Adam (Genesis 2:22–24). *Chokmah* (Wisdom) is the second of the *Sefirot*, which emerged from *Keter*, and represents the divine female. The third *Sefirah* (*Binah*/Understanding) represents the point where the two worked together to create the physical world, in accordance with the pattern of the below being a reflecting of the above. *Chavah* was taken directly from the same being as Adam, with the purpose of them reuniting and working together as one (Genesis 2:24).

Gimel represents divine parenting; as children progress through life, they are recompensed (rewarded) with different levels of wealth or poverty in order to stimulate and reinforce growth and change. The camel is symbolic of the Spirit of Wisdom, who guides/carries us on our journeys (Wisdom 10:1–18); she is the camel who can pass through the eye of a needle and helps humans accomplish what might otherwise seem impossible (John 14:26).

The binding of Isaac occurred on the third day (Genesis 22:4). It was also on the third day that Levi and Simeon rescued their sister Dinah from her abductors (Genesis 34:25). The third day was the day of the burnt offering, which completed the sacrifice (Leviticus 7:17), and on the third day the Lord came down from Sinai in the sight of all the people (Exodus 19:11). On the third day, Esther went before the king and was granted life before going on to save her people (Esther 5:1), and the apostles taught that on the third day, God raised Jesus from the dead and caused him to be seen (Acts 10:40).

The value of the three letters that spell *Gimel* (*Gimel, Mem, Lamed*) equals 73, which reduces to 10, the number of *Sefirot*, the number for a minyan, and the number of righteous needed for a city to be escape judgment (Genesis 18:32). The third commandment is not to use *HaShem*'s name in vain. The word used in the verse (Exodus 20:7) means *emptiness*, *deception*, *falsehood*, or *worthless* and means not to falsely swear in *HaShem*'s name, use it for deception, or treat it with disrespect. The verse includes the statement that those who disrespect the name will not go unpunished.

The third *Sefirah* is *Binah* (Understanding / Intuitive Intelligence), which deals with creation and *HaShem*'s plan being put into motion (Matthew 13:35). Within the plan, the Holy Spirit guides *HaShem*'s followers. This cycle is repeated by each generation as they embark on their own journey of self-discovery, learning to discern between good and evil, facing discipline, and growing through adversity. While challenges are inevitable during the journey (1 Peter 4:12), those who are given the gift of the Holy Spirit are guided along their path as a camel carries its rider across the desert or through the eye of the needle. When Abraham obeyed *HaShem*'s calling and began his journey to the Promised Land, a camel served as his vehicle (Genesis 12:16, 24:61).

The *Sefer Yetzirah* lists *Gimel* as one of the seven double letters, because it can make the sound of either a *G* or a *J*. The opposite attributes associated with *Gimel* are *wealth* and *poverty*, which are indicative of the blessings and curses one might experience while trying to navigate through the world. On the Lurianic Tree, *Gimel* represents the Path connecting *Binah* and *Geburah* and provides either strength (*Geburah*) and understanding (*Binah*) or recompense and correction (spiritual wealth/poverty). On the Hermetic Qabbalah, *Gimel* connects *Keter* and *Tiferet* and is associated with the High Priestess card. It shows the connection between Heaven and Earth, and God (*Keter*), the Spirit of Wisdom (High Priestess), and mankind (*Tiferet*) working together as partners in creation.

The Hebrew letter *Gimel* is constructed out of a *Vav* with a *Yod* attached to it, so that it appears to be a person walking (the *Yod* as the person's foot). The person's heart devises his/her way, but it is the LORD who directs the person's steps (Proverbs 3:6, 16:9). The combination of the *Yod* and *Vav* equals 7, which is the number of perfection, completion, and rest (Genesis 2:2, Revelation 5:6). In some styles of Hebrew lettering, *Gimel* appears to be constructed of *Yod* (hand) and *Zayin* (sword) and would represent the recompense associated with the Path connecting *Geburah* (Strength/Justice) and *Binah* (Understanding) on the Lurianic Tree. The value of *Yod* and *Zayin* is 8 (10 + 7 = 1 + 7 = 8), the same value as the Tetragrammaton.

On a dreidel, the letter *Gimel* stands for *GaDeL*, which means *great*, *grow*, or *develop*. When playing the game of dreidel, *Gimel* is the winning letter that allows the player to collect all the *gelt* (gold/chocolate coins) in the pot. The four letters on the dreidel are *Gimel*, *Nun*, *Shin*, and *Hei* and serve as abbreviations for the words *NeS*, *GaDeL*, *HaYaH*, *SheM* (a Great, Miracle, Happened, There), which refers to the miracle of Hanukkah and the liberation of the Temple. In later folklore, the miracle was said to be in relation to a single day's oil burning for eight days, but the original miracle was that the Maccabees where able to retake and rededicate the Temple of God in order to celebrate the eight-day holiday of *Sukkot*. Thus, the letter *Gimel* can represent God helping you obtain victory.

Talisman Symbolism: The divine name on the Talisman is YHVH *Elohim*, which in Jewish mysticism represents the union of the divine male and female, with YHVH representing the male aspect and *Elohim* representing the divine feminine. *Elah* (*Alef*, *Lamed*, *Hei*) is the Hebrew word for goddess, which is the root word of *Elohim*. The word *Binah* (the third *Sefirah*) is also written in Hebrew. Below the masculine triangle (with the point at the top) are the letters that spell *Gimel*. Camel is the meaning of the Letter, Benefactor is the attribute/concept associated with it, and the contrast between *Wealth* and *Poverty* is the opposite traits listed in the Sefer Yetzirah in relation to the letter *Gimel*. The Three Mother Letters (*Alef*, *Mem*, *Shin*) are at the corners of the triangle, which could also represent the Supernal Triangle of the Kabbalah, consisting of *Keter*, *Chokmah*, and *Binah*. These letters can represent the heavenly couple (*Alef*/Male, *Shin*/

Union, *Mem*/Female), or the *Fire* can represent the earthly male, *Water* with the earthly female, and the Air could represent the divine Spirit (YHVH *Elohim*) overseeing the union of the earthly couple.

THE LETTER *Dalet*

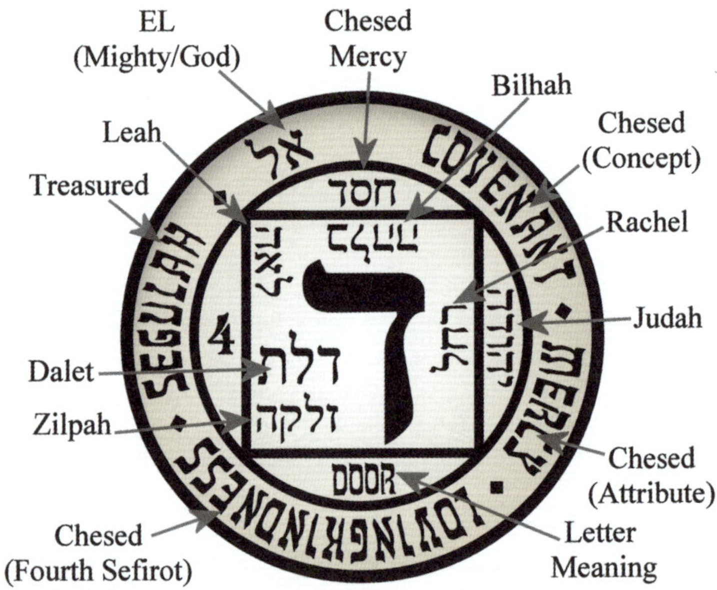

Letter: Dalet, Lamed, Tav

Transliteration: Dalet

English Letter: D

Sound: Door

Gematria Value: 4

Etz Chayim Sefirot: Chesed

Ten Commandments: Remember the Sabbath

Name Value: 4 + 30 + 400 = 434 = 4 + 3 + 4 = 11 = 1 + 1 = 2

Name Meaning: Door/poor/humble

Sequential Number: 4

Sefer Yetzirah Classification: Double

Sefer Yetzirah Attribute: Fruitfulness/impotence

Hermetic Tree Path: Chokmah-Binah

Hermetic Tarot: Empress

Lurianic Tree Path: Keter-Tiferet

Kabbalah Cube: East

Numerical Tarot: Emperor

Constructed Gematria: Vav, Vav (12 = 3)

Prefix/Suffix: N/A

Mystical Associations: The fourth letter in the Hebrew *Alef-bet* is *Dalet*, which means *door*, *poor*, or *humble*. The word *Dalet* is a feminine noun and represents women being the literal *doorway* into the physical world (they create life). Jesus taught both that he was the door for the lost sheep, and the concept that salvation comes from the Jews (John 4:22, 10:3, 7). He described the entrance to the kingdom as a narrow door/gate that people must strive to enter (Luke 13:24), and he assured that the door will be opened for those who seek (Matthew 7:8).

The Tanukh and Kabbalah teach that Jews are in a special covenant with God and serve as priests for the rest of the world (Exodus 19:6). Jews (Yehudim) are descendants of Israel's son Judah, whose name means "*praise*," and his mother Leah named him that because "*she conceived again and bore a son, and said, 'This time I will praise the Lord'; therefore she called his name Judah; then she ceased bearing*" (Genesis 29:35). The word Judah (YHVDH), is constructed in Hebrew by adding a *Dalet* to the *Name of God* (YHVH), representing that the Jews provide a *doorway* to *HaShem*, just as Jesus (who was a Jew from the line of Judah) taught (John 4:22) in the New Testament.

The value of the letter *Dalet* is 4 and is with the fourth commandment and the instruction to *remember the Sabbath and keep it holy* (Exodus 20:8). The fourth *Sefirah* is *Chesed* and represents *HaShem*'s loving kindness and mercy expressed to those in a covenant with him. Remembering the Sabbath is an aspect of the Covenant, which was compared to a marriage relationship (Jeremiah 31:32). On the Lurianic Tree, the letter *Dalet* is on the Path connecting *Tiferet* and *Keter*. The Major Arcana Tarot card with the numeric value of 4 is the Emperor card, which represents the Messiah serving as the doorway to heaven. On the Hermetic Qabbalah, the High Priestess fills that role. The Sabbath provides us with a taste of Heaven, and the *Olam HaBa* (world to come) is said to be an Eternal Sabbath that will be ushered in by the Messiah (a descendant of Judah/YHVDH).

On the Lurianic Tree of Life, the letter *Dalet* is represented by the Path connecting *Tiferet* and *Keter*. The Major Arcana Tarot card with the numeric value of 4 is the Emperor card, representing the Messiah (anointed ruler) having had all authority delegated to him (Ephesians 1:10; 1 Corinthians 15:27), so that the anointed king in the line of David (Luke 2:4) connects *Tiferet* and *Keter* and serves as the doorway to heaven—as the High Priestess (Spirit of Wisdom) does on the Path in the Hermetic Qabbalah.

On the Hermetic Tree, *Dalet* is on the Path connecting *Chokmah* and *Binah* and is associated with the Empress card. The Empress represents the *Shekinah*, who is the Anointing Spirit that guides the human Messiah (Emperor card). The Empress card can also represent femininity or women in general, who are the doorway into the physical world. It is through the doorway of the Empress that humans enter the physical world, and it is through the doorway of the Emperor (who grows out of the Philosopher's Stone) that they enter the Olam HaBa.

The value of the letters that spell *Dalet* equals 434, which reduces to 2 (*Chokmah*/Wisdom). The letter can be mystically viewed as being constructed of an upright *Vav* with a sideways *Vav* above it; this can be viewed as an open door, with the 12 Tribes (*Vav* + *Vav* = 6 + 6 = 12) being the doorway. The Empress is the Doorway to Life, the Emperor/Messiah is the Doorway to *Olam HaBa*, and the letter *Dalet* inserted in the name YHVH spells Judah (YHVDH). The Tribe of Judah is the doorway of the Messiah according to the promises made to David and Solomon. Four is the number of letters in the great name (Tetragrammaton), and these letters are associated with the Court cards and all four the suits of the Tarot (Yod/Wands, Hei/Cups, Vav/Swords, and Hei/Pentacles). The fourth *Sefirah* is *Chesed*, which means *Loving kindness* or *Mercy*. It is an attribute that is shown to those who are in a Covenant with *HaShem*. Four could also represent the four levels of interpretation of scripture (PaRDeS). In the *Sefer* Yetzirah, *Dalet* is listed as a Double Letter and is associated with the opposites of *Fruitfulness* and *Impotence*. It represents production, opening doors for success, or of the womb.

Talisman Symbolism: The divine name associated with the fourth *Sefirah* is *EL*, which refers to God as the Mighty One. *Segulah* is the word used to describe those in a covenant with God as being a "*Special Treasure*" to him. Above the square is the word *Chesed* (loving kindness), which is the title of the fourth *Sefirah* and expresses the concepts that those in a Covenant with God will be shown Mercy. On the right side (right hand) of the square is the Hebrew word Judah. To the left of the *Dalet* in a larger font are the three letters that spell *DaLeT*. Around the inside of the square (starting from the bottom and moving clockwise) are the words Zilpah, Leah, Rachel, and Bilhah, which are the four wives of Jacob who served as doorways (gave birth) to the 12 Tribes of Israel.

THE LETTER *Hei*

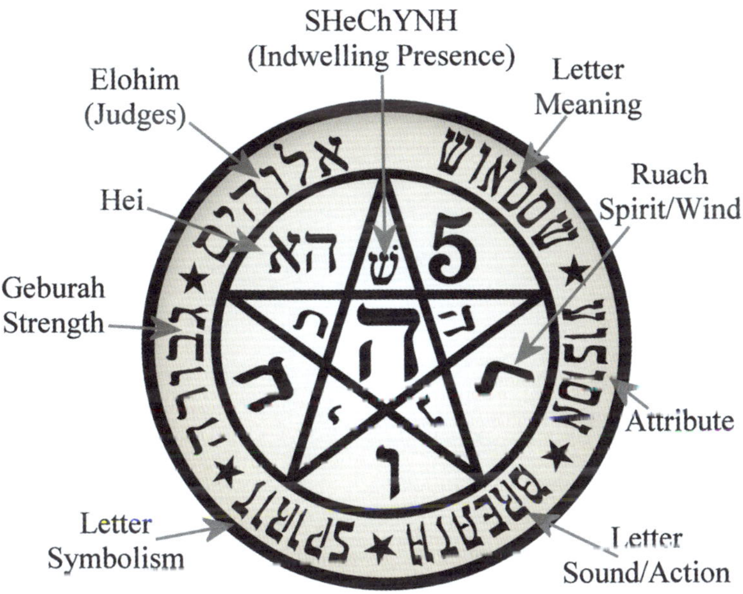

Letter: Hei, Alef

Transliteration: Hei/Hey/Heh Alef

English Letter: H

Sound: Hay

Gematria Value: 5

Reduced Value: 5

Etz Chayim Sefirot: Geburah

10 Commandments: Honor one's mother and father

Name Value: 5 + 1 = 6

Name Meaning: Breath/spirit/behold

Sequential Number: 5

Sefer Yetzirah Classification: 12 Single/Simple

Sefer Yetzirah Attribute: Speaking

Hermetic Tree Path: Chokmah-Tiferet

Hermetic Tarot: Emperor

Lurianic Tree Path: Keter-Chokmah

Kabbalah Cube Path: Chokmah-Tiferet

Numerical Tarot: High Priest

Constructed Gematria: Dalet supported by Yod (4 + 10 = 5)

Prefix/Suffix: Prefix, definite article / suffix, feminine gender of noun

Mystical Associations: The Hebrew Letter *Hei* can be used as the exclamation *Behold!* It draws one's attention and alerts them to something important that might have otherwise gone unnoticed. The Hebrew letter *Hei* has a value of 5, which is associated with the five times on the first day of creation (Genesis 1:3–5) that the word *Light* is mentioned. The letter *Hei* is constructed by adding a *Yod* to support a *Dalet*. The letter is associated with the Spirit of Wisdom (*Shekinah*), who opens a *Window* into the Mysteries of God and enlightens those who are in union with her (Wisdom 9:17–18). As a prefix, the letter *Hei* serves as the definite article. It endows the object with uniqueness and transforms it from an indefinite article into something specific. Taking the *Hei* from the last letter of the word *AdamaH* and breathing the *Breath* of Life into him transformed Adam from Red Clay into a *Living Soul* (*Chaiyim Nefesh*).

The letter *Hei* was added to the names of *AbraHam* and *SaraH* once they received the blessings of God. The letter *Hei* by itself is also used as an abbreviation for God (as a shortened form of *HaShem*). As a suffix, the *Hei* can denote the feminine gender of words, such as in *ShekinaH* (Indwelling Presence), *ChokmaH* (Wisdom), or *AdamaH* (Earth/Ground/Land). The Hebrew letter *Hei* is also used to represent *Breath* (*Ruach*) because the letter makes the sound of a strong exhalation. It is the *breath* that gives *life* to the spoken word.

The fifth *Sefirah* of the Kabbalah is *Geburah*, which represents *strength*, *justice*, or *judgment*. It is through the guidance of the Spirit of Wisdom that humans are able to master judgment and discernment (Proverbs 8:15–16). The fifth commandment is to love one's mother and father, which comes with the blessing of a long life. This commandment is applied to our human parents, but by PaRDeS, it can also reference our heavenly parents, God and his *Shekinah*, YHVH *Elohim*, YaH, *Yod Hei*, all of which have been mystically interpreted to represent the union between the Creator God (*Eheieh Asher Eheieh*) and his first creation Wisdom (Proverbs 8:22–23, Sirach 1:9–10).

The letter *Hei* is spelled *Hei Alef*, which has a Gematria value of 6 (*Hei* 5 + *Alef* 1 = 6 *Vav*); this too suggests that the union of the divine male and female working together brings about balance through humankind—who were created on the sixth day. *Alef* is male and represents God, and the *Hei* is female and represents the *Shekinah*. The name of God, *YaH*, is viewed similarly, with the *Yod* representing the divine masculine and the *Hei* representing the Spirit. When *Yod* and *Hei* are combined, they also produce the *Vav* (*Yod* 10 + *Hei* 5 = 15 = 1 + 5 = *Vav* 6), just as the *Elohim* created humankind in their image, male and female (Genesis 1:27). The *Vav* is associated with the *Sefirah* of *Tiferet* and humans, who were created on the sixth day.

The Sefer Yetzirah classifies the letter *Hei* as one of the 12 simple letters and associates it with *Speech*. *Hei* is the sound of breath/speech, expressing intention and manifesting one's thoughts/purpose. It can also represent the inner voice of divine guidance, the Spirit speaking to you from within. *Hei* symbolizes a *window*; the Spirit provides a *window* for humans to peer behind the veil and be enlightened.

On the Hermetic Tree of Life, the *Hei* is found on the path connecting *Chokmah* and *Tiferet*, and is associated with the Emperor card. This is reference to the Spirit of Wisdom guiding humans to master their domain. On the Lurianic Tree of Life, the *Hei* is found on the path connecting *Keter* and *Chokmah*. The fifth card of the Major Arcana is the High Priest card and would represent the High Priest making intercession before God. Mystically, the Hebrew letter *Hei* is said to be constructed of a *Dalet* being supported by a *Yod*. A *Dalet* and *Yod* combine to produce a gematria value of 5 (Dalet 4 + *Yod* 10 = 14, and 1 + 4 = 5), which is value of the *Hei*. The image of the constructed *Hei* can symbolize God (as the *Yod*) supporting the Door (*Dalet*), through the support of the Holy Spirit (*Hei*). The *Breath of Life* is added to the womb of a woman (doorway) to give the baby life, and so the Holy Spirit is added to the Soul of the believer to produce rebirth and spiritual life.

On a dreidel, the letter *Hei* represents the word *Hayah* (*Hei, Yod, Hei*), which is a conjugation of the verb "to be" (the same word used to form God's two most holy names, YHVH and AHYH, and the same word that the *Sefer Yetzirah* says *HaShem* used to speak the universe into existence). It is used to mean "*was*" or "*happened*" when describing the Great/*Gadol* Miracle/*Nes* that *Happened/Hayah* There/*Sham*. Like the *Hei* and *Alef* or the *Yod* and *Hei*, the Gematria of *Hayah* (*Hei* 5 + *Yod* 10 + *Hei* 5 = 20, and 2 + 0 = 2) can demonstrate *HaShem* and the Spirit of Wisdom working together, when the two of them created the world together (Wisdom 9:9, Genesis 1:27). The second *Sefirah* is *Chokmah*/Wisdom, who *Was*/*Hayah* with God during creation (Proverbs 8:30, Sirach 1:4). The *Hei* has a value of a *Yod* divided in *half* (10 *Yod* ÷ 2 *Chokmah* = 5 *Hei*). When the dreidel lands on *Hei*, the player wins *half* of the pot of gelt.

Talisman Symbolism: The talisman includes both the divine name *Elohim* as well as *Geburah*, written in Hebrew. The letter meaning *Window*, the Sefer Yetzirah attribute of *Vision*, and the mystical symbolism of *Breath* and *Spirit* are written in English. Starting from the inside of the top point of the Star and read in a counterclockwise direction are the Hebrew letters that spell *Shekinah*. There is a 5 to the right of the top point, and the word *Hei* (*Hei, Alef*) is on the left. Below the right point of the Star and read in a clockwise direction are the letters *Resh*, *Vav*, *Chet*, which spells *Ruach* (Spirit/Breath). This *Goral/Kame'ah* can be used as a reminder of the gifts of life, intuition, and the strength that is received by the Spirit. It provides a window into the secrets of God and represents Strength, Judgment, and Justice.

THE LETTER *Vav*

Letter: Vav, Vav

Transliteration: Vav

English Letter: V/W

Sound: Vine/victory

Gematria Value: 6

Reduced Value: 6

Etz Chayim Sefirot: Tiferet

Ten Commandments: Do not murder

Name Value: 6 + 6 = 12 = 3

Name Meaning: Peg/nail/hook

Sequential Number: 6

Sefer Yetzirah Classification: 12 Single/Simple

Sefer Yetzirah Attribute: Thinking

Hermetic Tree Path: Chokmah-Chesed

Hermetic Tarot: High Priest

Lurianic Tree Path: Keter-Binah

Kabbalah Cube Path: Chokmah-Chesed-Netzach

Numerical Tarot: Lovers

Constructed Gematria: Yod stretched down to reach from Heaven to the earth

Prefix/Suffix: prefix, conjunction / suffix, third-person possessive (his)

Mystical Associations: the Hebrew Letter *Vav* means *hook*, *peg*, or *nail.* It corresponds to the English letter *V* and *W* and in Hebrew is used as both a vowel (making the sounds oo and oh). As a prefix, it is used as a conjunction, similar to the English word *and.* The first time the letter *Vav* appears in the Bible is in the first verse of Genesis, where it is used as a conjunction to connect Heaven and Earth. The letter performs a similar function on the Kabbalistic Tree; it is associated with the *Sefirah* of *Tiferet* at the center of the Middle Pillar, where it connects *Keter*) and *Malkut.*

The Gematria value of *Vav* is 6, which associates it with the sixth *Sefirah* of *Tiferet*, which means *glory*, *adornment*, *beauty*, *honor*, or *source of pride and joy.* The name of the letter *Vav* is spelled "V" followed by another "V," which provides a Gematria breakdown of 12 and 3 (*Vav* 6 + *Vav* 6 = 12, and 1 + 2 = 3). The *Sefer Yetzirah* lists *Vav* as one of the 12 Single/Simple Letters and associates it with the attribute of *thinking.* It represents the need to contemplate and comprehend how everything fits together within providence, fate, and grand design. The Messiah is prophesied to come out of the 12 Tribes and the line of Judah, who is the head of the Tribe that received the birthright after his three brothers were passed over, making Judah (YHVDH) the door (Dalet) to *HaShem.*

The first three of the 12 Sons/Tribes of Israel were named after selfish concepts and negative feelings: at Reuben's birth, Leah believed that she was unloved (Genesis 29:32), at Simeon's birth she believed she was hated (Genesis 29:33), and Levi was named in hopes that she would finally be considered a companion to her husband (Genesis 29:34). When Judah was born, Leah moved her thoughts away from her concern for herself and unfair treatment but instead said, "*This time I will praise the Lord*" (Genesis 39:35). Her focus shifted away from herself and onto God. *Vav* means tent peg and is symbolic of the *Sefirah* of *Tiferet* holding the Tree of Life together, similar to how a tent peg supported the Tabernacle—it is not the primary purpose of the Tree, but without it, the Tabernacle could not stand. The sixth commandment is not to murder, which was the first sin in the Bible after the expulsion from the Garden of Eden, when Cain killed his righteous brother, whose offerings God preferred (Genesis 4:7). The response to the murder requires a balance of justice and mercy, which is what the *Sefirah* of *Tiferet* aims to do. In scripture, God curses Cain (Genesis 4:11–12), but he also protects him by placing a curse on anyone who would harm him (Genesis 4:15). The parents of the two boys would have faced similar choices when balancing justice and mercy for their only remaining son.

On the Hermetic Tree, the letter *Vav* is associated with the path connecting *Chokmah*/Wisdom and *Chesed*/Kindness. The Tarot card associated with that path is the High Priest or Hierophant card, representing the role of the High Priest who makes the Wisdom of God (John 14:26) accessible to all who are willing to enter into a covenant with God, symbolized by the *Sefirah* of *Chesed*. On the Lurianic Tree, *Vav* is on the path connecting *Keter* and *Binah*. Since *Keter* represents *HaShem* and *Binah* is associated with the *Ruach Elohim*, this path can be viewed as representing *HaShem* and Wisdom working together to bring forth humankind, who become their partners in creation—just as *YaH* (*Yod* 10 and *Hei* 5 = 1 + 0 + 5 = *Vav* 6) represents the divine male and female uniting to produce the *Vav*.

The sixth Tarot card in the Major Arcana is the Lovers Card, which shows Adam and Eve in the Garden of Eden, symbolizing the state of being that humans are to return to in the *Olam HaBa* (world to come) as a reward for practicing *Tikkun Olam* (repairing the current world). Mystically, the *Vav* is said to represent the *Yod* being stretched down to reach from Heaven to Earth. The *Vav* is first used in the Bible as a prefix to unite Heaven *And* (Vav) Earth. As a suffix, *Vav* represents the third-person possessive (his) and reminds us that in relation to *HaShem*, humankind are His, "*Know that YHVH is Elohim, and we are His people*" (Psalm 100:3).

The *Shema* has six words in it: "*Shema Israel Adonai Elohenu Adonai Echad*" (Hear O'Israel, the LORD is our God, the LORD is One), representing the above (higher) aspects of Israel (*Tiferet*). The second portion of the *Shema*, "*Baruch Shem Kavod Malkuto L'Olam Vaed*" (Blessed be his Name, his glorious kingdom is forever and ever), represents the below aspects of Jacob (Kingdom on Earth/

Malkut), which also consists of six words. Together the *Shema* contains 12 words, representing the 12 Tribes of Israel, who recite that prayer twice each day. The *Sefer Zohar* (Book of Splendor) expounds on the first word of the Bible, "*B'reishit*" (In the Beginning / BRAShShTh), and reads it as "*Bara Shishith*" (He Created Six / BRAh ShShTh), which connects to the concept within the *Sefer Yetzirah* of God creating the universe by sealing it in six directions (in front of him, behind him, to his right, left, above, and below).

Talisman Symbolism: The talisman includes both the divine name YHVH and *Tiferet* written in Hebrew on the left side of the outer circle. The English word *Connection* refers to the function of the letter *Vav* as a prefix; *Balance* and *Adornment* represent its attributes associated with the sixth *Sefirah*. The symbol at the center of the talisman is the Star of David, which is created by combining the male (upright) triangle and the female (downward pointing) triangle. The symbol represents the perfect balance of male and female (since humans were made on the sixth day). Around the outside of the Star (starting from the top right and read in a counterclockwise direction) is the word Adam (*Alef, Dalet, Mem*), and starting from the middle right (and read clockwise) is the word Eve (*Chet, Vav, Hei*). Inside the top point of the Star is the divine name YaH (*Yod, Hei*), representing the unity of the divine couple. The values of *Yod, Hei* (10, 5) are on the left of right points of the female triangle. At the bottom of that triangle is the number 6, which is the reduced value of 10 and 5 (10 + 5 = 1 + 0 + 5 = 6) and the value of the letter *Vav*. At the lower points of the male triangle are the letters *Vav, Vav*, which spell the letter and their combined gematria value (6 + 6 = 12 / Tribes / Disciples / Months). Around the inside of the Star are the names of the three patriarchs, written in the positions of the *Sefirot* they are associated with. In Kabbalah, Abraham is associated with *Chesed* and the original covenant (circumcision), mercy, and hospitality. Isaac is associated with *Geburah*, due to his ability to use judgment and to restrain his emotions, and he demonstrated strength in his willingness to serve as a sacrifice to *HaShem*. *Tiferet* is associated with Jacob, who balanced the attributes of *Geburah* and *Chesed*, while also balancing his earthly nature (Jacob) with his spiritual self (Israel). The lot/talisman can represent a perfect balance of the physical and the spiritual, a stable relationship, or completion in a matter.

THE LETTER *Zayin*

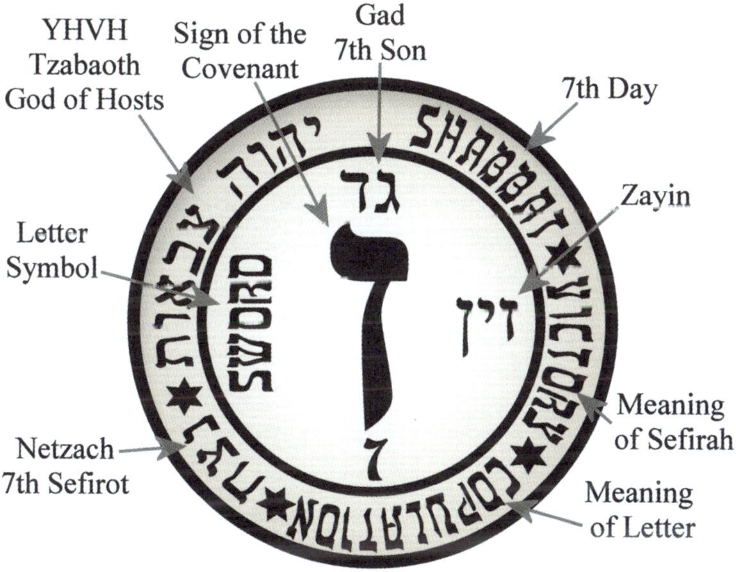

Letter: Zayin, Yod, Nun

Transliteration: Zayin

English Letter: Z

Sound: Zealot

Gematria Value: 7

Etz Chayim Sefirot: Netzach

Ten Commandments: Do not commit adultery

Name Value: 7 + 10 + 50 = 67 = 6 + 7 = 13 = 1 + 3 = 4

Name Meaning: Sword/arrow/penis/intercourse

Sequential Number: 7

Sefer Yetzirah Classification: Single/Simple

Sefer Yetzirah Attribute: Movement/advancement

Hermetic Tree Path: Binah-Tiferet

Hermetic Tarot: Lovers

Lurianic Tree Path: Chokmah-Geburah

Kabbalah Cube Path: Netzach-Malkut

Numerical Tarot: Chariot

Constructed Gematria: V, Y = 6 + 10 = 16 = 2 + 6 = 7

Prefix/Suffix: N/A

Mystical Associations: The Hebrew letter *Zayin* means *sword, penis*, or *intercourse* and makes the sound of the English letter Z. It has a Gematria value of 7, which is the number of perfection. On the seventh day, God rested from his work. Humans were created on the sixth day, and they were given the first instruction to being fruitful and multiply; the husband and wife are to come together as one flesh.

Kabbalistic practice of the Sabbath Bride involves a husband and wife being united on Friday night or Saturday morning in fulfillment of the first mitzvah. This practice was considered a Double Mitzvah, because not only was the couple observing the first mitzvah, they were also practicing *Oneg Shabbat* (enjoying the Sabbath). Their union on the seventh day (Shabbat) is symbolic of uniting *HaShem* and his Shekinah. Uniting on Friday night is associated with Jacob lying with Leah and brings favor to one's family, marriage, and household. Connecting on Saturdays is said to improve the passion of the couple, since Jacob married Rachel after Leah and had more passion for her.

The *L'Shem Yikhud* is a customary blessing that is said before performing certain Mitzvot, but it is particularly related to the practice of the Shabbat Bride. *L'Shem Yikhud* is the beginning of the blessing/prayer that reads, "*L'Shem Yikhud ([I perform this action] in order to unify the name) Kodasha (of the Holy One) Baruch Hu (Blessed be He), U'Shekintei (and his Shekinah): L'Yikhud Shem (to unite the name) Yod Hei (Y, H) B'Vav Hei (In V, H).*" In relation to the Shabbat Bride, an earthly couple becoming one flesh is said to inspire the heavenly union of *HaShem* and his Shekinah, and it represents the earthly couple doing their part in *Tikkun Olam* (repairing the world). In less mystical religious practices, Orthodox, Conservative, and Reform Jews welcome the Shabbat Bride as a representation of the *Ruach Elohim* (Spirit of God) descending onto and dwelling with the Nation of Israel during the Shabbat, sanctifying them and the day, as a part of the eternal covenant that *HaShem* made with them (Exodus 31:16).

The seventh *Sefirah* is *Netzach*, which means *Victory* and represents success in all endeavors, just as *HaShem* succeeded in creating the world, and Shabbat observers celebrate having made it through the workweek and reaching the day of rest. Seven is a number of perfection, which has many correspondences. The Woman Wisdom (Shekinah) built her house on Seven Pillars:

Seven Pillars of Wisdom

- Wisdom/Prudence/Cunning/Craftiness
- Knowledge/Perception/Skill/Foresight/Purpose
- Council/Advice/Resourcefulness
- Understanding/Discernment
- Courage/Strength/Might
- Justice
- Righteousness

These can also represent the seven lower *Sefirot* of the Kabbalah: *Chesed, Geburah, Tiferet, Netzach, Hod, Yesod,* and *Malkut*. There are 7 Seven Spirits of God that are associated with the 7 Branches of the Menorah, there are 7 Angels of the Churches in John's Revelation, and the book of Enoch provides a list of seven Archangels: Uriel (2 Esdras 4:1), Raphael (Tobit 5:4), Raguel, Michael (Revelation 12:7), Saraqael, Gabriel (Daniel 8:16), and Remiel.

The seventh commandment is not to commit adultery, which is directly related to all of the above information. Sex and marriage relationships are meant to be holy. Marriage is sacred and is a holy union, which serves as an analogy of our union with the Creator (Isaiah 54:5). Through marriage, we are able to comprehend our relationship/covenant with God, who is a husband to us (Jeremiah 31:32). The Sabbath Bride is also symbolically understood by the relationship between Israel as the Bride of *HaShem*, while the Shekinah represents both *HaShem*'s Bride and the Sabbath Bride of Israel.

Committing idolatry and worshiping foreign gods were symbolic of a cheating spouse. By comparing Israel's relationship with God to the concept of human marriage, we can comprehend the gravity of such offenses (Ezekiel 23:16–21, Hosea 3:1). Israel is in a spousal covenant with the Creator and is a special treasure to him; serving other gods would be an act of adultery.

The Gematrical value of the Hebrew letters that spell *Zayin* (*Zayin, Yod, Nun*) reduce to four (7 + 10 + 50 = 13 = 4) and can be thought of as (7 *Zayin*/

Intercourse) opening the Door to Life (4 *Dalet*/Door), or uniting the four letters of the *L'Shem Yikhud.*

The Sefer Yetzirah classifies the letter *Zayin* as one of the *single letters* and associates it with the attribute of *movement/walking.* On the Hermetic Tree, *Zayin* is on the Path connecting *Binah* and *Tiferet.* The placement of the *Zayin* on this path expresses the concept of the *L'Shem Yikhud,* where the union of the *Yod Hei* (*Keter* and *Binah*) must be united with the *Vav Hei* (*Tiferet/Malkut,* Messiah/Bride). A. E. Waite provided an alchemical representation of the kabbalistic practice of the Sabbath Bride on his Three of Cups card, which shows the Chymical Wedding of the Red King (human male), White Queen (Spirit of God), and the Gold/White Queen (human woman).

The Tarot card associated with that path on the Hermetic Tree is the Lovers card, which in the Rider-Waite Tarot deck shows Adam and Eve's union being blessed by a divine being. The connection between the Creation aspect of *Binah* and the balancing aspect of *Tiferet*, reflects humans becoming partners in creation and rectifying (*Tikkun Olam* / repairing the world) the sins of the word to restore their connection with God. The conjunction of the *Vav* and this holy unification connects the *Yod Hei* (God/Wisdom) with the *Vav Hei* (Messiah/World), as in the *L'Shem Yikhud.* All of this is done through committed relationships and covenants, between earthly couples, the divine, and how they treat their fellow humans.

On the Lurianic Tree, the letter *Zayin* is on the Path connecting *Chokmah* and *Geburah.* Since Wisdom is associated with the Shekinah, the *Zayin* on this Path can be understood as the Sabbath Bride giving Strength to a holy union that began in *Chesed.* Wisdom built her house on Seven Pillars, which can represent the 7 lower *Sefirot*, with *Chesed* representing the Eternal Covenant (Marriage/Sabbath) and the first of the lower 7 *Sefirot. Geburah* is the fifth *Sefirah*, representing the union being blessed by the Shekinah. The effects of that Covenant/Marriage result in the *Yod Hei* being united with the *Vav Hei* (the 7 lower *Sefirot* combining with the 3 higher *Sefirot*), which is what the Sabbath Bride practice representations.

The numeric Tarot card would be the Chariot card, which in the Rider-Waite deck shows the purified Soul of an alchemist growing out of the Philosopher's Stone following the Chymical Wedding. The Hebrew letter *Zayin* is mystically constructed by a *Yod* being added to the top of the *Vav*, which gives the letter the appearance of the *Vav* having been circumcised—another reference to the Eternal Covenant. The *Yod* and *Vav* work together to produce Victory/Success/*Netzach* (*Yod* 10 + *Vav* 6 = 1 + 6 = 7), and mankind (created on the sixth day) celebrates *Yod* (representing the Tetragrammaton) by remembering (*Zachor*) and engaging in joy (*Simchat*) on the Sabbath (seventh day).

Talisman Symbolism: The talisman includes the divine name YHVH Tzabaoth (God of Hosts/Armies), and the seventh son of Israel was Gad, which means Good Fortune or a Troop is coming. The seventh *Sefirot* is *Netzach*, and the letter *Zayin* can be sword. The God of Armies, Troops, Swords, and Victory makes this talisman a symbol of success during conflicts. It also contains sexual connotations, with *Zayin* representing a circumcised penis and being associated with copulation. The number seven represents perfection and is a day of rest and rejoicing. Both circumcision and remembering the Shabbat are related to covenants with God. The talisman can symbolize success in conflict or success with relationships.

THE LETTER *Chet*

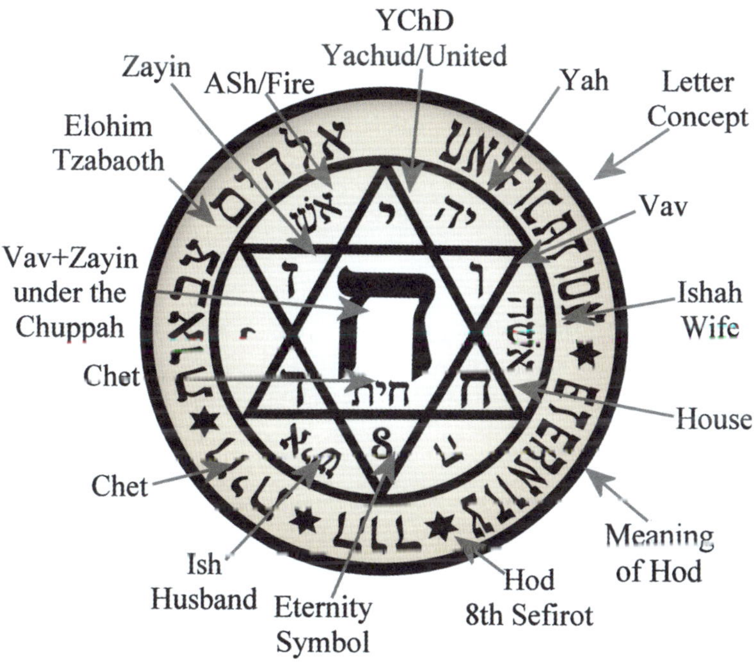

Letter: Chet, Yod, Tav

English Letter: Ch

Transliteration: Chet

Sound: BaCH

Gematria Value: 8

Reduced Value: 8

Etz Chayim Sefirot: Hod (glory/eternity)

Ten Commandments: Do not steal

Name Value: 8 + 10 + 400 = 418 = 4 + 1 + 8 = 13 = 1 + 3 = 4

Name Meaning: Beast/animal/life

Sequential Number: 8

Sefer Yetzirah Classification: Single/Simple

Sefer Yetzirah Attribute: Seeing

Hermetic Tree Path: Binah-Geburah

Hermetic Tarot: Chariot

Lurianic Tree Path: Chesed-Tiferet

Kabbalah Cube Path: Binah-Tiferet

Numerical Tarot: Strength (Shekinah strengthening the Lion of Judah)

Constructed Gematria: Vav, Zayin

Prefix/Suffix: N/A

Mystical Associations: The Hebrew letter Chet means beasts/animal/life, and the sound it makes is like the ending of the English words BaCh or LoCh. The first time the word appears in the Tanakh is in Genesis 1:25. The word is used again in Genesis 2:19 when God brought each animal to Adam in order for him to give them a name. The act of naming is part of creation. Adam declared that Eve was bone of his bone and flesh of his flesh and should be called Woman (*Alef, Shin, Hei*) because she was taken out of Man (*Alef, Yod, Shin*).

The letters of the word *Fire* (*Alef, Shin*) are found both in the words *Man* (*Alef, Yod, Shin*) and *Woman* (*Alef, Shin, Heh*) and symbolize the passion (fire) between them. This passion is on a *Chet* (undomesticated animal) level of the psyche/*NeFeSh* (soul) and represents the animal magnetism between male and female that people such as Dr. Franz Anton Mesmer contemplated. On a mystical level, the relationship of the human male and female is a shadow of the relationship between the divine masculine and feminine within the YaH, which are the divine masculine and feminine letters (*Yod, Hei*) that were added to *Fire* (*Alef, Shin*) in order to produce human *Male* and *Female* (*Ish/Ishah*, Husband/Wife). Since the Hebrew letter *Hei* (*Hei, Alef*) was taken from the word *Earth/Ground* (ADaMaH) and *Breathed* into Adam in order to give *life* (*Chet, Yod, Hei*) to his *soul* (NeFeSh), the letter *Hei* (feminine suffix) was added to the *Fire* (*Alef, Shin*) of *Man* (*Alef, Yod, Shin*) in order to produce *Woman* (*Alef, Shin, Hei*)—they are soulmates.

The verses go on to state that *Man* should leave his father and mother and cleave (be connected/glued) to (in/with) his *Woman/wife*, and they were both *Naked* (*Ayin, Resh, Vav, Mem*) and unashamed. At the *surface* (PeSheT) level of interpretation, this statement might describe the unification of a husband and wife in marriage, which is a concept directly related to the letter *Chet*. However, at the *ReMeZ* (Hinted/Symbolic) or *SVD* (Secret/Mystery) level of interpretation, the mystical concepts could be understood in relation to Adam leaving his divine Father and Mother (YaH) in order to join with *his woman/wife* (Ishto) when she shared the forbidden fruit with him.

The next verse following the statement that the man and woman were *naked* and unashamed describes the *Serpent* (*Nun, Chet, Shin*) as being more *naked* (*Ayin, Resh, Vav, Mem*) than any *beast* (*Chet, Yod, Tav*) of the field that *HaShem* had created. The letter *Ayin* means *Eye*, and the root letters of the word ARVM (naked), *Ayin Resh*, mean *Awake/Alert*. Adam and Eve were *aware* (able to see things clearly) and were unashamed, but the *Serpent* (NChSh), who was the most of insightful of the *beasts* (*Chet*), would bring an awareness of the *evil* (*Resh Ayin*) *inclination* (*Yod, Tzadi, Resh*) to the human *soul* (NeFeSh). It is as if Adam, by leaving the instructions of the YaH (his divine father and mother) and joining his *woman* (*Alef, Shin, Hei*) in following the most *naked* (*Ayin, Resh, Vav, Mem*) of the *beasts* (*Chet, Yod, Tav*), took on the *Chet* (animal instincts) of the *serpent* (*Nun, Chet, Shin*) and mixed it with the *Pei/Fei* (*Pei* = 80, which is an expanded value of *Chet* 8) of his *soul* (*Nun, Fei, Shin*).

As their *eyes* (*Ayin, Yod, Nun*) were opened, they were aware of both *good* (*Tov, Tet Vav Bet*) and *evil* (*RA, Resh Ayin*). Because of this, humans are born both with the *Yetzer Hara* (Evil Inclination) and *Yetzer Tov* (Good Inclination). In the Talmud, Avot D'Rabbi Natan (chapter 16) states that the *Yetzer Ra* (Evil Inclination) dominates a child's behavior until they reach the age of Bar/Bat Mitzvah (the ceremony representing the time when the youth is responsible for observing the commandments). From then on, the *Yetzer Tov* (Good Inclination)—stemming from the awareness of accountability for one's actions—will be released from its captivity within the heart and able to dominate their behavior. The person can then live with *Wisdom (Chokmah, Chet Kaf Mem Hei)*.

Wisdom (*Chokmah*) takes the *Animal* (*Chet*) *Instincts* (*YTzR*) and with the *Palm* (*Kaf*) of *Elohim* purifies/washes (*Mem*) it with the *Hei* (Breath/Spirit) of God, so that the *Ruach* (Spirit, *Resh Vav Chet*) enables the *Head* (*Resh*) to be *Connected* (*Vav*) with the *Chet* (Animal) in perfect balance. The word *Elohim* means *Judges*, and our ability to obtain a correct understanding, control, and balance of the *Yetzer Tov* and *Yetzer HaRa* is what allows us to become "*Like God*" (Genesis 3:5). The *Kaf-Elohim* implies that humans can become *like the divine judges* (Kaf as a prefix means *as* or *like*). The *Ruach Elohim* (Spirit of God) symbolizes the *Head* (*Rosh*) and (*Vav*) *Animal* (*Chet*) nature in perfect *Judgment* (*Elohim*).

The Gematria value of *Chet* is 8, which is also the reduced value of the Tetragrammaton (Y 10 + H 5 + V 6 + H 5 = 26 = 2 + 6 = 8). The eighth *Sefirot* is *Hod* (Glory/Eternity), which refers to the Eternal Glory of the Most High God. The English number 8 when rotated at a 90-degree angle is the symbol of eternity, and the proper name of God means the Eternally Existing One. The name revealed to Moses at the Burning Bush (Genesis 3:14) was *Eheieh Asher Eheieh* (*Alef Hei Yod Hei, Alef Shin Resh, Alef Hei Yod Hei*), which means "*I will exist, therefore I will exist*" as stated in the first person. The Tetragrammaton (*Yod, Hei, Vav, Hei*) is the third-person future conjugation of *exist*, meaning "*He will always Exist / He is the Eternal One*."

The bush was burning because the Tetragrammaton is described (Deuteronomy 4:24) as a consuming *fire* (*Alef, Shin*) and was visible to Israel as a Pillar of Fire (Exodus 13:21). Just as the worldly couple is a reflection of the heavenly couple, the *fire* (*Alef, Shin*) that connects the earthly couple is a reflection of the divine *Fire* (*Alef, Shin*). In the Three Mother Letters of the Sefer Yetzirah, the letter *Shin* by itself represents the Primordial Fire and symbolizes the Shekinah (*Shin*) as a reflection (Wisdom 7:26) of the Eternal One (*Alef*), who empowers the Fire (Air is the fuel of Fire). Just as the *Yod* and *Hei* of YaH represent the Divine Masculine and Feminine, the *Alef* and *Shin* of ASh do likewise, and it is a combination of these sacred letters (*Alef, Shin, Yod, Hei*) that produced the human Male (*Alef, Yod, Shin*) and Female (*Alef, Shin, Hei*).

To better understand the *fire* (*Alef Shin*) aspect of the Creator, we will contemplate the word *AShR*, which is interpreted as "*who*" in the phrases "I Am *Who* I Am," or "I Will Exist, *Therefore* I Will Exist" (Exodus 3:14). The word *Asher* (*Alef, Shin, Resh*) also means *Happiness* or *Bliss*, and its anagram "*Rosh*"

(*Resh, Alef, Shin*) means *Head*. Similar to how the word "*Elohim*" means *judges/gods* but there is a Most High God (*El Elyon*) and Ultimate Judge among the Elohim, there is a *Head* of the *Divine Fire*.

If *HaShem* is thought of in light of this concept, the name might suggest "*I am the highest fire for eternity*." Adding the feminine suffix *Hei* to AShR+H produces Asherah, which was the name of the consort/spouse of the Tetragrammaton among the Israelites between their Exodus for Egypt and their Exile to Babylon. The goddess Asherah was associated with trees, just as Wisdom (*Chokmah*) is referred to as a Tree of Life (Proverbs 3:18). Asherah (AShRH) is the female counterpart of AShR, and the Holy Fire (Matthew 3:11, Luke 3:16), sent to dwell within and give life to humans in order to make them friends and prophets of God (Wisdom 7:27). The *Shekinah* made her dwelling with Israel as a Pillar of Cloud and Fire (Sirach 24:4) provided by God (as Air/*Alef* fuels Fire/*Shin*), similar to how it is stated that when a man acquires a wife, he obtains a good thing (Proverbs 18:22), for she is a pillar of support (Sirach 36:24).

The Gematria value of the word *Chet* (*Chet, Yod, Tav*) is 418 (*Chet* 8 + *Yod* 10 + *Tav* 400 = 418 = 4 + 1 + 8 = 13 = 4), which reduces to 13 (the same value as AHAVAH/Love) and then to 4. The fourth *Sefirah* is *Chesed* and represents the Covenant established between God and Israel and the human covenant of marriage. The letter *Chet* represents the covenant of marriage and represents the *Chuppah* (Wedding Canopy, *Chet Vav Pei Hei*) a husband and wife are united beneath, which symbolizes the *Shekinah* overshadowing, covering, blessing, and protecting their union. Sometimes a *Tallit* is used as the Wedding Canopy, and in some traditions a Jewish male does not wear a *Tallit* unless he is married (other traditions allow one who has had a Bar/Bat/Bnai Mitzvah to wear a *Tallit*). The letter *Chet* is constructed of the letters *Zayin* and *Vav* (intercourse and connection) being united under the *Chuppah*.

The Hebrew *Alef-bet* tells the story of this union, with *Alef* representing *HaShem* (AHYH) prior to creation. *Bet* represents his first Creation, the Woman Wisdom, represented on the Kabbalah Tree by *Chokmah*, and the woman being the home. *Gimel*, the third letter, represents the *Sefirah Binah* and their unity during creation (Proverbs 8:22). *Dalet* would represent the doorway created to enable the manifestation of the seven lower *Sefirot*. *Hei* would represent the Breath of Life being given to all creatures. *Vav* symbolizes the sixth day and the creation of humans in the image of the divine (*Ish, Ishah, Yah, Ash, Asher, Asherah*). *Zayin* represents the first instruction given to the Lovers (to be fruitful and multiply). *Chet* represents the marriage covenant by which they are joined into a holy union.

The eighth commandment is not to steal, which is a sin that is motivated by selfish desire. In contrast, the holy union and covenant of marriage is the opposite of selfishness; it is commitment, unity, sharing, and the desire to love someone and treat them with equal regard to oneself. The result of this holy union is the creation of new life, and the human male and female becoming partners with the divine in the continuation of creation. On the eighth day of life the *Bris* (Covenant/Birth) occurs, which is the ritual circumcision of a male child into the Eternal Covenant that God made with Abraham (Genesis 17:9–10).

The letters *Vav* and *Zayin* united under the wedding canopy (*Vav* 6 + *Zayin* 9 = 13) combine to the number 13, which is also the number of *love* (*Alef, Hei, Bet, Hei*) and to be *One* (*Alef, Chet, Dalet*). Jewish males are circumcised into the Covenant on the *eighth* (*Chet*) day of *life* (*Chet Yod*), and at age 13 they have a *Bar Mitzvah*. From that day onward they are responsible for obeying *Mitzvot* (commandments/precepts). At age 13, the *Yetzer Tov* (good inclination) begins to overcome the *Yetzer Hara* (evil inclination).

In ancient Israel, people married earlier than in modern times. Following one's *Bar Mitzvah*, the male was treated as an adult, able to be married and enter into the holy union. The Covenant of circumcision, which had previously represented a private bond between the individual Jew and *HaShem*, is now shared with his wife, and the two become one (*Echad*/13) flesh in union with each other and with the divine.

Strength Tarot card, Rider-Waite deck

The Sefer Yetzirah classifies the letter *Chet* as one of the single letters and associates it with the attribute of *seeing*, which has both objective and subjective aspects. One can see the objective letter *Chet*, but one can also visualize the subjective construction of the letter as representing a couple entering into the covenant of marriage under the *Chuppah*, which can symbolize the relationship of a human couple, or the relationship of humans with the divine. The path associated with the letter *Chet* in the Lurianic Tree connects the *Sefirah* of *Chesed* with *Tiferet*. The numeric value of *Chet* would be the Strength Tarot card, which shows the White Queen (*Shekinah*) strengthening/supporting the Lion of the Tribe of

Judah (a symbolic portrayal of the connections between male and female and humans with the divine).

Chariot Tarot card, Rider-Waite deck

The associated Path to the letter *Chet* on the Hermetic Tree connects *Binah* (Understanding/Creation) and *Geburah* (Strength/Judgment)—each an element that has already been discussed in relation to the letter *Chet*. The Tarot card associated with this path is the Chariot, depicting the *soul* (NeFeSH) growing out of the Philosopher's Stone beneath the *Chuppah* (Wedding Canopy). This card shows the results of the Chymical Wedding of Alchemy, when the alchemist's Soul/Sulfur has been united with the Spirit/*Ruach* (*Shekinah*/White Queen) and the purification process (overcoming the *Yetzer Ra* with the *Yetzer Tov*) has started. The card shows one black and one white sphinx, as well as a lingam and a yani, representing that the union of opposites (male and female) has already taken place.

The letter *Chet* is used as a *talisman* (*Kame'ah, Qof, Mem, Yod, Ayin*) and expression of one's faith (*Emunah, Alef, Mem, Vav, Nun, Hei*). The word *Chai* (*Chet, Yod*), which means *life*, is symbolic of choosing to enter into a covenant with *HaShem* and obey his commandments (*Mitzvot*). After declaring a series of blessings and curses to the Israelites, *HaShem* told them that he was placing before them (Deuteronomy 30:15) *life* (*Chet Yod*) and *good* (*Tet, Vav, Bet*) as well as *death* (*Mem, Vav, Tav*) and *evil* (*Resh, Ayin*). Therefore, they should choose *life* (*Chet Yod*). Those who elect to wear such a talisman do so as a statement that they have chosen *life* and have entered into a covenant with God.

The value of *Chai* is 18, which is considered a lucky number in Judaism. The reduced value of 18 is 9, representing the *Sefirah* of *Yesod* (Foundation). *Yesod* is the mystical location of the Chymical Wedding of Alchemy, situated just above the physical world of *Malkut*. In Kabbalah, it depicts the Wedding of the Bride (*Malkut*) and Messiah (of *Tiferet*). It represents the union of the divine and human male and female (Strength Tarot card), and the results of this connection are represented by the Chariot Tarot card and a purified *soul* (NeFeSh) receiving new *life* (*Chet, Yod*) growing out of the Philosopher's Stone. Seven is the number of completion and perfection, while eight is the number of rebirth and the start of a new cycle/generation.

Talisman Symbolism: The talisman includes the divine name *Elohim Tzabaoth*, meaning God of Hosts or God of Armies. The word *Elohim* is usually associated with the Creator aspects of God, but it also means *Judges* and relates to the justice aspect of his nature. *Hod* (Eternity, Glory, and Majesty) is the eighth *Sefirah*, which is also the reduced gematria value of the Tetragrammaton. The letter represents the *Chuppah* (Wedding Canopy) and signifies the union of a couple and the consummation of the covenant (the wedding night). Within the top left and right points of the Star of David are the letters *Zayin Vav*, which form the letter *Chet*, symbolizing the connection (union/marriage) and its consummation. The top point and the lower left and right points of the Star include the letters *Yod, Chet, Dalet*, spelling the word *Yachud* (united), representing the couple becoming one under the *Chuppah* (*Chet*), with the result of their union providing a doorway (*Dalet*) to life. Around the outside of the star are separated and combined letters *Yod, Hei*, a name of God, which mystically represents the union of the divine masculine and feminine, and the words *ASh* (fire), *Ish* (husband), and *IShaH* (wife)—constructed by mixing the letter of *YaH* with *ASh*. This talisman might be used to symbolize a strong marriage or union, either physically or spiritually.

THE LETTER *Tet*

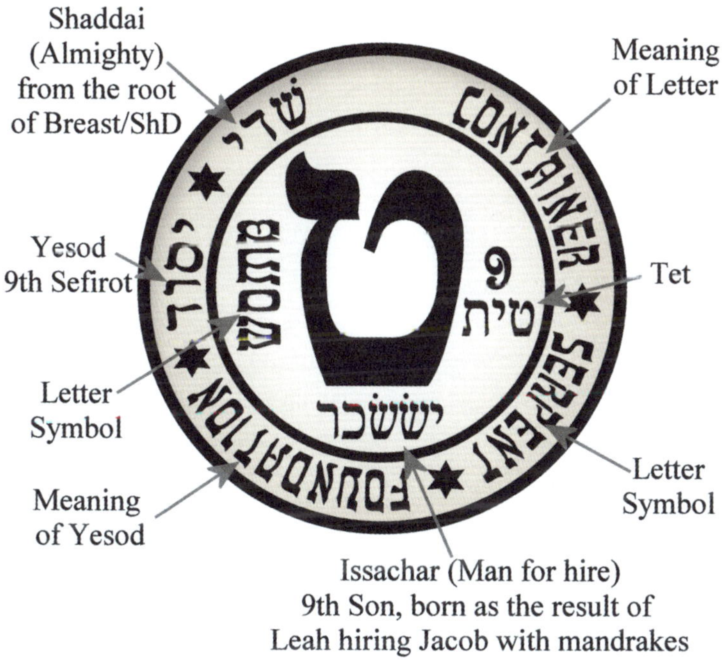

Letter: Tet, Yod, Tav

Transliteration: Tet

English Letter: T

Sound: Temple

Gematria Value: 9

Etz Chayim Sefirot: Yesod (Foundation)

10 Commandments: False Witness

Name Value: 9 + 10 + 400 = 419 = 4 + 1 +9 = 14 = 1 + 4 = 5

Name Meaning: Serpent/container/womb

Sequential Number: 9

Sefer Yetzirah Classification: 12 Single/Simple

Sefer Yetzirah Attribute: Hearing

Hermetic Tree Path: Geburah-Chesed

Hermetic Tarot: Strength

Lurianic Tree Path: Chokmah-Tiferet

Kabbalah Cube Path: Tiferet-Malkut

Numerical Tarot: Hermit

Constructed Gematria: Zayin, Kaf (7 + 20 = 9)

Prefix/Suffix: N/A

Mystical Associations: The Hebrew letter *Tet* resembles a *container/basket* or *serpent*. It makes a sound like the English letter T in the word *temple*. When the Tabernacle and the Temple existed, they served as a container of the Shekinah (Sirach 24:9–10, Ezekiel 43:5), just as our bodies do now (Wisdom 7:27, 1 Corinthians 6:19). Its gematria value is 9, which associates it with the *Sefirah* of *Yesod* and means *Foundation*. The *Foundation Stone* is said to be the location where the world first began (Bamidbar Rabbah 12:4, Midrash Tehillim 91:5); it is believed to be the location where Abraham was about to sacrifice Isaac, where the Temple of Solomon was built (Isaiah 28:16), and the Ark of the Covenant is said to have rested upon it.

On the Tree of the *Sefirot*, *Yesod* represents the location of the marriage of *Tiferet* and *Malkut*, the union of the Sun and the Moon, the Messiah and his Kingdom/Bride (Ephesians 5:31–33), and location of the Chymical Wedding of Alchemy. *Tiferet* represents the Messiah and"*the unification of Yesod and Malchut—this is one of the principal missions of Mashiach ben Yosef: to unify heaven and earth, to unify the two meshichim, which means the tree of Yosef with the tree of Judah during the awakening from below with the joining of Jerusalem above with Jerusalem below*" (Kol HaTor 2:56). The two meshichim represent the unifying efforts of the Messiah of the Line of Joseph (who rebuilds the Temple) and the Messiah in the Line of David/Judah (who will establish the Messianic Age). *Tiferet* connects Heaven and Earth, and *Yesod* is the location where the union/wedding is consummated.

When the Kabbalistic Tree of Life is superimposed on the human body (Adam Kadmon), *Yesod* is in the region of the sexual organs and is the point where the union takes place. *Chesed* and *Geburah* are the arms, "*Tiferet (harmony) is the torso. Netzach (dominance) and Hod (empathy) are the two legs, and Yesod (foundation or channel) is the body's extremity, the sign of the Holy Covenant. Malchut (kingship) is the mouth of the holy covenant. It is therefore called the 'Oral Torah.' Above these 'limbs' is the 'head' in which Chokmah (wisdom) is the right brain, the seat of thought, and Binah (understanding) is the left brain and the heart, the heart's ability to discern*" (Tikkunei Zohar 17a:20–22). The sign of the covenant is the circumcision, and although *Malkut* is referred to as a mouth and Oral Torah, the "*mouth that is below*" can also refer to the womb; that is, "*the mouth that is below, a euphemism for healing the womb of a barren woman*" (Sanhedrin 100a:11).

This union is the foundation that produces life, and the results of the union grow in the *container* of the *womb*. After God created Adam and Eve, they became God's partners in creation, and the future of humankind rested upon their willingness to obey God's first commandment, to become one flesh and to multiply. The letter *Chet* represents the couple being joined together in a covenant, and the letter *Tet* symbolizes the results of that union growing in the womb.

In alchemy, the Chymical Wedding represents the union of the Red King (Adam) and the White Queen. The result of that union is the development of the Philosopher's Stone, which ferments in the philosopher's egg (allegorical of the womb). The apostles encouraged their coverts to become living stones, and for their bodies to become spiritual houses/temples (1 Peter 2:4–5, 1 Corinthians 3:16). The bodies of those indwelt by the Shekinah are containers of the Holy Spirit, just as the Ark of the Covenant or the Temple of Solomon was in the past.

Noah was saved by an Ark, and Moses likewise escaped death by being floated down the Nile River in a basket/container. Similar to the miracle of life requiring the union and efforts of a human couple, the salvations of Noah, Moses, and the Israelites were also a unified effort of divine will and intervention with human effort. Noah had to build the Ark, and Moses had to first leave everything he knew, confront Pharaoh, and finally spend the remainder of his life leading the Israelites in the desert. During *Chatzi Kaddish* (the blessing over the bread), we praise God for bringing forth bread from the earth, but bread does not grow in loaves. God provides the raw material and potential, but he relies on human partners to do their parts for the miracles to take place. Men and women are capable of baking bread or creating new human life, but in order to do so they must fill their roles as partners in creation.

Vav is the connection between heaven and earth; *Yesod* is where the connection takes place. Nine is also the average number of months of pregnancy—the time the seed is contained in the womb. *Zayin* represents joy, inspiration, and sexual desire. *Chet* is the commitment to the covenant, where the couple advances their relationship beyond the physical. *Tet* is the container that collects and accumulates the efforts to bring about success. The *Yod* represents the *Hand* of God supporting the vessel and doing his part to support his partners in creation (Jeremiah 1:5; Psalm 139:13).

The ninth commandment is not to bear false witness, which relates to the attribute of *hearing*, ascribed to the letter *Tet* by the Sefer Yetzirah. The Hebrew word for *truth* (EMeT) has a gematria value of 9 (*Alef* 1 + *Mem* 40 + *Tav* 400 = 441 = 4 + 4 + 1 = 9). We are to refrain from falsehood and cling to the truth, which is the call of Wisdom (Proverbs 8:7, 1 Esdras 4:38–40, John 14:17). The letter *Tet* is also said to resemble a serpent. The Serpent was the first to spread falsehood (Genesis 3:4). Due to this deception, God put enmity between the offspring of the serpent and of woman (Genesis 5:15). While on Earth, humans are to choose good and resist evil (Amos 5:15), and their effort at *Tikkun Olam* and overcoming the *Yetzer Hara* is an ongoing process.

When the Israelites were fulfilling their commitments, *HaShem* was with them, but when they became impatient and began to complain about their situation, they were plagued by fiery serpents. It was only after *HaShem* commanded Moses to erect a Bronze Serpent in the desert that the people were saved from their sins (Numbers 21:8). Anytime an Israelite was bitten by a serpent (inflicted by evil), they could look to the mounted serpent (which reminded them of their *nakedness* / caused them to be *aware*), and they would survive their battle against the venom that came from the serpent's mouth to inflict them. The serpent on a pole was a reminder of God's promise of salvation, which gave the Israelites faith to encouragement to press on—they stopped their complaining and advanced forward in battle.

The letter *Tet* first appears in the Bible in the word *good* (*tov*). On the first day, God saw that the light was good, and he separated light from darkness (Genesis 1:4). The first thing that the Bible states was *not good* (*lo tov*) was for man to be alone (Genesis 2:18), but when he who finds a wife, he finds good and obtains favor from God (Proverbs 18:22), and the couple is blessed by their union. Rabbi Yehoshua stated that even "*if one sees the letter tet in his dream, it is a good sign for him*" (Bava Kamma 55a:4). The *Tet* container collects one's blessings like a *Tzedakah Box*. The letter *Tet* is constructed by combining a *Zayin* and a *Kaf*, which can represent a *Sword* in the *Palm* of the hand. The letter *Kaf*, like *Bet*, is predominantly a feminine letter, and the *Zayin* is masculine, so the *Tet* can represent the womb being the result of the union of the male and female opposites. The gematria of *Zayin* and *Kaf* equals *Tet* (7 + 20 = 2 + 0 + 7 = 9).

The letter *Tet* can be thought of as the midpoint of the effort, the liminal stage of an endeavor, when you keep working, collecting, and building while you patiently wait for the time of reward. The nine months of pregnancy are not the most pleasant, but they result in a tremendous blessing. Do not become impatient (as the Israelites did) or fall prey to the venom of the serpent's mouth. Pursue good, overcome evil, and continue to gather the sparks of light; transform bitterness to sweetness.

Strength and Hermit Tarot cards, Rider-Waite deck

On the Hermetic Tree, *Tet* is on the path connecting *Geburah* and *Chesed*, which can represent the two arms of Adam Kadmon carrying a basket/container full of the attributes of justice and mercy. This path is associated with the Strength card, which shows the White Queen supporting the Lion of Judah, symbolizing the Shekinah being present with the people as they wander through the desert of diaspora. On the Lurianic Tree, *Tet* is on the path connecting *Chokmah* and *Tiferet*. The numerical Tarot card would be the Hermit card, which shows Moses, with his staff that can transform into a serpent, as he stands in the Manna (Bread from Heaven) and holds the light (the first thing declared to be good) in the form of a Magen David.

Talisman Symbolism: The talisman contains the divine name *Shaddai* (Almighty), which is usually combined with *El Shaddai* (God Almighty). The word *Shaddai* comes from the root word meaning *Breast* and represents the feminine, mothering, and nurturing nature of the White Queen as she is depicted on the Strength

Tarot card. *Yesod* is the ninth *Sefirot* and means Foundation. *Yesod* is the location of the Chymical Wedding. The Foundation Stone represents the Beginning of Creation. The letter can mean either serpent or container; each brings with it unique attributes for contemplation. Issachar was the ninth son of Jacob, and he is the result of Leah trading mandrakes with Rachel in order to unite with Jacob and become pregnant. The meaning of *Issachar* is *Man for Hire*, and his tribe is associated with labor and working. This talisman can be used to encourage or support pregnancy, or as a reminder to put in the work and endure the labor, because as you perform *Mitzvot*, you are accumulating blessings in your container.

THE LETTER *Yod*

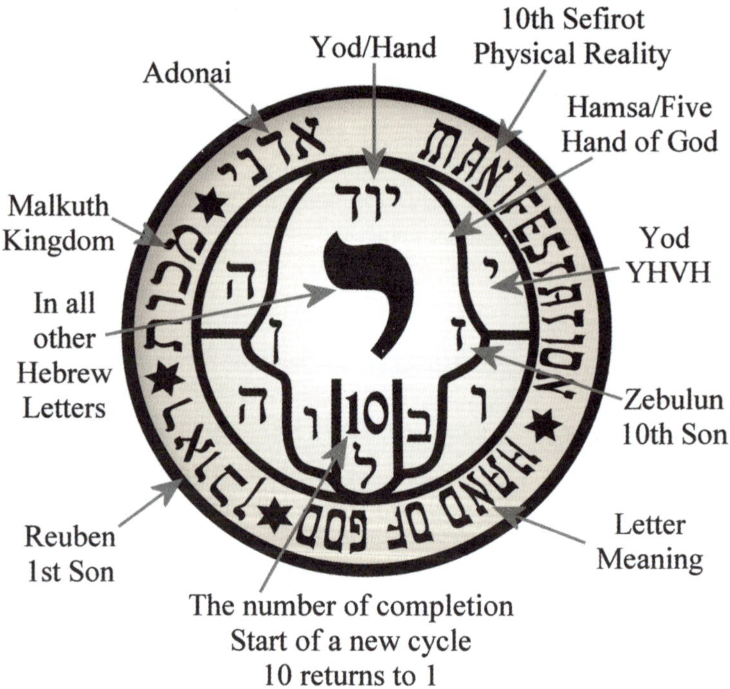

Letter: Yod, Vav, Dalet

Transliteration: Yod

English Letter: Y (J/I)

Sound: You

Gematria Value: 10

Reduced Value: 1

Etz Chayim Sefirot: Malkut (kingdom)

10 Commandments: Do not covet

Name Value: 10 + 6 + 4 = 20 = 2 + 0 = 2

Name Meaning: Hand

Sequential Number: 10

Sefer Yetzirah Classification: Single/Simple

Sefer Yetzirah Attribute: Working

Hermetic Tree Path: Chesed-Tiferet

Hermetic Tarot: Hermit

Lurianic Tree Path: Tiferet-Netzach

Numerical Tarot: Wheel of Fortune

Kabbalah Cube Path: Hod-Malkut

Constructed Gematria: N/A

Prefix/Suffix: Prefix, third-person future verb conjugation (He will) / suffix, first-person possessive (my)

Mystical Associations: The Hebrew letter *Yod* means *hand* and represents the *Hand of God* at work within the world. All things are the work of his hands (Jubilees 12:20): "*If He desireth, He causeth it to rain, morning and evening; and if He desireth, He withholdeth it, and all things are in His hand*" (Jubilees 12:19). The blessings one receives are their portion, from the hand of God (Ecclesiastes 2:24, 8:9). The *Yod* can be represented in English as a Y, J, or I, but within Hebrew words it can make additional sounds in conjunction with vowels.

The value of *Yod* is 10, which is the number of completion. The universe was created with 10 utterances, and "*these Ten Utterances are a Yod*" (Likutei Moharan 97:1–17). Each suit of the Tarot has cards numbered from 1 to 10, which represents the differing levels of the attributes of the particular suit, cumulating in the 10th card. Ten also represents the number of commandments (Deuteronomy 9:20) or the 10 Plagues of Egypt that were attributed to the finger/hand of God (Exodus 8:19, 9:3). Ten is the amount of righteous people that will allow a city to be spared (Genesis 18:32), which is also why a *minyan* is required for certain prayers, because "*when ten assemble for prayer, the Shekinah is in their midst*" (Berakhot 6a:9).

The letter *Yod* is the first letter in the name of God (YHVH), and it represents the fullness the attributes of God contained in the 10 *Sefirot*. The Ten Emanations are aspects of a single God, since 1 is the reduced value of 10 (10 = 1 + 0 = 1). *Malkut* is the 10th *Sefirah* and the final emanation from the one in *Keter*. The value of the three letters that spell *Yod* (*Yod, Vav, Dalet*) equals 20 (10 + 4 + 6 = 20), the value of the letter *Kaf*, which means *palm/hand* and reduces to 2 (*Chokmah*). The *Yod* and the *Kaf* represent the hands of the divine male and female working together in *yachad* (Proverbs 3:9). Two *Yod* written together (representing the first letter in YHVH and the last letter in Adonai) are used to abbreviate the name of God, which would also have a gematria value of *Kaf* (20).

The *Yod* and its gematria value of *10* are also related to Abraham, Sarah, and Isaac. It is said that the *Yod* was taken from the name "*Sarai*" and then divided between her and Abram so that each received a *Hei*—with the value of five—added to their names (Bamidbar Rabbah 18:21). After dividing the *Yod* and adding the *Hei* to their names, God said that *Sarah* would have a son that they would name Isaac (Genesis 17:19). The value of the name Isaac adds up to 208, which reduces to 10 (Midrash Tanchuma Shemot Siman 4:1). In the name Isaac, the "*Yod corresponds to the ten trials* [*of Avraham*]. [*The letter*] *tsadi,* [*since*] *Sarah was ninety when he was born. Chet,* [*since*] *he was circumcised on the eighth day. And the letter kof,* [*since*] *Avraham was a hundred years old when he was born*" (Bamidbar Rabbah 18:21).

The letter *Yod* was also added to the name Joshua, and he received the "*reward* [*that would have gone to the other*] *ten* [*spies*], *in that a Yod* [*which stands for*] *ten was added to his name*" (Midrash Tanchuma Sh'lach Siman 6:15), similar to how the faithful servant received the 10 talents of the unfaithful in Yehshua's Parable of the Talents (Matthew 25:21). The tenth commandment is not to covet anything belonging to one's neighbor. Instead, people should have *bitachon* (trust in God) that he will provide for their needs (Matthew 6:33, Ecclesiastes 5:18, Deuteronomy 12:7) and guide their paths (Proverbs 3:6, Jeremiah 29:11).

Yod is one of the "*father*" letters—the three letters in the Tetragrammaton. The *Sefer Yetzirah* lists it as a one of the 12 single/simple/plain (that make a single sound) letters and associates it with the attribute of working/action. When used as a prefix, *Yod* is the third-person masculine future verb tense (He will), which is how it is used with the verb "*to be*" in the Tetragrammaton (He will be). As a suffix, *Yod* is the first-person possessive (my), and in *AdonaY*, which means "*My Master*."

On the Hermetic Tree, *Yod* is associated with the path connecting *Chesed* and *Tiferet* and is represented by the Hermit card, which shows Moses lighting the way for Israel while holding the staff of God in his *hand* (Exodus 4:20), with the manna from heaven at his feet, as an example of *bitachon* and trusting his fate into the hands of God (Deuteronomy 5:15, Luke 23:46).

On the Lurianic Tree, *Yod* is on the path connecting *Tiferet* and *Netzach*. The numerical Tarot card associated with it would be Wheel of Fortune card, which is symbolic of God's providence. On the Cube of Kabbalah, *Yod* is on the path connecting *Hod* and *Malkut*, eternity and the physical world.

Talisman Symbolism: The talisman contains the name *Adonai*, which means *My Master* and is used in place of the Tetragrammaton during prayer. Also in Hebrew are the words *Malkut* (Kingdom), which is the 10th *Sefirah*, and Reuben, who was the first Son of Jacob. In the blessing Jacob gave Reuben, he associated him with water (Genesis 49:9). Water is also what God separated at the beginning of creation. On the fingers of the Hamsa are the Hebrew letters that spell Zebulun, who was Jacob's 10th son and would become a safe harbor on the sea (Genesis 49:13). Both Reuben and Zebulun are on this talisman, because it represents 1 and 10, as well as the amateur (Reuben) and the adept (Zebulun). The letter *Yod* is spelled at the top of the hand, and at its center is the letter. The shape of the letter *Yod* is contained in all other letters, as the hand of God is within all of creation. Manifestation represents the *Hand of God* at work within the world Outside the Hamsa are the letters of the Tetragrammaton, with *Yod Hei* above and *Vav Hei* below, suggesting the need to unite the above and below (Heaven and Earth) in order to bring unity to the name, as in the *L'Shem Yikhud*. Finally, there is a downward-facing Hamsa (fingers reaching down), which is used as a symbol of blessing from above or being supported by the *Hand of God*. A Hamsa with its fingers above shows a raised hand, which is used to ward of evil. The different hand positions can be remembered by imagining someone raising their hand in preparation to strike someone (the evil/danger), or reaching down to help lift someone off the ground (receiving luck or blessings). Whether facing upward or downward, the Hamsa can be used to symbolize the *Hand of God* either providing blessings or protecting those in his hand. This talisman can serve as a reminder that God is with you (Judith 13:11) as you make the most of the situation his hand has placed you in (Judith 13:3). Esther was taken to the king's palace in the 10th month, and her fate led to the Jews being protected from the hands of Haman (Esther 8:7) and his 10 sons (Esther 9:13). Do not be unstable, like water (Reuben), but master it (like Zebulun) and separate the above and below (Genesis 1:7), the light from the darkness, and the holy from the profane. This talisman is about taking action to manifest one's destiny, and reaching down to help others who are less fortunate (Deuteronomy 10:18, Isaiah 1:17)

THE LETTER *Kaf*

Letter: Kaf, Fei

Transliteration: Kaf

English Letter: K/F

Sound: baCH/Kid

Gematria Value: 20

Reduced Value: 2

Etz Chayim Sefirot: Chokmah

Ten Commandments: Do not create or worship idols

Name Value: 100 + 20 = 120 = 1 + 2 + 0 = 3

Name Meaning: Palm, Spoon

Sequential Number: 11

Sefer Yetzirah Classification: 12 Double

Sefer Yetzirah Attribute: Life and death

Hermetic Tree Path: Chesed-Netzach

Hermetic Tarot: Wheel of Fortune

Lurianic Tree Path: Chesed-Netzach

Kabbalah Cube of Space: West

Numerical Tarot: Justice

Constructed Gematria: Second form is of Dalet

Prefix/Suffix: Prefix, preposition (as, like)

Mystical Associations: The Hebrew letter *Kaf* means *palm* or *spoon* and can be thought of as the female counterpart of the *Yod*. The *Yod* and the *Final Kaf* (*Kaf Sofit*) look very similar to a *Yod* and a *Dalet*, which spells *hand* in Hebrew. Since the Hebrew *Alef-bet* is written and read from right to left, the *Kaf* would represent the left hand and the *Yod* would represent the right hand. The *Yod* male and the *Kaf* female work together.

In the Torah, the right side was associated with the masculine, and during sacrifices the priests would put blood on the ear, thumb, and big toe on the right side of the body (Exodus 29:20, Leviticus 8:23). Since east is the direction *HaShem* faced in the *Sefer Yetzirah* when creating the world, and also the direction we face when praying or when magicians perform the Lesser Banishing

Ritual of the Pentagram, south is associated with the right direction and north is with the left. The Archangel Michael is associated with the right, and Gabriel is to the left (HaBahir 11, Zohar 116a:4).

On the Tree of the *Sefirot*, Michael is associated with *Hod* (Exodus 15:6) and would represent the right hand of Adam Kadmon, the Pillar of Severity. The Archangel Gabriel is associated with *Yesod*, which is to the left of the right hand (*Hod*) in the genital area—where the Chymical Wedding takes place and the marriage of the Sun and the Moon is consummated. The left hand of Adam Kadmon would be associated with *Netzach* and the archangel Haniel, who is associated with Venus, joy, grace, and pleasure.

Michael represents the male attribute and Haniel the female. Gabriel means *Man / Strength of God* (Daniel 8:16), but this angel is also associated with feminine qualities. Gabriel is the Angel of Fertility, who announced to Mary that she was pregnant (Luke 1:26–27). Gabriel is said to go into the Garden of Eden, retrieve a soul from the treasury of souls, and would then entrust it to Laylah, the Angel of Conception, who watches over it in the womb. The name Gabriel can be used for either males (Gabe) or female (Gaby), depending on how the vowel is stressed. So, in relation to the hands of Adam Kadmon, the right hand is associated with the male, Michael, and the Pillar of Severity. The left hand is associated with the female, Haniel, and Pillar of Mercy, and the genital region is associated with the union of male and female, Gabriel, the Pillar of Mildness, and procreation.

The *Kaf* is the 11th letter in the Hebrew *Alef-bet*, with a gematria value of 20. It reduces to the number 2, which connects *Kaf* to the letter *Bet*; these two letters resemble and are often confused for each other. The *Kaf* is the first letter to have two different forms. When *Kaf* is written at the beginning or within a word, it resembles a less rigid *Bet*, but when at the end of a word, the *Final Kaf* resembles to elongated *Dalet*. The value of *Kaf* reduces to 2, which associates it with the *Sefirah* of *Chokmah*, the Pillar of Mercy, and feminine attributes of wisdom and contemplation.

Bet is the *house* of Wisdom (Proverbs 9:1) and is associated more with thought and intension. *Kaf* is the evolved form of *Bet*, and when the *Ein* (*nothing/* zero) is added to two, it becomes 20. Hands are used to manipulate physical objects in manifested reality. The two hands (male/female, right/left) work together in union, with the left palm supporting the oil and the right hand sprinkling the blessing (Leviticus 14:14–16). The gematria value of 20 is connected with the *Yod*, not only because it is a double value of *Yod* (two *Yod* serve as an abbreviation for the Name of God), but it is the value of letter *Yod* (*Yod* 10 +

Vav 6 + *Dalet* 4 = 20). Since Wisdom is a Mirror of God (Wisdom 7:26), *Kaf* is a reflection of *Bet*, and the palm is an aspect of the *Hand of God* at work within the universe. The *Yod* and *Kaf* are the two hands at work within manifested reality and are an evolution of the *Alef* (male aspect of God) and the *Bet* (his first creation). *Chokmah* emanates from *Keter*, and *Keter* (*Kaf, Tav, Resh*) starts with a *Kaf*.

Kaf, with a value of 20, is a doubled value of *Yod*, which is 10. When *Kaf* 20 is reduced to 2 (*Bet*), and *Bet* 2 is then doubled, it equals 4 (*Dalet*). *Dalet* represents the Door to the Holy of Holies—the special chamber that only the High Priest enters in the Temple of the Body of Adam Kadmon (*Yesod*). This is where the *Shekinah* dwells within those who have begun the Chymical Wedding and embarked on the Great Work, or where the angel Laylah guards the soul of a new creation as it passes through the doorway into physical life. When performing the Priestly Blessing, the Kohen displays his palms to those being blessed. Each hand (*Yod*) has a value of 10 and together equals *Kaf* (Palm). The two Yod (hands) being lifted up represent an abbreviated name of God, so that in doing the Priestly Blessing, God's name is put on the people (Numbers 6:27). The gematria value of the letters that spell *Kaf* is 120 (*Kaf* 20 + *Pei* 100), which reduces to 3 (*Gimel*) and can represent the Spirit of Wisdom guiding you to your destiny, with your fate having been written on the palm of your hand (Job 37:7, Isaiah 49:16, Exodus 13:9). Chiromancy (Palmistry) was an aspect *Merkabah Mysticism*, which was pre-Kabbalah Jewish mysticism. In modern palmistry, the individual's nondominant hand (usually a person's left) represents the potential the person is born with; the dominant hand is contrasted against the opposite hand in order to compare how the individual has utilized their potential. Comparing the two palms allows the reader to contrast free will and destiny in order to interpret progress and estimate possibilities.

The Sefer Yetzirah classifies *Kaf* as a double letter, due to it making two different sounds. If the letter has a *dagesh* (dot) in it, it makes a hard sound like the K in king. If the dagesh is absent, it makes a weaker sound like the CH in BaCH. The Sefer Yetzirah associates it with the duality of Life and Death and with Venus, Wednesday, and the left eye. On the Hermetic Tree, *Kaf* is on the path connecting *Chesed* and *Netzach* and is associated with the Wheel of Fortune card—representing one's ability to choose between life and death (Deuteronomy 30:19).

The numerical Tarot card corresponds to Justice, and the consequence of being judged according to one's choices. On the Lurianic Tree, *Kaf* is also on the path connecting *Chesed* and *Netzach*. On the Kabbalah Cube, *Kaf* is associated with the west, which is the direction Abraham traveled when he answered the call of *Lech-Lecha* (go forth) and is also the destination of the setting Sun; the direction that kabbalists face as they sing *Lecha Dodi* (come my beloved) to welcome the *Shabbat Bride* (the chorus of *Lecha Dodi* contains 26 letters, the value of the Tetragrammaton, and is sung 10 times, once for each of the *Sefirot*).

The *Final Kaf* is constructed by extending the *Dalet* to reach farther below, the fourth *Sefirot* (*Dalet*) reaching down the path of *Kaf* to bring *victory* to *Justice*. *Kaf* reduces to 2 (*Chokmah*), *Bet* connects *Chokmah* (Bet/2) and *Chesed* (Dalet/4), and *Kaf* connects *Chesed* and *Netzach*, linking the entire Pillar of Mercy together. The *Kaf* can also be viewed as a bow, which joins with the arrow (*Zayin/Netzach*), showing the need for the male and female natures to function in unity to be effective. As a prefix, the *Kaf* is used to mean *as* or *like* and is used in Genesis 3:5 to say that after eating from the Tree of Knowledge of Good and Evil, humans would become *Like God/Judges* (*Kaf-Elohim*).

Talisman Symbolism: This talisman contains the divine name YaH, which is a shortened form of the Tetragrammaton and can represent the divine masculine and feminine working together in unity. Together the *Yod* and *Hei* make six, representing the six days of creation. *Chokmah* means Wisdom and refers to the first creation that emanated from *Keter* (Proverbs 8:22, Psalm 104:24, Wisdom 9:1). Life and Death are the contrasting attributes associated with *Kaf* in the *Sefer Yetzirah*. A person's destiny being engraved on the palms of their hands, or everything being in the hands of God, can symbolize divine providence or fate working within one's life. The Hamsa on this *kame'ah* is upright, which wards off evil, or it can be viewed as a hand of blessing. The gematria value of *Kaf* is 20. Above the dividing line on the outside of the Hamsa are the two versions of *Kaf* (standard and final). Below the dividing line (as if the waters were dividing Heaven and Earth) are letters that appear as reflections of the *Kaf*, with *Bet* below *Kaf*, and *Dalet* below the *Kaf Sofit* (divine female above, earthly female below). This talisman can serve as a reminder of the delicate balance between free will and fate, and the life-and-death decisions that are left in our *hands*, now that we have become *Kaf-Elohim* (Like Judges / Like God).

THE LETTER *Lamed*

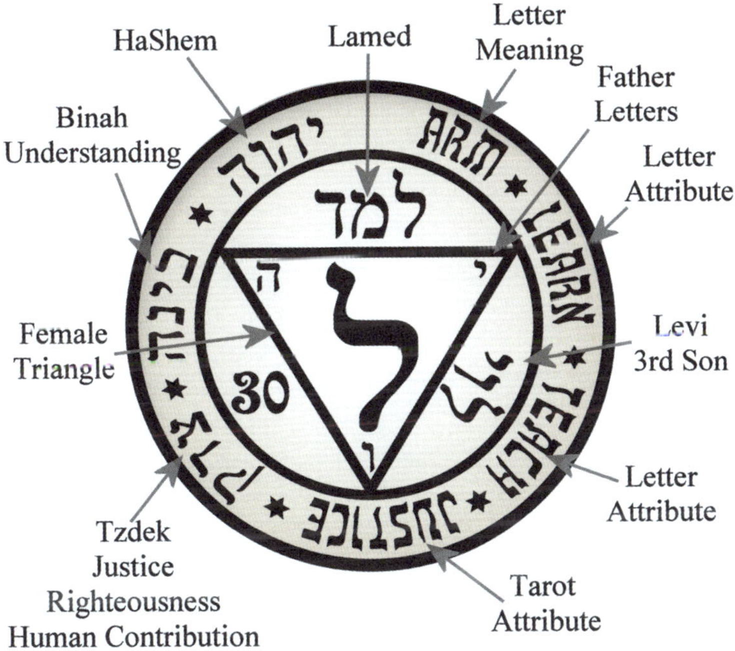

Letter: Lamed, Mem, Dalet

Transliteration: Lamed

English Letter: L

Sound: Lamb

Gematria Value: 30

Reduced Value: 3

Etz Chayim Sefirot: Understanding

Ten Commandments: Do not misuse the name

Name Value: 30 + 40 + 4 = 74 = 7 + 4 = 11 = 1 + 1 = 2

Name Meaning: Learn, ox, arm

Sequential Number: 12

Sefer Yetzirah Classification: Single/Simple

Sefer Yetzirah Attribute: Coitus

Hermetic Tree Path: Geburah-Tiferet

Hermetic Tarot: Justice

Lurianic Tree Path: Hod-Yesod

Kabbalah Cube Path: Keter-Binah

Numerical Tarot: Hanged Man

Constructed Gematria: Vav and Kaf

Prefix/Suffix: Prefix, preposition (to, for)

Mystical Associations: The Hebrew letter *Lamed* is the 12th consecutive letter and means *learn*, *ox*, or *arm*. Its gematria value is 30, which is the age that priests could perform holy service (Numbers 4:3). Joseph was one of the 12 Tribes of Israel and was appointed to his position by Pharaoh at age 30 (Genesis 41:46). Jesus also started his teaching at age 30 (Luke 3:23), and he selected 12 Disciples. The gematria value of the letters that spell *Lamed* equals 74 (Lamed 30 + Mem 40 + Dalet 4 = 74 = 11 = 2), and these letters reduce to 2, which points to *Chokmah*. When *Lamed* is combined with *Bet*, it spells *Heart* (*Lamed Bet*) and is the first and last letters of the Torah.

> *And the Torah in its entirety is called lev (heart), because it begins with a Bet and concludes with a Lamed. [The heart] is the dwelling place of the spirit "which blows in the six sections of the arms and the six sections of the legs"—i.e., in the revealed and the hidden.* (Likutei Moharan 10:7:2)

The Torah begins with the word *B'reishit* (Genesis 1:1) and ends with the word *IsraeL* (Deuteronomy 34:12). The value of *Lamed Bet* is 32, which refers to the 32 Paths of Wisdom found in the Kabbalah. Jesus of Nazareth taught that the greatest and first commandment was to love *HaShem* with all one's heart, which is the beginning of *Shema* (Deuteronomy 6:4). The instruction we are to take to our *hearts* and *learn* (Deuteronomy 6:6). We are to *teach* them to our children (Deuteronomy 6:7) and have them inscribed on our houses and hands and visible between our eyes. They should be part of are foundations (homes), and the *Mitzvot* should be visible in what we see (eyes) and do (hands).

Lamed is roughly in the center (at the heart) of the *Alef-bet*. The Heart of Adam Kadmon is *Tiferet*, which has a value of six and represents humanity. The value of *Tiferet* is 1,081 (*Tav* 400 + *Fei* 80 + *Alef* 1 + *Resh* 200 + *Tav* 400 = 1,081 = 10 = 1), which equals both 10 and 1, since humans were created to be *Kaf-Elohim* (Like God) and share the same attributes as God. Humans serve as the *arm* of the *HaShem* on the earth. Adam was created to tend to the garden (Genesis 2:15), and humans were created in order to procreate (Genesis 1:28). Humans are God's Partners in Creation. The *Lamed* embodies all of these concepts because through *learning*, *teaching*, and serving as the *ox* (workers) and *arm* of God on Earth, humans do their parts in *Tikkun Olam* (repairing and perfecting the world).

The letter *Lamed* is constructed by adding a *Vav* to a *Kaf* (*Vav* 6 + *Kaf* 20 = 26), which is the same value as the Tetragrammaton. As *Tiferet* (which equals both 10 and 1) is at the Heart of the Kabbalah, *Lamed* is at the Heart of the *Alef-bet*. *Lamed* is the only letter that goes above the line; it reaches higher than any other letter, as if humans (*Vav*) are stretching out their arms to reach toward heaven. The Torah is the Heart, and those who receive its instruction (John 12:36–40, Jeremiah 31:33) serve as the Arm of the Lord and God's partners on Earth.

The Heart is the dwelling place of the Spirit (Likutei Moharan 10:7:2). Just as the *Bet* is compared to a House, the *Kaf*, as an evolved form of the *Bet*, can be superimposed over the Tree of the *Sefirot*, representing the divine feminine supporting the Heart of Adam Kadmon (humans) in her Palm (*Kaf*)—with the Heart of Adam Kadmon is embraced and housed by the *Shekinah*. When superimposed on the Kabbalah, *Kaf* supports the Heart (*Tiferet*) and the reset of the other six sections (*Geburah* / Right Hand, *Chesed* / Left Hand, *Tiferet*/ Heart/Torso, *Hod* / Right Leg, *Netzach* / Left Leg, *Yesod*/Extremities) of Adam Kadmon (*Tikkunei Zohar* 17a:20–22). When the *Vav* is added to the *Kaf*, it reaches toward Heaven and touches *Binah* (Understanding); by standing up, it connects its learned understanding and is able to serve as the Arm of the Lord (or God's worker/ox) on the earth (*Malkut*). When the *Lamed* is superimposed on the Tree of Life, it brings Understanding down from *Binah*, balances Justice (*Geburah*) and Mercy (*Chesed*) in the Heart (*Tiferet*), and brings Victory (*Netzach*) to the Kingdom (*Malkut*) by becoming a Partner in Creations (*Yesod*).

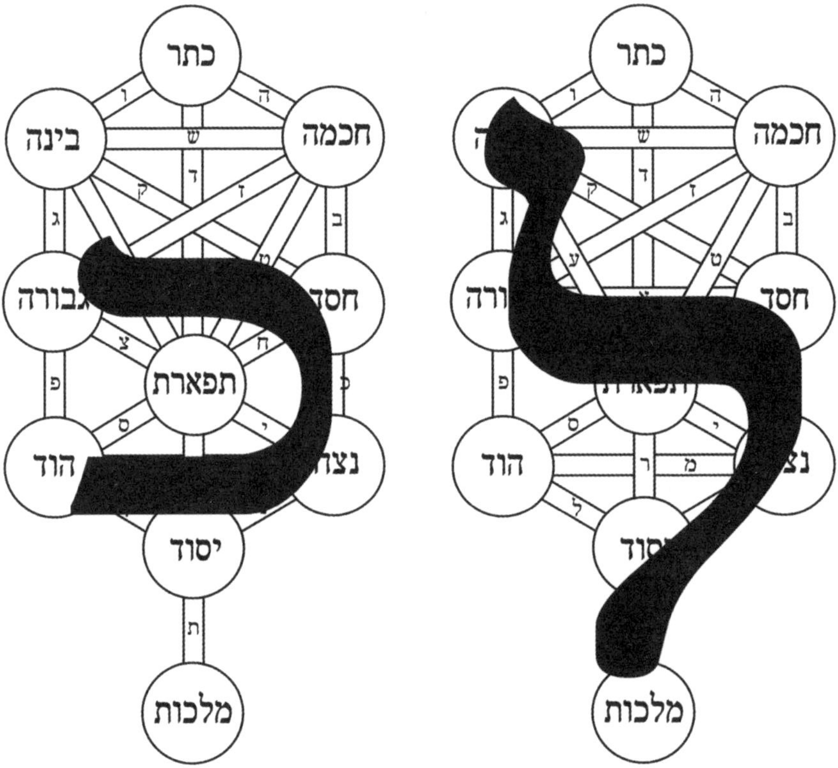

Kaf and *Lamed* superimposed on the Kabbalah

Heaven and Earth are the products of *Chokmah* and *Binah* (Proverbs 3:19, Jeremiah 10:12), and the meditation of one's heart brings understanding (Proverbs 24:3, Psalm 49:3). Understanding (*Binah*) is the third *Sefirah*, which is the reduced value of *Lamed*. The third commandment is not to profane the name of God. When examining the commandments listed in the *Shema*, the first is to love *HaShem* with all one's *heart*, soul, and might/abundance; the second is to receive the commandments upon your *heart*; and the third is to *teach* them to your children.

The Sefer Yetzirah classifies *Lamed* as a Single Letter and associates it with *coitus* (sexual desire) and Libra (the Scales of the Zodiac). On the Hermetic Tree, *Lamed* is on the path connecting *Geburah* and *Tiferet*, and the Tarot card associated with that path is the Justice card. The Justice card in the Rider-Waite deck shows the Red King (Adam or Solomon) holding a scale in his left hand, and a sword in his right hand reaches toward heaven just as the *Vav* does in the construction of the *Lamed*. On the Lurianic Tree, *Lamed* is on the path connecting *Hod* and *Yesod*; since the constructed value of the *Lamed* is the same as the Tetragrammaton (26), its reduced value is 8 (*Hod*). On the Kabbalah Cube, *Lamed* is on the path connecting *Keter* and *Binah*, the divine masculine and feminine. The numerical Tarot card would be the Hanged Man, who *learns* and receives enlightenment due to his experiences (actions in the world).

Talisman Symbolism: This talisman contains the divine name of *HaShem* (the Tetragrammaton). *Lamed's* value is 30, and its reduced value points to the *Sefirah* of *Binah*. *Tzedek* (Justice/Righteousness) is its core attribute, and *Lamed* represents serving as the Arm of the Lord, or his ox (laborer) on Earth. The letter is also associated with *learning* and *teaching*. Jacob's third son was Levi, which means Companion. The Tribe of Levi is God's companions/representatives on Earth, and they acted as his priests and intermediaries. The Tribe of Dan was the judges of judicial matters, and the Tribe of Levi were the judges of spiritual matters. The inverted triangle is the female triangle of the Kabbalah (connecting *Binah*, *Chokmah*, and *Tiferet*), and within it are the Father letters that were used to seal the universe in six directions, providing a symbolic representation of the divine masculine and feminine. This talisman can be used as a reminder of one's partnership in creation. Humans, as God's companions, are to *learn* and *teach* his mitzvot with all our *hearts*, souls, and strength. This talisman can be used to encourage learning or teaching, or as a reminder of one's role as a light worker in the universe. "*Justice, Justice, you shall pursue*" (Deuteronomy 16:20). There is suffering and injustice in the world, but God does not ignore it, he sent his companions and partners into the world to establish justice, to have dominion over the earth, and to subdue it (John 17:17–18, Genesis 1:28); this talisman reminds you to do your part.

THE LETTER *Mem*

Letter: Mem, Mem

Transliteration: Mem

English Letter: M

Sound: Mother

Gematria Value: 40

Reduced Value: 4

Etz Chayim Sefirot: Chesed

Ten Commandments: Remember/Keep the Sabbath

Name Value: 40 + 40 = 80 = 8 + 0 = 8

Name Meaning: Water

Sequential Number: 13

Sefer Yetzirah Classification: 3 Mothers

Sefer Yetzirah Attribute: Water/passiveness

Hermetic Tree Path: Geburah-Hod

Hermetic Tarot: Hanged Man

Kabbalah Cube: Water-Earth

Numerical Tarot: Death

Constructed Gematria: Vav 6, Kaf 20 = 26

Prefix/Suffix: Prefix (from) / suffix, YM dual form (two)

Mystical Associations: The letter *Mem* is the 13th consecutive letter in the Hebrew *Alef-bet*; it means *water* and has a numerical value of 40. At age 13, boys have a *Bar Mitzvah* and become responsible for keeping the commandments (girls have their *Bat Mitzvah* at age 12). The gematria value of the words *Ahavah* (love) and *Echad* (one) is 13. The Sefer Yetzirah lists *Mem* as one of the three Mother Letters and associates it with Primordial Water. In alchemy, it is the *Prima Materia* from which everything else was created. The world was formed by water and out of water (2 Peter 3:5). In the beginning, God separated the waters and brought forth dry land (Genesis 1:2–10). Both water and the number 40 are associated with purification.

The reduced value of 40 is 4, and *water* serves as a means (doorway) of transformation. Water rained upon Noah's Ark for 40 days in order to purify the world (Genesis 7:12), Moses met with God at the top of Mount Sinai for 40 days (Exodus 34:28), Goliath challenged the armies of Israel for 40 days (1 Samuel 17:16), Jonah preached against Nineveh for 40 days (Jonah 3:4), and Jesus was tempted by the Devil in the desert for 40 days (Mark 1:13). In Christianity, one must be reborn through water and Spirit (John 3:5), and in Judaism, a *mikvah* is also used in the conversion process (40 *se'ah* of water is the minimum requirement for a *mikvah* immersion). Water purification is associated with the receiving the Spirit (Ezekiel 36:25–26, Isaiah 44:3, Acts 2:38), and 40 is the traditional age when someone can begin studying the Kabbalah/Wisdom (Pirkei Avot 5:21). In alchemy, the Chymical Wedding refers to the soul of the alchemist being united with the Spirit of Wisdom, which represents the point when the alchemist begins the Great Work—this is accomplished in spagyrics with the Spirit Solvent/Water extracting and purifying the essential oils (soul) from the body (plant material).

The letter *Mem* is the second letter that transforms and is different at its beginning than it is in its final form (*Mem Sofit*). The open and closed *Mem* represents revealed and concealed truth (*Emet*). The letter *Mem* is in the *middle* of the word *Emet*, just as it is roughly in the center of the *Alef-bet*. The Talmud states that "*the open mem and the closed mem indicate that the Torah contains an open statement, understood by all, and an esoteric statement*" (Shabbat 104a:5). The reduced value of *Mem* (40) is 4 (*Dalet*), which can represent the *door* being either open or closed, just as the *Mem* can be open or closed. The *Mem* is a feminine letter that is associated with Wisdom, and it is part of the supernal triad, with the *Alef*, representing Air, being the fulcrum of the scale in *Keter*, the *Shin* in *Binah* representing fire, and the *Mem* being the counterbalance of water in *Chokmah*. The gematria of Jewess (*Yod Hei Vav Dalet Yod Hei*) is also 40.

As a Mother Letter, *Mem* is associated with *Chokmah*, and its reduced value of 4 is linked to *Chesed*. God has *mercy* on those in a *covenant* with him, and although they may face trials such as David did with Goliath, Noah did with the Flood, or Moses did during his 40 years wandering in the desert, God's *loving kindness* sustained them. The fourth commandment is to remember the Sabbath, which is part of God's eternal covenant with his people. The gematria value of the letters that spell *Mem* (*Mem Mem*) is 80, which reduces to 8 (the reduced value of the Tetragrammaton). The open *Mem* is constructed of a *Vav* 6 and a *Kaf* 20, which represents the divine Spirit (palm) supporting the *Vav* (humans) and helping them to stand. Once the *Vav* is standing straight up, it is united with the *Kaf* as one (*Echad*/13) and forms the *Mem Sofit*. In the Rider-Waite Tarot deck, the Star card (XVII = 1 + 7 = 8) portrays the divine feminine as Mother Nature, who replenishes the earth (*Adamah*) with *water*.

The attribute listed in the Sefer Yetzirah with *Mem* is *water*, which is passive; like electricity, water takes the path of least resistance. Water flows as it is directed; those who are guided by God allow their paths to be directed by the Spirit (Proverbs 3:6, Numbers 9:20). On the Hermetic Tree, *Mem* is on the path connecting *Geburah* and *Hod* and is associated with the Tarot card Hanged Man, which represents a disciple (Peter was crucified upside down) obtaining enlightenment through suffering. On the Lurianic Tree, *Mem* connects *Hod* and *Netzach*, revealing the connection between honor and victory; it is through our trials that we obtain victory and receive glory. On the Kabbalah Cube, water is one of the primordial elements that everything is created *from*. When *Mem* is used as a prefix, it means *from*. As a suffix it represents the masculine plural (a grouping of males and females). The numerical Tarot card would be Death, which is symbolic of rebirth through baptism/mikvah (Romans 6:3).

The Talisman: This *Kame'ah* contains the divine name *EL*, which means *mighty*. The names of angels usually end in *el* (Michael, Gabriel, Uriel, Raphael), and human names such as Daniel (God is my Judge), Ezekiel (God will strengthen), or Azriel (God is my help) all have meanings that are related to God. *Chesed* is the fourth *Sefirah* and represents one's covenant with God and loving kindness. *Chesed* is at the center of the Pillar of Mercy (which is crowned by *Mem*), just as *Mem* is in the middle of the *Alef-bet* and at the center of the word *truth* (*EMeT*). "*And he separated the water*" is written in Hebrew, and the waters are symbolically separated by a line at the center of the talisman, which represents the heavens and the earth, the above and below. Purification and Holiness are key aspects of *Mem*, as is the concept of transformation. The closed *Mem* is below, implying that some of the mysteries are hidden from those on the earth, but the *Mem* above has an opening at its bottom, allowing the water and spirit to pour down blessings on those below. This talisman can be used as a reminder that overcoming adversity leads to personal growth, and that victory (*Netzach*) leads to glory (*Hod*). The *Vav* is guided and supported by the *Kaf*, which later unites with it, becoming one with the Spirit (*Mem Sofit*), and thereby the *Vav* (humanity) finds their connection with the Tetragrammaton (26).

THE LETTER *Nun*

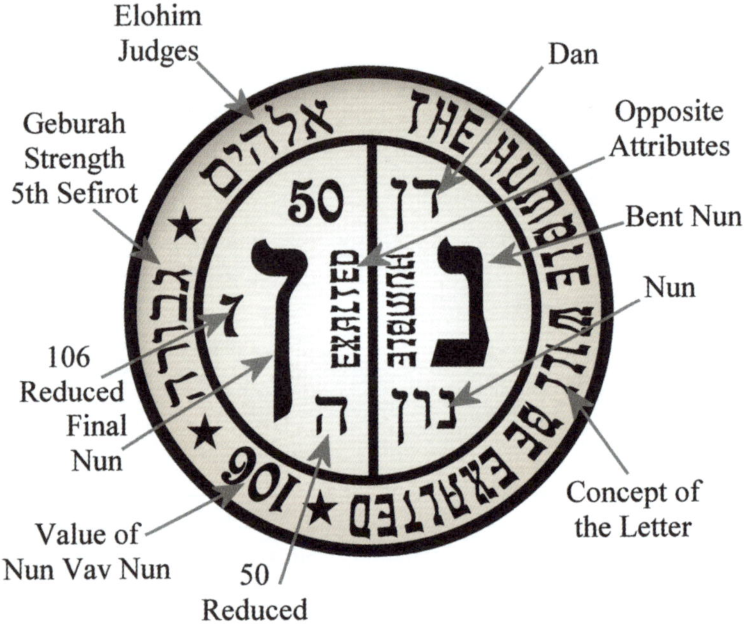

Letter: Nun, Vav, Nun

Transliteration: Nun

English Letter: N

Sound: Noon

Gematria Value: 50

Reduced Value: 5

Etz Chayim Sefirot: Strength

Ten Commandments: Honor (higher) parents for a long (eternal) life

Name Value: 50 + 50 + 6 = 106 = 1 + 0 + 6 = 7

Name Meaning: Failure, fish, kingship, or miracle

Sequential Number: 14

Sefer Yetzirah Classification: Single/Simple

Sefer Yetzirah Attribute: Smell

Hermetic Tree Path: Tiferet-Netzach

Hermetic Tarot: Death

Lurianic Tree Path: Yesod-Netzach

Kabbalah Cube Path: Binah-Geburah-Hod

Numerical Tarot: Temperance

Constructed Gematria: Bent and erect Vav 6

Prefix/Suffix: Prefix, verb conjugation (We will) / suffix, VN, third-person female possessive

Mystical Associations: The Hebrew letter *Nun* is the 14th consecutive letter; it means *failure* or *fish* and has a value of 50. On the Dreidel, the *Nun* represents *Nes* (miracle). *Nun* is the third letter with a *Sofit*, and it is compared to a humble person who is later exalted (1 Samuel 2:7, Job 5:11, Proverbs 29:23, Luke 14:11, 1 Peter 5:6). The bent *Nun* represents someone bowing, and the straight *Nun* at the end of a word represents the person standing tall with renown (Shabbat 104a:5).

Similar to the purification and transformation aspects of the *Mem*, the *Nun* can represent a period of trial followed by reward. The 50th year is referred to as the Jubilee (Yovel), during which all lands and the slaves are set free. The word for land (*Adamah*) has a gematria value of 50. Following Passover and the death of the firstborn in Egypt, the Israelites spent 50 days traveling across the desert to Mount Sinai, where they received the Torah and were transformed from being slaves in Egypt into a Kingdom of Priests and a Holy Nation (Exodus 19:6).

On the 10th day of Nisan, a yearling male lamb or goat was selected, and it was sacrificed on the 14th day of Nisan (Exodus 12:6). Beginning on the second night of Pesach, Jews count the *Omer* (a unit of measurement of grain) for 49 days until reaching the holiday of *Shavuot* (weeks), which celebrates the spring harvest and commemorates receiving the Torah at Mount Sinai. Counting the *Omer* is a biblical commandment (Leviticus 23:15–16) and is therefore a *Mitzvot* and *Segulot*. Christianity observes this same period of time, which roughly coincides with the seven weeks following Easter Sunday to Pentecost (50th day). On Pentecost, the Apostles received the Holy Spirit (Acts 2:1). The reduced value of 50 is 5, which represents the Spirit/Breath (*Hei*). The Spirit of

Wisdom is synonymously with the Torah (five books of Moses): "*She is the book of the commandments of God, and the law that endures forever. All who hold her fast will live*" (Baruch 4:1). The Festival of Unleavened Bread commemorates the first seven days of the Israelites' journey out of Egypt, until they crossed the Red Sea (Sea of Reeds) and were freed from their oppressors. The Chymical Wedding of Christian Rosenkreutz also begins on Passover, and his journey of spiritual growth takes place over the next seven days.

Counting the Omer is associated with the house of Wisdom, which is built on seven pillars (Proverbs 9:1) and is referred to as the 50 Gates of *Binah*. The Talmud states, "*Fifty gates of understanding were created in the world, and all of them were given to Moses, except for one gate, for it is stated: 'The words of the Lord are purified shivatayim,' which he understands to mean seven times seven, i.e., forty-nine, and it is stated: 'And You have made him a little less than God' (Psalm 8:6). God created fifty gates of understanding, but He made man a little lower than God, giving him only forty-nine of them*" (Rosh Hashanah 21b:11). Counting the Omer can be done using an Omer Counter, such as the one in the following table, which is arranged into seven pillars.

The calendar is arranged according to the seven lower *Sefirot* (below the Supernal Triad) and is arranged vertically from top to bottom as *Chesed*, *Geburah*, *Tiferet*, *Netzach*, *Hod*, *Yesod*, and *Malkut*. The same order is assigned horizontally from right to left (as Hebrew is read), with each day/square given a consecutive number from right to left and top to bottom. Starting from the top right, the first day would be counted by verbally stating

> "*Today is _______ day(s), which is _________ week(s), and ________ days of the Omer,*" which in Hebrew would be "*HaYom ____ Yom, Shehem ______ V'_____ Yomim L'Omer.*"

If one can count in Hebrew, that is preferred; however, performing the *Mitzvot* in English is better than not at all. In addition to counting the Omer, one can meditate on the mixed properties of the two concerned *Sefirot* and the lessons that can be learned from them. For example, day 1 combines *Chesed* and *Chesed*, day 2 combines *Chesed* and *Geburah*, and day 3 is a mixture of *Chesed* and *Tiferet*. Each day provides an opportunity to meditate on specific attributes of the Kabbalah, which can be combined with numerology/gematria for even-deeper contemplations.

Days ←

	Malkuth	Yesod	Hod	Netzach	Tiferet	Geburah	Chesed	
Chesed	חֶסֶד 7 ז מַלְכוּת	חֶסֶד 6 ו יְסוֹד	חֶסֶד 5 ה הוֹד	חֶסֶד 4 ד נֶצַח	חֶסֶד 3 ג תִּפְאֶרֶת	חֶסֶד 2 ב גְבוּרָה	חֶסֶד 1 א חֶסֶד	Week 1
Geburah	גְבוּרָה 14 יד מַלְכוּת	גְבוּרָה 13 יג יְסוֹד	גְבוּרָה 12 יב הוֹד	גְבוּרָה 11 יא נֶצַח	גְבוּרָה 10 י תִּפְאֶרֶת	גְבוּרָה 9 ט גְבוּרָה	גְבוּרָה 8 ח חֶסֶד	Week 2
Tiferet	תִּפְאֶרֶת 21 כא מַלְכוּת	תִּפְאֶרֶת 20 כ יְסוֹד	תִּפְאֶרֶת 19 יט הוֹד	תִּפְאֶרֶת 18 יח נֶצַח	תִּפְאֶרֶת 17 יז תִּפְאֶרֶת	תִּפְאֶרֶת 16 טז גְבוּרָה	תִּפְאֶרֶת 15 טו חֶסֶד	Week 3
Netzach	נֶצַח 28 כח מַלְכוּת	נֶצַח 27 כז יְסוֹד	נֶצַח 26 כו הוֹד	נֶצַח 25 כה נֶצַח	נֶצַח 24 כד תִּפְאֶרֶת	נֶצַח 23 כג גְבוּרָה	נֶצַח 22 כב חֶסֶד	Week 4
Hod	הוֹד 35 לה מַלְכוּת	הוֹד 34 לד יְסוֹד	הוֹד 33 לג הוֹד	הוֹד 32 לב נֶצַח	הוֹד 31 לא תִּפְאֶרֶת	הוֹד 30 ל גְבוּרָה	הוֹד 29 כט חֶסֶד	Week 5
Yesod	יְסוֹד 42 מב מַלְכוּת	יְסוֹד 41 מא יְסוֹד	יְסוֹד 40 מ הוֹד	יְסוֹד 39 לט נֶצַח	יְסוֹד 38 לח תִּפְאֶרֶת	יְסוֹד 37 לז גְבוּרָה	יְסוֹד 36 לו חֶסֶד	Week 6
Malkuth	מַלְכוּת 49 מט מַלְכוּת	מַלְכוּת 48 מח יְסוֹד	מַלְכוּת 47 מז הוֹד	מַלְכוּת 46 מו נֶצַח	מַלְכוּת 45 מה תִּפְאֶרֶת	מַלְכוּת 44 מד גְבוּרָה	מַלְכוּת 43 מג חֶסֶד	Week 7

Omer Calendar

The attributes of humility and being exalted reflect a repeating pattern within the universe. We overcome difficulties while learning and growing through our experiences. Sometimes we are at the bottom of the wheel and sometimes we are at the top. We might seem to be *failures*, but then *miracles* can take place, and the slaves can be freed. Those who felt forsaken or abandoned can receive divine blessing. The great *miracle* that the *Nes* on the Dreidel commemorates is that a defeated people (viewed as *failures* by their enemies) received the blessing of God, who gave them strength through their struggles and enabled them to retake the Temple and obtain *victory*.

The fifth *Sefirah* is *Geburah* and represents the attributes of strength and judgment sustaining a person during troubling times. The fifth of the Ten Commandments is to honor one's parents. The gematria value of the letters that spell *Nun* (*Nun Van Nun*) equals 106 and reduces to 7 (*Netzach*/Victory). The conjunction *Vav* reminds the two *Nun* that they are connected, and the humble state is linked with its final exalted state. Those who have overcome trials are able to stand proud.

The Sefer Yetzirah classifies *Nun* as a single/simple letter and associates it with *smell* and the zodiac sign Scorpio. In Aramaic and the original pictograph, the *Nun* meant *fish*, which is used as a remedy against evil. Fish are said to be immune from the Evil Eye (*Ayin HaRa*), which is why in addition to the Hamsa, a blue fish eye is used to ward off the Evil Eye. The Zohar states, "*I am not afraid of an evil eye, for I am the son of a great and precious fish, and a fish does not fear from the evil eye, as it is written: 'and they shall multiply abundantly like fish upon the earth' [Genesis 48:16]*" (Zohar 3:187a:7). In the book of Tobit, the angel Raphael instructed Tobias to burn parts of a fish to ward of the demon Asmodeus (Tobit 6:16–17), which combines the attributes of both *fish* and *smell*.

On the Hermetic Tree, *Nun* is on the path connecting *Tiferet* and *Netzach*, which would be on the 18th day of the *Omer*. This path might symbolize that balance brings victory. This path is associated with the Tarot card of Death, which represents change and the need to face trials in order to obtain victory. Moses went before Pharaoh to save the children of Israel and struggled with Pharaoh prior to obtaining victory and receiving the Torah. Esther likewise went before the king in order to save the Jews, and recognizing that she might be killed for her efforts, she stated, "*I will go before the King, and if I die, I die*" (Esther 4:16). Through her bowed/difficult times, she obtained miraculous victory.

On the Lurianic Tree, *Nun* is on the path connecting *Yesod* and *Netzach*. On the Kabbalah Cube, *Nun* connects *Binah*, *Geburah*, and *Hod* and represents the Pillar of Severity and learning through adversity (by facing hardships). The numerical Tarot card would be Temperance, which shows the angel of the LORD, balancing two cups, representing opposites, which in association with *Nun* might represent adversity and reward, hardships and honor, or perseverance and glory.

The letter *Nun* is constructed by a bent *Vav* (which is also the letter that connects the two *Nun* in the word describing the letter) and an extended *Vav*, representing humankind both in their humbled and exalted states. When *Nun* is used as a prefix, it modifies a verb to denote "*We will,*" as seen in Exodus 19:8, where it was added to *Oseh* to mean *We will do*: "*And all the people answered together, what HaShem has said, We will do.*" As a suffix, *Nun* serves as the second- or third-person feminine possessive.

The Talisman: The talisman contains the divine name *Elohim*, which is usually associated with the Creation or Judgment aspects of God. *Elohim* can also refer to angels or humans as judges. *Geburah* is the fifth *Sefirah* and is associated with strength, justice, and judgment. The value of the word *Nun* is 106, which reduces to 7. Seven is the day for rest after a week of work. It is the *Shabbat*, which multiplied by 7 would represent the Jubilee. The seventh *Sefirah* is *Netzach*, which begins with the letter *Nun*, and 50 reduced is the value of *Hei* (Breath/Spirit). Written above the bent *Nun* is the name Dan (*Dalet Nun*), which means Judge. Dan was the fifth son of Jacob. This talisman can be used as a reminder of the need for perseverance during troubling times, which are linked to future successes. The path may be difficult, but you will eventually reach the land of milk and honey.

THE LETTER *Samech*

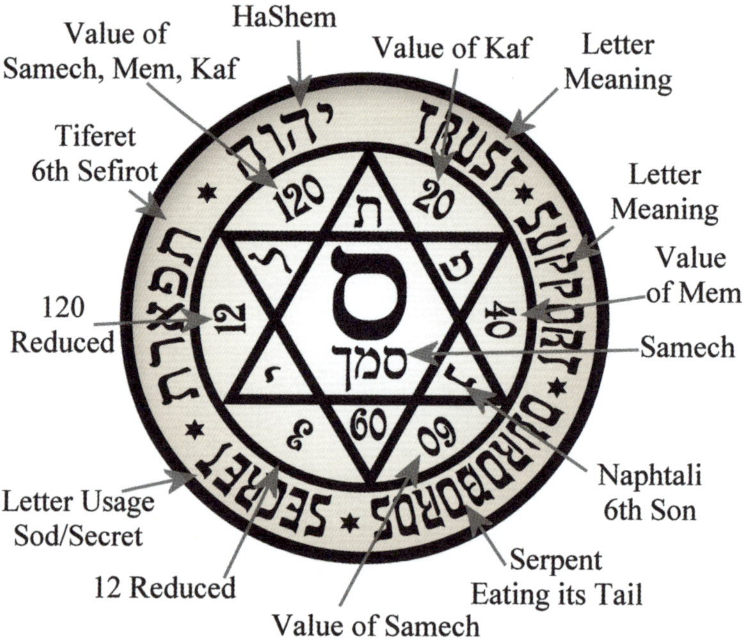

Letter: Samech, Mem, Kaf

Transliteration: Samech

English Letter: S

Sound: Serpent

Gematria Value: 60

Reduced Value: 6

Etz Chayim Sefirot: Tiferet

Ten Commandments: Do not murder

Name Value: 60 + 40 + 20 = 1 + 2 = 3

Name Meaning: Trust, depend on, lean on, support

Sequential Number: 15 (YaH)

Sefer Yetzirah Classification: Single/Simple

Sefer Yetzirah Attribute: Sleep

Hermetic Tree Path: Tiferet-Yesod

Hermetic Tarot: Temperance

Lurianic Tree Path: Tiferet-Hod

Kabbalah Cube Path: Yesod-Hod

Numerical Tarot: Devil

Constructed Gematria: Closed circle (infinity)

Prefix/Suffix: N/A

Mystical Associations: The Hebrew letter *Samech* is the 15th consecutive letter; it means *support* or *trust* and has a gematria value of 60. The Priestly Blessing (Numbers 6:23–27) consists of 15 words, with a total of 60 letters. *Samech* is closely related to *Nun*, the 14th letter. On the 14th day of Nisan, the Passover Lamb is sacrificed, and it is eaten on the 15th of Nisan (which begins at sunset). The 15th of Nisan also begins the Festival of Unleavened Bread, which lasts for seven days and commemorates the Israelites journeying out of Egypt to the Red Sea. Passover is associated with the 10th Plague of Egypt, which is what caused Pharaoh to let the Israelites go. At the conclusion of the seventh day of Unleavened Bread, the Red Sea was parted and Israel was freed from their oppressors; both of these evens were miracles.

The word for *miracle* is *Nes* (*Nun Samech*) and represents the bent *Nun* (humbled) being *supported* by the *Samech*, so that it can stand tall. The three letters of the *Alef-bet*, starting from *Samech* and read left to right (*Samech, Nun, Mem*), spell the plural form of *Nes* (Nisim) and remind us of the Morning Prayers, *Nisim B'Chol Yom* (Miracles in All Day), which thank God for Daily Miracles. The *Nisim B'Chol Yom* consists of 14 or 15 *Barchu* (Blessings), starting with the mind being given *Binah* and concluding with us being sanctified by the words of Torah (Mishkan T'Filah for Shabbat; Central Conference of American Rabbis 2007). In addition to the prayer mentioning *Binah* (Understanding), *Geburah* (Strength), and *Tiferet* (Splendor), it reminds us that *HaShem* lifts up the fallen, referencing *HaShem Somaech* (Supporting/ Upholding) the fallen and raising those who are bowed down (as the *Nun*) (Psalm 145:14).

The number 15 is one of two numbers that are written in a different format in order to avoid profaning the name of God (Leviticus 22:32). Instead of 15 being written using a *Yod Hei* (the divine name YaH), the letters *Tet Vav* are used to produce the same gematria value. The gematria value of *Aviv* (spring) is also 15 and marks the beginning of the religious new year. Nisan is the first month of spring (*Aviv*), and on the 15th of that month the Festival of Unleavened Bread begins and lasts for seven days. The *15th* of Av (Tu B'Av) is also a celebration of love and renewal, wherein the daughters would go to the vineyards and dance where the males would go to find brides.

The shape of the *Samech* is of a closed circle; it resembles the ouroboros (the serpent who eats its own tail) and represents eternity and cycles. *Aviv* and *Nisan* represent the first month of spring and the beginning of a new year/cycle. The Magician in the Rider-Waite Tarot wears an ouroboros as his belt and holds a wand in his hand. The Passover Meal is to be eaten with one's loins girded (wearing a belt) and with a staff in one's hand (Exodus 12:11). The enclosed circle can also symbolize a wedding band, which represents God's covenant with his people.

Following the counting of the *Omer*, which begins on the second night of Passover and lasts seven weeks (seven sets of seven), the Israelites received the Torah at Mount Sinai, which is symbolic of God giving a *Ketubah* (Marriage Contract) to his bride (Jeremiah 31:32, Isaiah 54:5, Ezekiel 16:8). The wedding band is a symbol of *trust* and *support*. During a wedding, the bride walks around (encircles) her husband seven times under the *Chuppah*. Similarly, on the seventh day, the Israelites circled around Jericho seven times (seven times on the seventh), which caused the walls around Jericho to collapse (Joshua 6:15). Rahab was rescued from inside its walls, and she later married Joshua, and her descendants include the prophets Jeremiah, Baruch, Huldah, and Ezekiel and other noteworthy people such as Boaz, King David, King Solomon, and Jesus (Matthew 1:5). The bride walking around the husband seven times can be symbolically viewed as removing his emotional walls/barriers, so that their souls can be joined in perfect union.

The Torah was given at the completion of the Counting of the Omer, during the Festival of Sukkot. The Torah included four levels/layers of truth (Flames of Faith 10:17). The four levels of truth (PaRDeS) are associated with the four worlds of the Kabbalah (*Atziluth*, *Briah*, *Yetzirah*, and *Assiah*). Each of the four worlds is associated with one of the letters of the Tetragrammaton and the different types of interpretations (PaRDeS). *Samech* is the first letter in the word *Sod* (secret); it is shaped as a closed circle, similar to how the *Mem Sofit* is used to represent concealed *truth* (EMeT). Without the *Samech* (*Sod*), PaRDeS spells only *Pered* (*separated*).

Both the *Samech* and the *Mem Sofit* are closed letters, and they resemble each other. Together *Samech Mem* is the word for medicine or potion. *Samech Mem* is also used as an abbreviation of *Samael Malakh* (the angel Samael), who is said to be the Guardian Angel of Esau, the counterpart of Lilith, and the Serpent from the Garden of Eden, who deceived Eve with the venom (*Samech Mem* / potion) of his mouth. Samael is the accusing angel, is associated with the *Yetzer HaRa* (evil inclination), and is the equivalent of the Devil in Christianity.

According to Rashi, it was the angel Samael that Jacob wrestled with prior to confronting Esau the next day. In addition to the number 666 representing the value of the different categories of the Roman alphabet being added together, the gematria value in Hebrew would be *Mem Sofit* (600), *Samech* (60), and *Vav* (6), which spells *V'SM*, meaning *And Samael Malakh* (and venom, drug, poison, toxin), representing that in addition to Rome, the false church would be led by the deceptive teachings of the Great Dragon/Serpent (Revelation 13:2–4).

The gematria value of 60 reduces to 6 and reminds us of the creation of man, and the events that took place in the Garden with the Serpent. The sixth *Sefirah* is *Tiferet*, which represents humans (Adam) having obtained Knowledge of Good and Evil and having become *Kaf-Elohim* (like the Angels/Judges). Having gained this knowledge, humans struggle with the *Yetzer HaRa* (evil inclination), just as Jacob did when he wrestled with Esau's Guardian Angel. The sixth commandment is to not murder, and the 15th of the 613 Mitzvot is the commandment not to hate one's brother in your heart (Leviticus 19:17); Jacob wrestled with the angel, the night before his brother sought to kill him.

The value of the letters that spell *Samech* is 120, which reduces to 12 and 3. The 12th letter is *Mem* and represents purification, and the third is *Gimel*, which represents the camel *supporting* its rider. The Sefer Yetzirah lists *Samech* as one of the simple letters and associates it with *sleep*. God speaks to his people in their sleep (Numbers 12:6, Genesis 15:12), and it was during the night that Jacob wrestled with the angel (Genesis 32:24). Sleep is a time when humans mentally process and compartmentalize the experiences they encounter during their waking states. It is a mental state that enables them to contemplate literal experiences metaphorically, and gives them the opportunity to comprehend *secrets*.

On the Hermetic Tree of Life, *Samech* is on the path that connects *Tiferet* and *Yesod*. This path is associated with the Tarot card of Temperance and the Chymical Wedding of alchemy. On the Lurianic Tree, *Samech* is on the path connecting *Tiferet* and *Hod*. On the Kabbalah Cube, it is on the path connecting *Yesod* and *Hod*; when these three different representations are combined, they form an oblique triangle that points toward *Chokmah*. The numerical Tarot card would be the Devil, which would represent the angel Samael and the need for humans to overcome the serpent and the *Yetzer HaRa*.

The Talisman: The Tetragrammaton is the divine name associated with *Tiferet* (the reduced value of 60) and represents the heart of the Kabbalah, the balance between Justice and Mercy, and the connection between Heaven and Earth. Written around the outside of the circle are the words *trust* and *support*, which is the meaning of *Samech*, and the ouroboros is the shape the letter resembles. The word *secret* begins with a *Samech* and represents the *Sod* of PaRDeS (the concealed meaning of a verse). The Hexagram represents the union of the male and female, representing the marriage of human couples or Israel receiving the Torah at Mount Sinai. Around the outside of the star (starting with 60) are the gematria values of the letters of *Samech* and their reduced values. Inside the points of the star are the letters that spell Naphtali, who was the sixth son of Jacob. Naphtali was given his birth name to represent Rachel having prevailed in her wrestling (just as Jacob did with the angel). Naphtali was an emissary and represents communication (Genesis 49:21). This **talisman** can be used as a reminder that you are being supported, even if it is being done only in secret. It also speaks to the need for clear communication (without deception) and balancing of the Pillars of Severity and Mercy. It can also represent spring, new relationships, or marriage, commitment, and support within a union or overcoming adversaries.

THE LETTER *Ayin*

Letter: Ayin, Yod, Nun

Transliteration: Ayin

English Letter: A

Sound: Silent (like Alef it takes on the sound of the vowels around it)

Gematria Value: 70

Reduced Value: 7

Etz Chayim Sefirot: Netzach

10 Commandments: Adultery

Name Value: 70 + 10 + 50 = 13 = 1 + 3 = 4

Name Meaning: Eye, look, study, consider, perception (good/evil eye)

Sequential Number: 16

Sefer Yetzirah Classification: Single/Simple

Sefer Yetzirah Attribute: Anger/wrath

Hermetic Tree Path: Tiferet-Hod

Hermetic Tarot: Devil

Lurianic Tree Path: Binah-Tiferet

Kabbalah Cube Path: Keter-Chokmah

Numerical Tarot: Tower

Constructed Gematria: Zayin, Nun, 57

Prefix/Suffix: N/A

Mystical Associations: The Hebrew letter *Ayin* is the 16th consecutive letter in the Hebrew *Alef-bet*; it means *eye* and has a gematria value of 70. The letter represents *perception* and includes and contrasts both the *Yetzer HaTov* and the *Yetzer HaRa*, the good and the evil inclinations. In Genesis 1:3, God created *light* (*Alef Vav Resh*) and saw that it was good (Genesis 1:4). God separated the light from the darkness, but after humans ate from the Tree of Knowledge of Good and Evil and became aware of good and evil (Genesis 3:22), God clothed them with garments of *skin* (*Ayin Vav Resh*) (Genesis 3:21) and sent them out of the garden. The words *light* (*Alef Vav Resh*) and *skin* (*Ayin Vav Resh*) sounds the same, but they have opposite meanings. Light allows people to see, but the word *skin* also means to conceal, hide, or blind. God clothes himself in a garment of *light* (Psalm 104:2), but humans were clothed in a garment of skins/blindness (Genesis 3:21). After they gained the ability to understand good and evil, God clothed them with a garment of blindness and sent them into the world to master their perception. As Solomon stated, "*It is the glory of God to conceal things, and the honor of kings to seek out a matter*" (Proverbs 25:2).

The Sefer Yetzirah classifies the letter *Ayin* as one of the 12 simple letters and associates it with *anger* or *wrath*; it can therefore be associated with the Evil Eye (*Ayin HaRa*), which describes an angry or jealous look. The gematria value of 70 reduces to 7 (*Zayin*) and connects it with the concept of lust, illicit sexual intercourse, or a sword/arrow (instruments of wrath). The seventh commandment is not to commit adultery, which is the result of lust or surrendering to the *Yetzer HaRa* (or both) and is part of the conflict between good and evil—faithfulness to God or being enticed into idolatry (Numbers 25:1–3, Revelation 2:14).

Ayin, like *Alef*, is a silent letter, and both represent humanity as an Image of God (*B'tzelem Elohim*). The *Alef* is the more ideal state of Adam Kadmon prior to his sin, and the *Ayin* symbolizes humanity after having become *Kaf-Elohim* (Like God/Judges) and having obtained an awareness of good and evil (*Resh ayin*). Although one's actions/choices may not be heard, that doesn't mean that they are not observed/perceived; for "*the eyes of the LORD are in everyplace, keeping watch on the evil and the good*" (Proverbs 15:3). Violating the seventh commandment is a transgression against both God and one's spouse; it is a sin against one's own flesh (1 Corinthians 6:18).

Of the 613 Mitzvot, the 16th is the commandment not to hate one's neighbor, and the obligation to correct one's neighbor when they are observed going astray (Leviticus 19:17). The 70th Mitzvot addresses the need to behave appropriately in the view of others (Deuteronomy 22:5). Both or these mitzvot are related; one mitzvah addresses one's response to his/her perception of others, and the other expresses the need for one to be cognizant of how one's actions are perceived by others.

The letter *Ayin* is constructed of the bent *Nun* with a *Zayin*. The value of these two letters is 57, which can be reduced to 12 or 3 (57 = 5 + 7 = 12 = 1 + 2 = 3). In Rambam's *Guide for the Perplexed* (part 2, 30:14), he discusses a Midrash that connects to the number 3 (*Gimel*/Camel) by stating, "'*The serpent had a rider, the rider was as big as a camel, and it was the rider that enticed Eve: this rider was Samaël.' Samaël is the name generally applied by our Sages to Satan.*" The serpent and its rider were equated with a camel (Pirkei DeRabbi Eliezer 13:2), and its rider was Samael, whom the Rabbis associated with the evil inclination (Sefer HaIkkarim, Maamar 1:11:7). Samael is the spirit of lechery, "*whose lecherous feelings were aroused by the sight of Adam and Eve copulating. The serpent which used to walk on legs was punished by having is legs cut off. The thigh joint (to which the legs are attached) is within the domain of the sexual organs*" (Shenei Luchot HaBerit, Torah Shebikhta, Vayishlach, Ner Mitzvah 5–6). This area (the socket of the hip) is what Samael targeted when he realized that he could not overpower Jacob (Genesis 32:25).

Samael is said to have been a great prince in heaven who had 12 wings. Out of envy, cupidity, and ambition he and other ministering angels determined to mislead humans, so they would sin against their Creator (Pirkei DeRabbi Eliezer 13:1–8). Samael descended from heaven and observed creation, and "*he found among them none so skilled to do evil as the serpent, as it said, 'Now the serpent was more subtle than any beast of the field. Its appearance was something like that of the camel, and he mounted and rode upon it*'" (Pirkei DeRabbi Eliezer

13:8). The Zohar equates the serpent with Lilith, Isheth Zenunim, or one of Samael's other female counterparts (Or HaChaim 49:11:3).

> *According to the Zohar the word* דבכ *does not merely mean liver but is a hyperbole for the male with whom Lilith consorts. The spiritually negative forces in this world are sometimes referred to as Samael, sometimes as the serpent. Samael is the male part of that team, Lilith, is the female. When adultery is committed, the female partner is released from the* דבכ, *i.e.* דבכה ןמ. *Having once been released it assumes a dominance over its former partner so that it will qualify for the description* דבכה לע, *"on top of the* דבכ*."* (Or HaChaim 49:11:3)

The *Sefer Yetzirah* associates the letter *Ayin* with *anger*, Capricorn (the Goat), and the *liver* of the soul. The letters *Kaf, Bet, Dalet* (*ka'veid*) mean *liver*, but when different *Niqqud* (vowel points) are used, the letters also spell *ka'vad*, which means heaviness, burdensome, or difficulty (the consequences of giving in to evil). The liver is the seat of life that the adulterous woman (contrasted against the Woman Wisdom in the book of Proverbs) uses persuasive words to take away (Proverbs 7:21–23). She takes away his life through deception, just as the serpent in the garden.

The Talmud also associates the liver with a source of anger (Berakoth 61b:1), and the *Zohar* contrasts the liver with the heart as metaphors for the good and evil inclinations; it compares them to the two nations (Esau and Jacob) within the womb of Rebecca. Esau and Jacob (and later Samael and Israel) struggled from the womb onward. Esau was angry and held a grudge against Jacob (Genesis 27:41), while Jacob was characterized by his love (Genesis 29:18). Jacob is associated with love and Esau with hate (Romans 9:13, Malachi 1:2).

The *Or HaChaim* (49:11:3) associates the liver as hyperbole of an adulterous male who is enticed by the Woman Folly (Proverbs 7:21), and compares the liver to the location where the (*Yetzer HaRa*) demons of anger, jealousy, lust, and vengeances reside in the body, stating that they are awakened and given power over the person when adultery is committed.

In Jewish folklore, *the Aleph Bet of ben Sira* creates an analogy where Lilith is said to be Adam's first wife, and the two argue as to who will be on top. If the Woman Folly (Proverbs 9:16–18) is successful, "*when adultery is committed, the female partner is released from the* [*liver*] דבכ, *i.e.* דבכה ןמ. *Having once been released it assumes a dominance over its former partner so that it will qualify for the description* דבכה לע, *on top of the* דבכ." (Or HaChaim 49:11:3), the demonic nature of *Yetzer HaRa* is released from liver, and Lilith wins her struggle against Adam, having dominated him and obtained the top position.

Lilith is also contrasted against Laylah, with Laylah being the Angel of Conception, and Lilith being the demon responsible for miscarriages and still births. Since Esau was envious/angry over Jacob obtaining the birthright, or since Samael and his band of angels resented the creation humans (Pirkei DeRabbi Eliezer 13:1), Lilith resented what Eve had and sought to destroy it, by causing husbands to commit adultery (Shabbat 151b:11), or by destroying their children. The character of Lilith is described in the *Testament of Solomon* as Obizuth/Abyzou (Abyss), who describes herself as "*by night I sleep not, but go my rounds over all the world, and visit women in childbirth. And divining the hour I take my stand; and if I am lucky, I strangle the child. But if not, I retire to another place. For I cannot for a single night retire unsuccessful. For I am a fierce spirit, of myriad names and many shapes.... For I have no work other than the destruction of children, and the making their ears to be deaf, and the working of evil to their eyes, and the binding their mouths with a bond, and the ruin of their minds, and paining of their bodies.*"

In the Testament of Solomon, she goes on to say that she is frustrated by the angel Raphael, "*by whom I am frustrated now and for all time. His name, if any man know it, and write the same on a woman in childbirth, then I shall not be able to enter her.*" In the *Aleph Bet of ben Sira*, Lilith promises the three angels appointed over healing (Sanoy, Sansanoy, and Semangalof) that whenever she sees their "*names or forms in a talisman, I will have no power over that infant.*" In both cases, it is an angel of healing they thwarts her efforts. Raphael is the Archangel of Healing, and he is the angel who protected Tobias and Sarah from the demon Asmodeus (Tobit 3:17), enabling their successful union.

The first instruction that God gave to humans was to be fruitful and multiply (Genesis 1:28). The ability of couples to unite as one enables them to create new life and to become partners in creation. Faithful relationships are holy unions that are blessed by God (Proverbs 5:18, 18:22; Tobit 4:12; Sirach 26:2–4). In his commentary on the Torah, Rabbi Horovitz (1611) associated the act with the mystical union of *Tiferet* and *Malkut*, he wrote, "*Sacred intentions during mating will bring about a union between the emanation of* **תראפת** *and* **תוכלמ**, *which represents the dual faced Adam before Eve was separated from him. These two emanations symbolize the mystical dimension of the* **גווז**, *physical union of man and wife*" (Shenei Luchot HaBerit, Shebikhtav, Ki Teitzei, Torah Ohr 13). Holy unions based on love and the *Yetzer HaTov* represent the ideal state of marriage, and its opposite is the *Yetzer HaRa*, which symbolizes lust, envy, and selfish sexual gratification and brings with it burdens, weightiness, and difficulties.

In the *Testament of the Twelve Patriarchs*, Benjamin advises his children to "*flee evil-doing, envy, and hatred of brethren, and cleave to goodness and love. He that hath a pure mind in love, looketh not after a woman with a view to fornication; for he hath no defilement in his heart, because the Spirit of God resteth upon him*" (Testament of Benjamin 8:1–2). Benjamin's statement provides an effective example of overcoming the *Yetzer HaRa* with love; he suggests overcoming the *Yetzer HaRa* (envy, hatred, fornication) with love, faithfulness, and a pure heart.

The letter *Ayin* is constructed by a bent *Nun* and a *Zayin*. The *Zayin* can represent intercourse or be viewed as an arrow, a sword, or a phallus, and the *Nun* represents a humble person. The two points of the *Ayin* can be understood as two eyes, or two opposite ways of thinking/perceiving. The right eye looks back toward *Samech*, and the supportive relationship of marriage symbolized by the wedding band and the seven times the wife circles her spouse under the *Chuppah*. The left eye looks toward *Pei*, which means to scatter.

The *Sefer Yetzirah* associates the right eye with the letter *Bet* and Wisdom (*Chokmah*), and the left eye with *Gimel* and *Health*. Although *Gimel* can be viewed as the *Shekinah* carrying its rider through the desert, the *camel* can also be associated with Lilith, the Serpent, and the angels of health as the means to bind her. When Yehshua described the coming of the Messiah, he said the King will separate the sheep from the goats, with the sheep going to the right and into the kingdom and the goats going to the left and to destruction (Matthew 25:32). The goat (Capricorn) is the zodiac sign associated with the letter *Ayin*. The scapegoat on *Yom Kippur* that is sent to *Azazel* (a fallen angel who led a group of angels to fornicate with human women in the book of Enoch) or Samael (Tomer Devorah 1:20; Shenei Luchot HaBerit, Vayishlach, Torah Ohr 63). The goats selected for *HaShem* and *Azazel* are selected by lot. Similarly, *HaShem* obtained Israel as His portion by Lot when He cast lots with 70 angels (Pirkei DeRabbi Eliezer 24:12).

The gematria value of *Ayin* is 70, which can represent the 70 nations of the world. The left eye of *Ayin* looks to the *Pei*, which represents the Jews being scattered among the 70 nations in the Diaspora. When the Kingdom of Judah was conquered by Babylon, they spent 70 years in captivity. There were 70 years before the destruction of the First Temple and the time it started to be rebuilt, and the Second Temple was destroyed in 70 CE. Seventy is also the number of people who traveled with Jacob to Egypt, when they left they homeland to eventually be enslaved (Genesis 46:27). Seventy is the number of Sages who translated the Hebrew Bible into the Greek Septuagint.

The Midrash Bamidar Rabbah contains many other associations to the number 70, such as there being 70 verses from the beginning of Genesis to the curse of the serpent, and in the book of Esther there are 70 verses between the time that Haman is promoted to the time he is a hanged. It also states that there are "*seventy days of goodness which the Holy One gave to Israel—seven days of Passover, eight days of Sukkot, Rosh HaShanah, Yom Kippur, Shavuot and the fifty two days of Shabbat in the solar year make seventy*" (Bamidar Rabbah 14:12).

The gematria of *Ayin* reduces to 7, which points to *Netzach* and the possibility of *victory*. It can also address concepts of sexuality, since *Netzach* is associated with Venus.

On the Hermetic Tree, *Ayin* is on the path connecting *Tiferet* and *Hod* and is associated with the Devil Tarot card, which represents the consequences of wrong choices. The Devil card in the Rider-Waite Tarot deck shows Adam and Eve in their fallen state, after having eating the forbidden fruit offered to them by Samael. On the Lurianic Tree, *Ayin* is on the path connecting *Binah* and *Tiferet* and represents humans gaining understanding over the knowledge (*Daat*) of good and evil that they have obtained. This path can represent comprehension of consequences and the ability to make good choices. On the Kabbalah Cube, *Ayin* is on the path connecting *Keter* and *Chokmah*, the divine male and female, as an example from the above for the below to imitate. The numerical Tarot card is the Tower, which shows the Red King and White Queen falling on two different sides of the Middle Pillar (Tower), representing Adam and Eve's fall from grace and the separation of the Pillars of Severity and Mercy, which need to be rectified within each individual.

The letter *Ayin* is all about perception, and the Kabbalah Tree of Life is a personality chart, which separates the attributes of God and each human into different traits. The diagram can be used to comprehend how Abraham, Isaac, and Jacob fit together on the Three Pillars, or how Boaz, Jachin, David, and Solomon built and supported the Temple and house of the *Shekinah*. The Tree of the Kabbalah is a unique psychological tool; however, the attributes of Matriarchs, Patriarchs, and the 12 Tribes also correspond to the personality types that have been identified through the sciences and modern psychology.

Modern personality classifications started with the work of Carl Jung, who classified people into two sets of opposites (rational and irrational) and (introverted and extroverted). These four categories were further delineated into eight psychological types. Briggs Myers and McCaulley (1985) expanded on Jung's work and produced four sets of opposites that can be mixed and matched into 16 personality types. Myers–Briggs Type Indicator examines a person's favored world, how a person takes in information, makes decisions, and interacts with the world (Briggs Myers 1995).

The favored world deals with a person's introverted or extroverted nature, which they classify as either E or I (extraversion or introversion). For the Learning/Processing categories, the S or N (sensing or intuition) deals with how a person comprehends new information, as to whether a person learns by analyzing concepts to understand the idea, or if they need to experience or engage in it (hands on). Decision-making is either T or F (thinking or feeling) and deals with how one makes choices: if they do so objectively, by examining statists, data, and best practices (thinking), or if they use a subjective approach and listen to their emotions. The final category looks at a person's preferred method of interacting with the world and classifies it by J or P (judging or perceiving); when one implements a decision or begins to pursue one's selected goal, do they trust their judgment and follow through with their thought-out plan, or do they perceive how things are going and make adjustments along the way until settling on something functional.

David Keirsey's temperaments (2006) builds on the Myers–Briggs model and adds keywords to each of the letter combinations of the Myers–Briggs personality types to make them easier to understand. Keirsey also examined if people preferred to work alone or with others, and if they preferred abstract or concrete concepts. In the following personality table, I have combined the works of Jung, Briggs Myers, Keirsey, and the Four Humors of ancient Greece with the personality attributes of the Matriarchs, Patriarchs, and 12 Tribes of Judah, which predate the Four Humors by more than a thousand years. As Solomon stated, there is nothing new under the sun (Ecclesiastes 1:9); people just organize the same information into a new models that they are more comfortable with.

In the personality table, the four categories are the intersection of the Left Brain and Right Brain columns and the introverted and extroverted rows. Sarah is in the top right, because she was more caring, she thought about Abraham and placed his needs over her own and believed that she was too old to have children, and she encouraged Abraham to father children with Hagar (Genesis 16:1–3). Rebecca was a thinker and strategizer, who instructed Jacob in how to obtain the blessing of the firstborn (Genesis 27:5–17). Leah was a devoted mother and is associated with structure, family, and dependability. Rachel was a fervent doer and was Jacob's passionate love, whom he met while she was shepherding her father's flock (Genesis 29:6). This covers the positions of the four Matriarchs who are represented on the talisman. The remainder of the attributes in the personality table will not be explained in detail but are made available to the reader as an avenue of contemplation; each of the 12 Tribes played a specific role in their society and is associated with specific character traits and attributes in relation to the blessings the received from Jacob (Genesis 49:1–27) and Moses (Deuteronomy 33:6–25). Other attributes listed in the table include the positions of the heavenly and earthly couples (YaH and Adam and Eve), the Worlds of the Kabbalah, the Suits of the Tarot, and the aspects of the Soul. Following the personality table is a representation of the Lurianic Kabbalah, with the consecutive/numerical Tarot, five aspects of the Soul, 12 Tribes, and Myers–Briggs typology and Maslow's hierarchy of needs divided among the *Sefirot*.

The Talisman: The talisman contains the divine name *YHVH Tzabaoth* (God of Hosts/Armies), a reminder that physical and spiritual battles that are taking place in the lower *Sefirot* are closer to the world of Action. The value of *Ayin* is 70, which reduces to 7. The seventh *Sefirot* is *Netzach* and is associated with Venus, the Roman goddess of love, desire, beauty, and fertility, which are attributes the *Ayin* needs to perceive and make choices regarding. The left and right sides of the *Ayin* represent the *Yetzer HaRa* and *Yetzer HaTov*, the *evil* and the *good* inclinations that are attributes all humans share. At the center of the talisman is a downward-facing Hamsa, which represents the blessings of God, or you reaching down to help someone in need (Tzedakah). The Hamsa is a talisman that protects against the Evil Eye, and the *Ayin* at its center means Eye and is used in place of the All-Seeing Eye that some Hamsa use a blue fish eye in place of. The Talmud links fish with the blessing of Jacob to Joseph's sons, where he compared them to fish. Just as fish are covered by water and not perceived, so that the evil eye has no power over them, the offspring of Joseph are said to be immune to the evil eye (Berakhot 55b:12). In relation to the evil eye, the Talmud instructs descendants of Joseph who enter a city and fear the evil eye to "*hold the thumb [zekafa] of his right hand in his left hand and the thumb of his left hand in his right hand and recite the following: I, so-and-so of so-and-so, come from the descendants of Joseph, over whom the evil eye has no dominion.*" Perception is a key attribute of *Ayin*. The letters that spell *Ayin* can be reduced to 4, which can represent the 4 Matriarchs (Sarah, Rebecca, Rachel, and Leah), who were the doorways (dalet) to life of the 12 Tribes, or 13 children (including Jacob's only daughter, Dinah). On the talisman, the names of the 4 Matriarchs are written around the Hamsa and are divided into quadrants to represent their unique attributes.

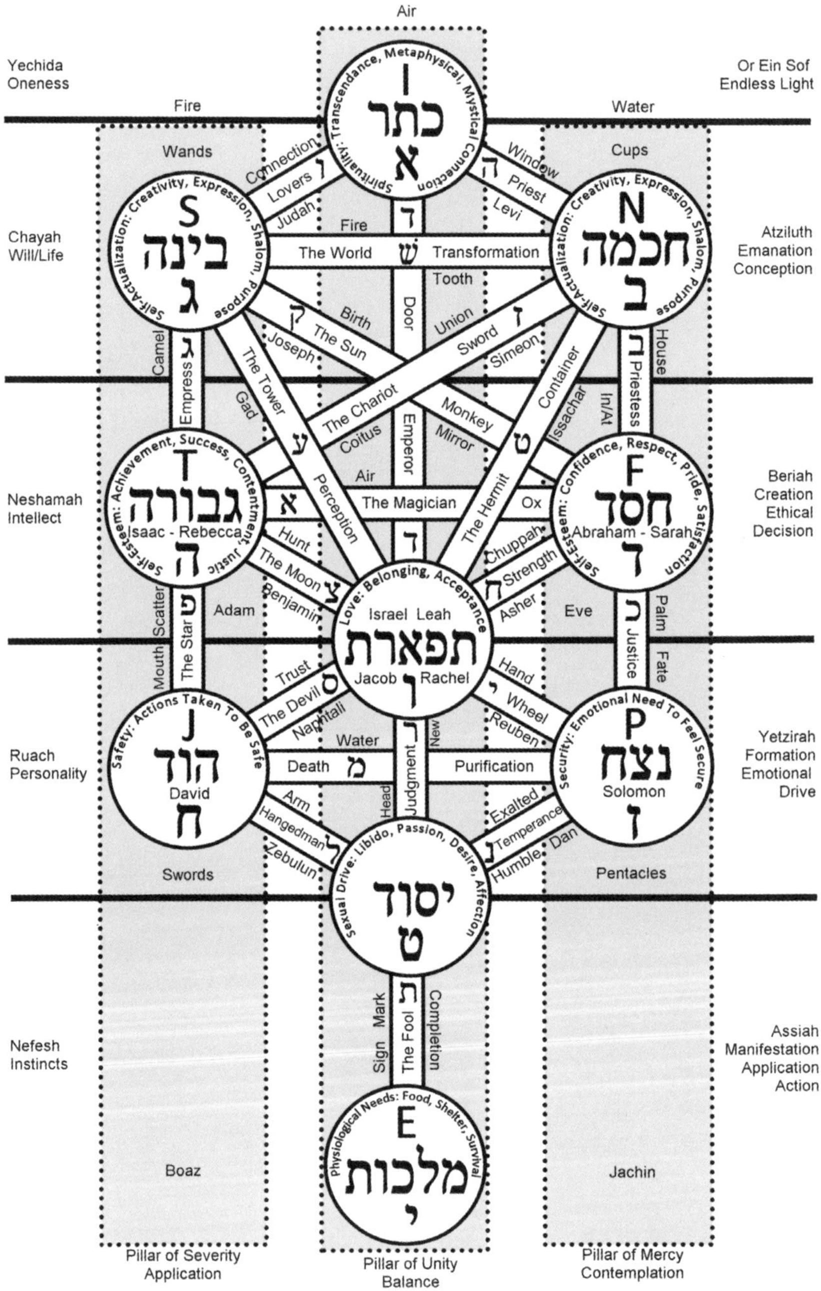
Air
Yechida
Oneness
Or Ein Sof
Endless Light
Fire
Water
Spirituality: Transcendance, Metaphysical, Mystical Connection
I
כתר
א
Wands
Cups
Connection
Lovers
Judah
Window
Priest
Levi
Creativity, Expression, Shalom, Purpose
Self-Actualization: Creativity, Expression, Shalom, Purpose
S
בינה
ג
N
חכמה
ב
Chayah
Will/Life
Atziluth
Emanation
Conception
Fire
The World
Transformation
Tooth
Door
Birth
The Sun
Joseph
Union
Sword
Simeon
Container
Camel
Empress
The Tower
Gad
House
Priestess
In/At
Issachar
The Chariot
Coitus
Emperor
Monkey
Mirror
Self-Esteem: Achievement, Success, Contentment, Justic
T
גבורה
Isaac - Rebecca
ה
Self-Esteem: Confidence, Respect, Pride, Satisfaction
F
חסד
Abraham - Sarah
ד
Neshamah
Intellect
Beriah
Creation
Ethical
Decision
Air
The Magician
The Hermit
Ox
Perception
Hunt
The Moon
Benjamin
Chuppah
Strength
Asher
Love: Belonging, Acceptance
Israel Leah
תפארת
Jacob Rachel
ו
Scatter
Mouth
The Star
Adam
Eve
Palm
Justice
Fate
Trust
The Devil
Naphtali
Hand
Wheel
Reuben
Safety: Actions Taken To Be Safe
J
הוד
David
ח
Security: Emotional Need To Feel Secure
P
נצח
Solomon
ז
Ruach
Personality
Yetzirah
Formation
Emotional
Drive
Water
Death
Judgment
New
Purification
Head
Arm
Hangedman
Zebulun
Exalted
Temperance
Humble
Dan
Swords
Pentacles
Sexual Drive: Libido, Passion, Desire, Affection
יסוד
ט
Sign
Mark
The Fool
Completion
Nefesh
Instincts
Assiah
Manifestation
Application
Action
Physiological Needs: Food, Shelter, Survival
E
מלכות
י
Boaz
Jachin
Pillar of Severity
Application
Pillar of Unity
Balance
Pillar of Mercy
Contemplation

PERSONALITY TABLE

	FIRE Left-Brain (Intellect) Sun	WATER Right-Brain (Emotion), Moon
AIR Reflection Contemplation Introverted Thought	REBECCA/ISAAC Strategic/Analytical/ Implementing Joseph (Tree) – Increaser, Provider Simeon (Sword) – Justice, Shrewdness Zebulun (Ship) – Dwelling, Safe Haven Kabbalah: Conception/ Emanation Tarot: King/Wands/Air Soul: Neshamah (Intellect) Subconscious Ideas YOD Left-Brain/Thinkers Jung: Thinking, Judging Humors: Choleric/Yellow Bile – Goals Keirsey: Rational – Abstract, Utilitarian Meyers-Briggs/Keirsey INTJ – Mastermind, Original Thought INTP – Architect, Logical Explanations ISTJ – Inspector/Realist, Dependability ISTP – Analyzer/ Developer, Cause/Effect	SARAH/ABRAHAM Emotional/Harmony/ Reactive Levi (Scales) – Companion, Priesthood Asher (Bread) – Cook, Business Reuben (Water) – Instability, Emotional Kabbalah: Creation Tarot: Queen/Cups/Water Soul: Ruach (Personality) Subconscious Feelings HEI Right-Brain/Feelers Jung: Feeling, Perceiving Humors: Phlegmatic/ Phlegm – People Keirsey: Idealist: Abstract, Cooperative Meyers-Briggs/Keirsey INFJ – Counselor, Relationships INFP – Healer/Harmonizer, Idealistic ISFJ – Protector/ Considerate/Conscientious ISFP – Composer/Artist, In the Moment

PERSONALITY TABLE *cont.*

	FIRE Left-Brain (Intellect) Sun	WATER Right-Brain (Emotion), Moon
EARTH Implementation Expression Extroverted Action	LEAH/ISRAEL Tradition/Dependability/Structure Judah (Lion) - Leadership, Government Dan (Horned Serpent) – Judge, Legal Naphtali (Deer) - Emissary, Expression Kabbalah: Formation/Foundation Tarot: Knight/Swords/Fire Soul: Chayah (Will) Conscious Mind Conscious Mind VAV/Adam Left-Brain/Planners Jung: Sensation, Judging Humors: Melancholic/Black Bile - Loyal Keirsey: Guardian – Concrete, Logistical Meyers-Briggs/Keirsey ENTJ – General/Field Marshall ENTP – Inventor/Explorer, Problem Solver ESTJ – Supervisor/Administrator, Results ESTP – Implementor/Promoter	RACHEL/JACOB Action/Sensation/Passion Gad (Tents) – Troops, Good Luck Issachar (Mule) – Worker, Labor Benjamin (Wolf) – Effort and Reward Kabbalah: Action/Manifestation Tarot: Page/Pentacles/Earth Soul: Nefesh (Instinct) Primitive Mind HEI/Eve Right-Brain/Doers Jung: Intuition, Feeling Humors: Sanguine/Blood – Optimistic Keirsey: Artisan – Utilitarian, Tactical Meyers-Briggs/Keirsey ENFJ – Teacher, Growth in Others ENFP – Champion/Campaigner, Improviser ESFJ – Provider/Needs of Others ESFP – Performer/Entertainer/Lover of Life

THE LETTER *Pei*

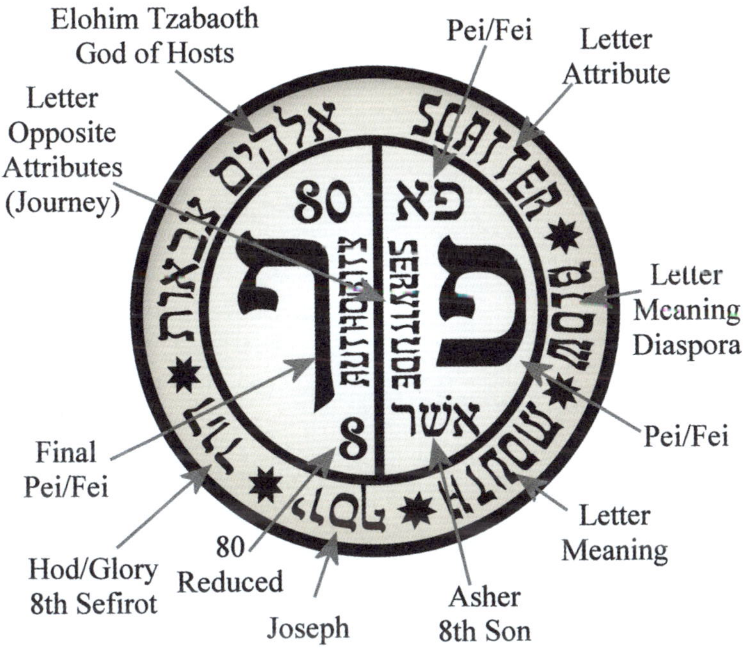

Letter: Pei/Fei, Alef

Transliteration: Pei/Fei

English Letter: P/F

Sound: Purpose/faith

Gematria Value: 80

Reduced Value: 8

Etz Chayim Sefirot: Hod

Ten Commandments: Do not steal

Name Value: 80 + 1 = 9

Name Meaning: Mouth, blow, scatter

Sequential Number: 17

Sefer Yetzirah Classification: 7 Double

Sefer Yetzirah Attribute: Authority/servitude

Hermetic Tree Path: Hod-Netzach

Hermetic Tarot: Tower

Lurianic Tree Path: Geburah-Hod

Kabbalah Cube: North

Numerical Tarot: Star

Constructed Gematria: Vav looking into Kaf (6 + 20 = 26)

Prefix/Suffix: N/A

Mystical Associations: The Hebrew letter *Pei/Fei* is the 17th consecutive letter in the Hebrew *Alef-bet*; it means *mouth*, *blow*, or *scatter* and has a gematria value of 80. At age 17, Joseph used his mouth to provide a bad report about his half brothers through Bilhah and Zilpah (Genesis 37:2), and that coupled with their jealousy / evil eye (Genesis 37:4) led to his brothers selling Joseph into slavery (Genesis 37:28). Scripture is full of warnings regarding the mouth and the use of the tongue (Psalm 34:13; 1 Peter 3:10; Proverbs 10:31, 15:2). Words are powerful and should be used with caution. Words were used by God to speak the universe into existence (Genesis 1:3, 2 Esdras 6:28, Hebrew 11:3). There is a time to speak and a time to keep silent (Ecclesiastes 3:7).

The Sefer Yetzirah classifies *Pei/Fei* as a double letter (it makes either a P or F sound) and associates it with the duality of *authority* and *servitude*. Joseph embodies both of these characteristics, because after being a slave and a prisoner, he also obtained authority that was second only to Pharaoh (Genesis 41:40). The letter *Pei/Fei* makes two sounds, but it also has two forms. The first form is bent, and like the bent *Nun* it represents the need to be humble. In relation to the mouth, it represents recognizing when to keep silent (keeping one's mouth shut) and when to speak up (mouth wide open). The *Pei/Fei Sofit* is firmly planted, representing that a person is in a position to express their opinions and open their mouth.

At the beginning of Joseph's life, he would have benefited from keeping his mouth closed and being humble around his brothers. As a slave, Joseph learned when to speak up at appropriate times, and he did the right thing, even if the consequences were detrimental to him. Eventually, it is through Joseph mastering his ability to use his mouth that he interpreted dreams and was given authority, so that everyone listened to what he had to say; like the *Pei/Fei Sofit*, he was firmly planted and able to be bold in his speech.

The letter *Pei/Fei* has a gematria value of 80, which reduces to 8. The eighth *Sefirah* is *Hod*, *glory/eternity*, and represents the honor received following the *victory* (overcoming one's struggles) in *Netzach*. According to the order listed on the Judaism 101 website (Rich 1996) of the 613 *Mitzvot*, the 17th is to circumcise all male offspring, which occurs on the eighth day. The 80th *Mitzvot* is the need to marry one's brother's widow if he dies childless (Rich 1996); this occurred in Genesis 38:8, which interrupted the story of Joseph in order to discuss events related to Judah and Tamar (Judah is the one who had the idea to sell Joseph into slavery in Genesis 37:26). Both Genesis 38 and 39 are about deception and righteousness, providing a contrast between Judah and Joseph as well as Tamar and Potiphar's wife.

Judah did not keep his word to Tamar, whom he promised would marry his youngest son (Genesis 38:11). Likewise, Joseph did not submit to the will of Potiphar's wife, who demanded sexual intercourse from her slave (Genesis 39:10). Both Tamar and Potiphar's wife responded with deceptions, with Tamar succeeding in becoming pregnant by Judah, and Potiphar's wife having Joseph sent to prison by falsely accusing him of attempted rape. Tamar was falsely accused of harlotry (Genesis 38:24–25) but was judged to be more righteous than Judah (Genesis 38:26), and the resultant descendants of their union included King David, Solomon, Daniel, and Jesus of Nazareth (Matthew 1:3). Potiphar's wife was also said to be unable to bear children, so by divine intervention the archangel Michael brought her the child of Joseph's older half sister Dinah to raise as her own daughter (Pirkei DeRabbi Eliezer 38:2). After Joseph was given authority by Pharaoh, he was given Potiphar's daughter Asenath (Dinah's child) in marriage (Genesis 41:45).

Jacob lived with Laban for 20 years (Genesis 31:41), and he did not start having children until he married Rachel and Leah in the seventh year (Genesis 29:20). During those 20 years, he fathered 12 children (including Dinah, but not Benjamin, who was born later), so starting at year eight, he had approximately one new child each year (for 12–13 years). This would mean that Dinah was Joseph's half sister, born about one year earlier through Leah. At age 12, Dinah was abducted and raped by Shechem (Jubilees 30:3), which means Dinah gave birth to Asenath around age 13.

Joseph was 17 when his brothers sold him into slavery, and he remained a slave until age 30 (Genesis 41:46). Joseph spent 13 years as a slave/prisoner before receiving authority. He was 30 years old when he married Asenath, who was approximately 13 years younger than him, which would mean that Joseph came to Potiphar's house as a slave when he was 17, and Asenath left Potiphar's house when she was around 17 (17 = 1 + 7 = 8). Asenath was the product of a rape, and Joseph was falsely accused of attempted rape by Potiphar's wife.

The name Joseph means *increaser*, and at his birth, Rachel stated, "*God has taken away my reproach*" (Genesis 30:23). Joseph spent 17 years in Canaan before being sold into slavery; he spent 10 years as a slave (the number of completion of a cycle), 3 years as a prisoner, and 80 years (the value of *Pei/Fei*) as a ruler of Egypt (Jubilees 46:7). At age 17 he was scattered from his home, and after God had removed his reproach, he spent 80 years with authority.

Asenath gave birth to Manasseh and Ephraim (Genesis 46:20), who received blessings (Genesis 48:9) and a share in the inheritance that would have otherwise gone to Simeon and Levi, but their blessings were *scattered* (Genesis 49:6–7) due to them murdering all the males of Shechem to avenge the rape of their sister Dinah (Genesis 34:25), who later gave birth to Asenath as a result of the rape. Simeon and Levi used their mouths to deceive Shechem's father (Genesis 34:13) into circumcising all the males in the city—an activity that normally occurs on the eighth day (Genesis 34:15, Judith 9:2–3). The sons of Israel wanted to have Asenath killed (Pirkei DeRabbi Eliezer 38:1), just as they originally wanted to have Joseph killed (Genesis 37:18); however, in the end God removed the reproaches of both Joseph and Asenath and gave them and their children authority over those who desired to harm them.

Of the Ten Commandments, the eighth is not to steal. Joseph went to prison because he would not take what belonged to his master (Genesis 39:9). The gematria value of the letters that spell *Pei/Fei* (*Pei/Fei Alef*) is 81 (8 + 1 = 9), which points to the *Sefirah* of *Yesod* (Foundation). The gematria of the word *Yesod* is also 80 (*Yod* 10 + *Samech* 60 + *Vav* 6 + *Dalet* 4). *Yesod* is the location of the Chymical Wedding, the womb in which the Spirit joins with the faithful and builds an eternal foundation (Sirach 1:14–15). *Pei/Fei* 80 is an evolved state of *Chet* 8, and just as the *Chet* alludes to the *Chuppah* and a physical union, *Pei/Fei* addresses the spiritual union of the soul. Although Joseph faced difficult trials, the Spirit of Wisdom was with him during his challenges. "*When a righteous man was sold into slavery, Wisdom did not desert him, but kept him from sinning. She was with him in prison and remained with him until she brought him the scepter of a kingdom and made him ruler over those who had oppressed him*" (Wisdom 10:13–14).

The letter *Pei/Fei* is constructed of a *Vav* and *Kaf* (6 + 20 = 26), which is the same value as the Tetragrammaton who directs one's path (Psalm 25:4, Proverbs 3:6, James 4:13–15). The *Vav* can represent humans (who were created on the sixth day) looking inward to the Spirit of Wisdom (*Kaf* / Divine Feminine) for intuitive guidance—just as Joseph was guided by his dreams. The *Vav* as a prefix can also denote connection and can refer to one's connection with the divine. Through Joseph's obedience—and recognition that the *Hand/Palm* of God was directing his fate (Genesis 50:20)—he earned authority, just as those in Yehshua's Parable of the Talents (Matthew 25:19–30), who earned *Glory* (*Hod*) through their suffering (Luke 24:26, Romans 8:18, 1 Peter 5:10).

In STaM the *Pei/Fei* is constructed with a *Vav* and *Kaf*, and within the white space of the letter a *Secret Bet* is formed, which reveals the connection between the *Kaf* and the *Bet*. Since *Pei/Fei* is an evolved form of *Chet*, the *Kaf* is an evolved form of *Bet*. The *Vav* resembles of *Zayin*, and they both can symbolize a male member, with the *Zayin* representing the circumcised version.

In Hebrew block lettering, the *Pei/Fei* is constructed by adding a *Yod* to a *Kaf*, which represents the hands/palms of the divine masculine and feminine. On the Lurianic Tree of Life, the *Kaf* is on the lowest vertical path on the Pillar of Mercy (the feminine side), and the *Kaf* with a *Yod* is immediately across from it on the lowest vertical path on the Pillar of Severity (the masculine side). In the pattern of Adam Kadmon that lists *Geburah* and *Chesed* as arms and *Hod* and *Netzach* as legs (Tikkunei Zohar 17a:20–22), the Paths of the *Pei/Fei* and *Kaf* would represent the hands. The Pillar of Mercy represents contemplation, and the Pillar of Severity is application. The *Kaf* represents thinking about what to say, and the *Pei/Fei* as application of speech involves using discernment as to what to say and when to speak—since one's words can lead to either Glory (*Hod*) or Judgment (*Geburah*).

The *Yod* added to one's fate to form a mouth can also represent those chosen as God's mouthpieces on Earth. Moses and Aaron served as God's agents to speak the words given to them (Exodus 4:30), as did the later prophets (2 Samuel 12:7, Isaiah 28:16, Jeremiah 2:2). After Moses fled Egypt and was scattered into the wilderness, God sent him back to Egypt to gather the Israelites, who had been shut in the wilderness by Pharaoh (Exodus 14:3). He then led them through the wilderness to the Promised Land (Deuteronomy 9:28). As they traveled through the wilderness, they were humbled and tested, much like Joseph was as a slave. But God was with them, just as the Spirit of Wisdom with was Joseph in prison, providing manna from heaven so that they might understand that humans do not live by bread alone, but "*by everything that proceeds out of the mouth of the* LORD" (Deuteronomy 8:1–3).

Similarly, Jesus of Nazareth was referred to as a "*Rabbi*" by his disciple (John 3:26, 11:8), and he taught in the synagogues of the Pharisees (Matthew 4:22, Luke 4:15). The people, however, thought of him as a prophet (Matthew 21:11–46, John 4:19). Jesus was filled with the Spirit of Wisdom as the Prophets (*Nevi'im*) were before him (Wisdom 7:27), and he stated that his teachings were not his own (John 7:16–17, 14:10, 14:24, 17:8). The Greek word "*Christ*" refers to one who is *anointed*, and in the case of Jesus, it is used to refer to him being *anointed* by the Spirit of Wisdom at his Baptism (Matthew 3:16); this anointing of the Spirit would play a central role in Christianity, as followers are also said to be indwelt and reborn by the Spirit at Baptism, similar to Chymical Wedding concept in alchemy. In ancient Israel, both kings and priests were anointed (Exodus 28:41), and the Apostle Paul considered Jesus anointed into the role of a Heavenly High Priest (Hebrews 3:1, 5:5).

During the Second Temple period, the Maccabees (Hasmonean) had succeeded in their revolt and gained their independence, but by the time of Jesus of Nazareth, the Israelites had been conquered and were under Roman domination. The descendants of the Priesthood were exiled to the Temple of Onias in Leontopolis, Egypt, while the Temple in Jerusalem was run by the Hellenistic Jews from the Hasmonean dynasty, who collaborated with Rome. This caused contention among the Jews, because they had a legitimate priesthood in Egypt without a legitimate Temple—and a legitimate Temple in Jerusalem without legitimate priests. Without legitimacy, the priestly sacrifices specified in the Torah could not be maintained. As alternatives, the Pharisees encouraged study of the Torah, and John the Baptist promoted baptism based on the practice of *Mikva* purification.

During the Second Temple period, the oppressed Jews hoped for the *Mashiach*, and the institution of the Messianic Age, with many hoping that Jesus of Nazareth would become the King of the Jews and lead a rebellion against Rome. However, Jesus said that he did not come to bring peace, but a sword (Matthew 10:34–36), which was an allusion to the Prophecy of Micah (Micah 7:6). Micah prophesied about a time of corrupt rulers (such as the Hellenistic Jews) that would cause the nation's downfall (Micah 3:1–12), and the remnant of the people would be scattered among the nations (Micah 5:7–8). Jesus restated this message and predicted the destruction of the Temple (Matthew 24:2) along with the people being scattered (Matthew 26:31, Psalm 44:11, Zechariah 13:7).

He taught a new way of worship while in the Diaspora, with each individual's body serving as a Temple of the Spirit (Matthew 26:61, John 2:21, 1 Corinthians 6:19), with prayer, righteousness, and keeping the commandments/*Mitzvot* replacing animal sacrifices (Matthew 9:13, 1 Corinthians 7:19, 1 John 5:3, Romans 12:1, Hosea 6:6, Psalm 51:16–17). As stated in the prophecy of Micah, *HaShem* does not desire burnt offerings or the blood of thousands of rams but desires for people "*to do justice, to love kindness, and to walk humbly with God*" (Micah 6:6–8), and neither a Temple nor a priesthood is necessary to accomplish it. A few decades later, the Jews did rebel against Rome, leading to the destruction of the Second Temple and the exile (scattering) of the Jews.

The Jews were scattered after the First Temple was destroyed (Esther 3:8), and following the destruction of the Second Temple, they were again scattered among the nations of the world. As Rabbinical Judaism developed, the Sages replaced Temple sacrifice with prayer and righteous living. They say the world is established on Three Pillars, which can represent Abraham (*Chesed*), Isaac (*Geburah*), and Jacob (*Tiferet*) (Shir HaShirim Rabbah 7:8), or Torah study (Pillar of Mercy), prayer/service (Pillar of Severity), and righteousness (Pillar of Unity) (Pirkei Avot 1:2, Hosea 14:3). In Diaspora they remain in the state of the bent *Pei/Fei*, but they have the promise of being restored (Ezekiel 28:25–26).

On the Hermetic Tree, *Pei/Fei* is on the path connecting *Hod* (Glory) and *Netzach* (Victory), associated with the Tower card in Tarot. The Tower card is a representation of the Kabbalah, with the Tower serving as the Pillar of Unity, and the Red King on the left side (Pillar of Severity) with the White Queen on the right side (Pillar of Mercy) representing the male and female opposites. This card shows people being scattered from the Tower, just as the people were scattered from the Tower of Babel (Genesis 11:8). The Kabbalah, symbolized by the Tower card, serves as a means for the seekers to return to God. Through struggle, one can obtain Victory and earn Glory.

On the Lurianic Tree, *Pei/Fei* is on the path connecting *Geburah* and *Hod*, representing the need to control one's speech, since it can lead either to glory or judgment. On the Kabbalah Cube, *Pei/Fei* represents north. In the numerical order of the Tarot, the eighth card is the Star, which shows the Shekinah replenishing the earth, demonstrating the distillation/purification process, and the cycles of life; water evaporates and is scattered across the earth, only to be gathered back and returned to a larger body of water (during the *Olam HaBa*).

The Talisman: The divine name *Elohim Tzabaoth* (God of Hosts) is rewritten on the *Kame'ah*, which is the divine name associated with *Hod*. *Elohim* is the name associated with judgment, which is a key aspect of controlling one's speech and the providence. Joseph is written on the outside of the ring, since he provides a prime example of the servant that is later exalted, which is the duality attributes associated with the letter *Pei/Fei* in the Sefer Yetzirah. The value of the letter is 80, and its meanings (*mouth, blow*, or *scatter*) refers both to speech as well as the Diaspora of being physically scattered among the nations, being blown over, or having one's life dramatically altered. Asher (happiness) is the eighth son of Jacob, and *Hod* is the eighth *Sefirah*. This talisman can be used as a reminder of rewards for effort, final rewards, achieving one's destiny, fulfillment of a promise, achievement of a goal, realization of potential, following inner guidance, listening to one's intuition, being led by the Spirit, or the providence of God. It reminds us that even when we are blown off course, with faith and endurance we can correct our course and manifest our goals, as Joseph fulfilled the dreams of his youth and achieved his destiny.

THE LETTER *Tzadi*

Letter: Tzadi, Dalet, Yod

Transliteration: Tzadi

English Letter: TS

Sound: Tz(Z)iTzit / nuTS

Gematria Value: 90

Reduced Value: 9

Etz Chayim Sefirot: Yesod

Ten Commandments: Do not bear false witness

Name Value: 90 + 10 + 4 = 104 = 5

Name Meaning: Side, flank, hunt, fishhook, righteousness

Sequential Number: 18

Sefer Yetzirah Classification: Single/Simple

Sefer Yetzirah Attribute: Taste

Hermetic Tree Path: Netzach-Yesod

Hermetic Tarot: Star

Lurianic Tree Path: Geburah-Tiferet

Kabbalah Cube Path: Keter-Yesod

Numerical Tarot: Moon (Reflection)

Constructed Gematria: Nun 50, Yod 10 = Samech 60 = Vav 6

Prefix/Suffix: N/A

Mystical Associations: The letter *Tzadi* is the 18th consecutive letter and has a gematria value of 90. It means *side*, *flank*, *hunt*, or *fishhook*, but since the letter *Qof* follows it, when repeating the *Alef-bet* in order the letters run together and sound like *Tzadik* (Righteousness). Holiness and righteousness are key aspects of this letter, which is used in words such as *mitzvot* (obedience to the commandments), *Tzitzit* (the tassels used to remind one of the commandments), *Tzadakah* (Justice/Charity), or *Zion* (Jerusalem / the Holy Temple). As the 18th letter, it is also associated with the value of *Chet Yod* (*Chai*), the word meaning *life* (Deuteronomy 30:19). The number 18 is also associated with the bridal canopy (Pirkei Avot 5:21), and the letter *Tet* contains the results of that union.

Tzadi is the evolved form of *Tet*, after it has been multiplied by *Yod* (10) and has mastered the 10 aspects of the *Sefirot*.

Like the *Nun* and the *Pei/Fei*, the *Tzadi* has two forms and conveys similar symbolism. The bent *Tzadi* resembles a bent *Nun* and represents a humble person having been purified (made righteous) by the waters of *Mem* (40 added to the *Nun* 50 = 90 *Tzadi*). The *Tzadi* is constructed of a *Nun* with a *Yod* on its back. The letters *Qof Dalet* spell to *bow* or to *bend* and have a gematria value of 90, as is the gematria of *water* (*Mem* 40, *Yod* 10, *Mem* 40). As the *Mem Sofit* represents the male and female uniting as one, the *Tzadi* represents the humble and exalted person being united with God (*Yod*). The *Pei/Fei* has the *Vav* (human) unite with the divine feminine (*Kaf*), and the *Tzadi* unites the humble person (*Nun*) with the divine masculine (*Yod*). The righteous person has learned to control their vision and the evil inclination (*Yetzer HaRa*) by advancing past the *Ayin* and has learned to control one's mouth at *Pei/Fei*, so that the person has removed sin from one's sight (*Ayin*) and speech (*Pei/Fei*) and now behaves righteously (*Tzadi*).

The value of the letters that spell *Tzadi* is 104 (*Tzadi* 90 + *Dalet* 4 + *Yod* 10 = 104, and 100 + 4 = 5) or 5 (*Hei*), representing this Spirit of Wisdom supporting the righteous person who stands tall (*Tzadi Sofit*). The shape of the *Tzadi Sofit* resembles the Middle Pillar (Pillar of Unity), with the firmly planted *Nun Sofit* representing the Middle Pillar, and the arm of the Yod forming the path connecting *Tiferet* (the Heart of Adam Kadmon) with *Chokmah* (Wisdom). On the Hermetic Tree of Life, the path connecting *Tiferet* with *Chokmah* is associated with the letter *Hei* (the value of the word *Tzadi*), and on the Lurianic Tree of Life, the same path is associated with the *Tet* (of which *Tzadi* is the evolved form); on both Trees, the *Tzadi Sofit* can be connected to that path.

The *Sefer Yetzirah* classifies *Tzadi* as a single/simple letter and associates it with Taste and Aquarius (the water bearer). Taste represents ingesting something, taking it in, or enjoying the fruits of one's labor (2 Samuel 22:21, Psalm 18:20, Matthew 10:41). Once Israel enters the Promised Land, they will enjoy a land flowing with milk and honey (Leviticus 20:24). The righteous will taste (ingest) the word of God, which will be sweeter than honey (Psalm 119:103). The righteous will be rewarded (Romans 5:21, Ephesians 6:14, Psalm 7:8). As stated in the Wisdom of Solomon, "*The righteous live forever, and their reward is with the Lord; the Most High takes care of them*" (Wisdom 5:15).

The concept of *Tikkun Olam* and repairing the world is done through acts of righteousness. The Torah says that you shall pursue *Tzedek* (Justice) (Deuteronomy 16:20). The world is supported by Three Pillars (Pirkei Avot 1:2): Studying Torah (*Ayin*—reading Torah), Prayer (*Pei/Fei*—verbal worship), and Righteous Deeds (*Tzadi*—Charity and Justice). Micah said "*to do justice, to love kindness, and to walk humbly with God*" (Micah 6:6–8), and Isaiah said, "*Learn to do good, seek justice, correct oppression, defend the fatherless, and plead for the widow*" (Isaiah 1:17). Establishing justice (Psalm 99:4, Amos 5:15) and loving God and one's neighbor as yourself (Leviticus 19:18) are key aspects of righteousness and fulfills the Torah and the teachings of the Prophets (Matthew 22:37–40).

Tzedakah (charitable giving / right acting) can involve helping others financially or donating your time and talents to repair the world. *Tikkun Olam* has come to represent social justice and righting wrongs. It involves caring for others and establishing justice for all. Performing *Tzedakah* (charity) is a *Mitzvot* (obligation), and going beyond what is expected of you is a *Segulah* (making you a special treasure to God). For God loves justice and he will reward the righteous (Psalms 11:7, 37:28; Proverbs 15:9). To do righteousness and to establish justice is better than sacrifice (Proverbs 21:3, 1 Samuel 15:22).

The same letters that spell *Tzadi* placed in a different order spell *Tzayid* (to hunt), and the letter is said to be shaped like a fishhook. The righteous will pursue *Tzedek* (justice) and will "*pursue Wisdom like a hunter (Tzayid), and lie in wait on her paths. He who peers through her windows (Hei) will also listen at her doors (Dalet); he who encamps near her house (Bet) will also fasten his tent peg (Vav) near her walls*" (Sirach 14:21–24). Wisdom is a Tree of Life to those who lay hold of her, and those who hold her fast are happy (Proverbs 3:18, Sirach 4:11–15).

The reduced value of 90 is 9, which points to the *Sefirah* of *Yesod*, the location of the Chymical Wedding, where the seeker first takes hold of the Tree of Life and begins climbing. The ninth commandment is not to bear false witness, which is an aspect of ensuring fairness, impartiality, and justice for all. On the Hermetic Tree, *Tzadi* is on the path connecting *Netzach* and *Yesod*. It is associated with the Star card of Tarot. The Star card shows the Spirit of Wisdom, pouring out water to replenish the earth, which resembles the water bearer of Aquarius and the concept of *Tikkun Olam* (repairing the world) through *Tzedakah* (sharing your blessings).

On the Lurianic Tree of Life, *Tzadi* is on the path connecting *Geburah* and *Tiferet*, representing strength and judgment of heart. In the numerical Tarot order, the 18th card of the Major Arcana would be the Moon card, which represents reflection and the divine feminine. On the Kabbalah Cube, *Tzadi* is on the path connecting *Keter* and *Yesod*, representing the Crown of Righteousness (Proverbs 16:31, 2 Timothy 4:8) obtained by those who succeed in the Chymical Wedding.

The Talisman: The divine name *Shaddai* (Almighty) is written on the talisman, which is the divine name associated with *Yesod* (Foundation). This name is abbreviated as a *Shin* and is written on the doorposts (*Dalet*) of the houses (*Bet*) and between the eyes (*Ayin*) of the righteous who follow the commandments (Deuteronomy 6:4–9). The *Shema* states to bind the commandments on one's hand (*Yod*) and to write them between one's eyes (*Ayin*) and on the doorposts (*Dalet*) of their houses (*Bet*). The letters *Yod Ayin Dalet Bet* mean "*will benefit*," and reciting the *Shema* will benefit and is a *Mitzvah* (Deuteronomy 6:4) that is said in the morning and at night. Also written in Hebrew are the words *Yesod* and *Tzedek Tzedek Tirdof* (Justice, Justice you shall pursue). The value of 90, the two forms of the letter, and the attributes of Righteousness and Justice are written on it as well. This lot/talisman can be used as a reminder to uphold all three pillars that support the world, to study righteousness, to speak righteousness, and to perform righteous deeds. It is only by the presence of the *Tzadikim* that the world is sustained (Sanhedrin 97b:11).

THE LETTER *Qof*

Letter: Qof, Vav, Fei

Transliteration: Kof

English Letter: K/Q

Sound: Kabbalah

Gematria Value: 100

Reduced Value: 1

Etz Chayim Sefirot: Keter

Ten Commandments: No other gods before me

Name Value: 100 + 80 + 6 = 186 = 15 = 1 + 5 = 6

Name Meaning: Monkey, ape, eye of the needle

Sequential Number: 19 = 1 + 9 = 10 = 1

Sefer Yetzirah Classification: Single/Simple

Sefer Yetzirah Attribute: Laughing/mirth

Hermetic Tree Path: Malkut-Netzach

Hermetic Tarot: Moon

Lurianic Tree Path: Binah-Chesed

Kabbalah Cube Path: Yesod-Netzach

Numerical Tarot: Sun

Constructed Gematria: Kaf 20, Vav 6 = 26 (Kaf and Zayin in STaM)

Prefix/Suffix: N/A

Mystical Associations: The letter *Qof* is the 19th consecutive letter and has a gematria value of 100. It means *monkey*, *eye of the needle*, or *reflection*. When the letter is spelled out, the *Final Fei*, *Vav*, and *Qof* give the appearance of a mirror image (**ףוק**), with the *Vav* representing the mirror in the center. This can represent humans being created in the image of God (Genesis 1:27), Wisdom being a mirror image of God's goodness (Wisdom 7:26), or the concept of duality, since Adam of Eve are said to have originally been created back to back (Kalach Pitchai Chokhma 135:8, The Beginning of Wisdom 7:12).

The phrase "*Monkey see, monkey do*" refers to mimicking someone's behavior, just as a monkey tries to imitate humans (Likutei Moharan 64:6:10). The word Kabbalah (to receive) begins with the letter *Qof*, as does *Kadosh* (Holy), *Kedushah* (Sanctification), *Kaddish* (the Mourners Prayer), and *Kiddush* (Blessing of the Wine). Kabbalah provides a system for the mystic to study attributes of God, and because humans were created in the image of God (*B'tzelem Elohim*), these attributes also exist in each human.

The Kabbalah can be used as a system for spiritual growth, as one seeks to imitate, mimic, and embrace the characteristics of God and to perfect those qualities in oneself. Even though a human compared to the Divine Presence is like a monkey compared to a human (Bava Batra 58a:6–7), that is not a reason to stop trying to improve. The above and the below are connected; the microcosm is an expression of the macrocosm, and just as a camel (*Gimel*) can pass through the eye of a needle (*Qof*), nothing is impossible with God's assistance (Matthew 19:24–26). Humans were created a little lower than the angels (Psalm 8:4–5) and were given the faculty of judgment (Genesis 3:5, 3:22). Humans became

Like-God (*Kaf-Elohim*), which "*every Hebrew knows that the term Elohim is a homonym, and denotes God, angels, judges, and the rulers of countries*" (*The Guide for the Perplexed*, part 1, chapter 2:1).

The purification of one's soul and the quest for righteousness are continual and ongoing processes of growth, which advance over time and go through cycles. The letter *Qof* begins the third cycle, or evolution, of the numbers (100–400). The first cycle of completion (1–10) describes the Beginning and explains how God created the universe and humans and established a system of universal laws that would allow the universe to continue to evolve and grow (become self-sustaining). The first cycle can also represent a human couple at the beginning of their lives, as they leave their parents' homes, unite with their partners, and start their own families (beginning a new cycle).

The second evolution (10–90) of numbers (in the *Alef-bet*) can be related to the spiritual and emotional maturity of the human couple, as they progress in life. They are initially supported by the hands of God (the *Yod* and *Kaf*), but they soon learn (*Lamed*) to serve as God's arms (*Lamed*) on the earth. As they mature and advance spiritually, they are purified (*Mem*), and their relationship connection intensifies so that they truly become one (*Mem Sofit*). They next come to recognize the different phases of life events—that sometimes they are humble and sometimes they are exalted (*Nun*). They learn to adapt and support each other and feel completion (*Samech*) in that area as they support each other through their worldly interactions.

Their next challenge is related to spiritual development. They must overcome the *Yetzer HaRa* and master their perceptions (*Ayin*). This is one of the Three Pillars that sustain the world (Studying Torah) and is associated with the Pillar of Mercy (Contemplation). The aspect to master is *Pei/Fei*, which involves both mastering one's speech (Prayer) and understanding the phenomenon of being scattered or overcoming unsuspected challenges. Since this involves obtaining balance on many different levels, it is associated with the Middle Pillar (the Pillar of Unity). The final level of development in the second evolution is righteousness (*Tzadi*). After thinking about what is right and saying what you plan to do to about it, one must put their thoughts and words into practice and do it. God first planned, then he spoke, and finally he manifested this vision into reality. Righteous actions are the Third Pillar, which sustains the world (Sanhedrin 97b:11), and are associated with the Pillar of Severity (Application).

Taking action without thought would make one only a laborer. This might reach the level of *Lamed* (serving as an arm), but it does not obtain the level of the *Tzadik*. Spending all of one's time at a college or university might allow the person to know what they should do, but without application, the knowledge is wasted. Discussing and talking about what should be done enables clarification and can obtain cooperation and buy-in with an idea, but unless action is taken to implement the concept, the words are empty. The ideal state involves a balance of all three—planning, proclaiming one's intension, and implementing the solution—each of these areas is an important aspect of *Tikkun Olam*. Without any one of these elements, there would be an imbalance. The following gematria provides a breakdown of the three different evolutions of the *Sefirot*, and they are divided among the *Alef-bet*:

First Cycle of Completion
1 + 0 = 1 (Alef)
1 + 2 = 3 (Bet)
1 + 2 + 3 = 6 (Gimel)
1 + 2 + 3 + 4 = 10 = 1 + 0 = 1 (Dalet)
1 + 2 + 3 + 4 + 5 = 15 = 1 + 5 = 6 (Hei)
1 + 2 + 3 + 4 + 5 + 6 = 21 = 2 + 1 = 3 (Vav)
1 + 2 + 3 + 4 + 5 + 6 + 7 = 28 = 2 + 8 = 10 = 1 + 0 = 1 (Zayin)
1 + 2 + 3 + 4 + 5 + 6 + 7 + 8 = 36 = 3 + 6 = 9 (Chet)
1 + 2 + 3 + 4 + 5 + 6 + 7 + 8 + 9 = 45 = 4 + 5 = 9 (Tet)
1 + 2 + 3 + 4 + 5 + 6 + 7 + 8 + 9 + 10 = 55 = 5 + 5 = 10 = 1 + 0 = 1 (Yod)

Second Evolution of the *Sefirot*
55 + 11 = 66 = 12 = 3 (Kaf)
66 + 12 = 78 = 15 = 6 (Lamed)
78 + 13 = 91 = 10 = 1 (Mem)
91 + 14 = 105 = 6 (Nun)
105 + 15 = 120 = 3 (Samech)
120 + 16 = 136 = 10 = 1 (Ayin)
136 + 17 = 153 = 9 (Pei/Fei)
153 + 18 = 171 = 9 (Tzadi)

Third Evolution of the *Sefirot*
171 + 19 = 190 = 10 = 1 (Qof)
190 + 20 = 210 = 3 (Resh)
210 + 21 = 231 = 6 (Shin)
231 + 22 = 253 = 10 = 1 (Tav)

Examining these calculations reveals patterns within the advancements of the numbers. We can see patterns of three sets of numbers being repeated starting from *Bet*: 136, 163, and 199. Each of these numbers equals 10 (1 + 3 + 6 = 10; 1 + 6 + 3 = 10; and 1 + 9 + 9 = 19 = 1 + 9 = 10). All these combinations return to the number 10, just as the *Sefer Yetzirah* linked the various letters/numbers of the Hebrew *Alef-bet* to the 10 *Sefirot*.

Another thing to notice in the calculations is the cycles of completion, where the value equals 10 and can be returned to the one occurs in every third calculation starting with *Bet*. This pattern helps us understand how the four-letter name of God represents his 10 attributes and oneness. The letters where we find tens or ones are *Alef*, *Dalet*, *Zayin*, *Yod*, *Mem*, *Ayin*, *Qof*, and *Tav*, offering an additional dimension to these letters that might not be apparent in their standard gematria.

The third and final cycle of emanations within the Hebrew *Alef-bet* begins with *Qof* and ends with *Tav*. The *Qof* has a gematria value of 100, which reduces to 1. The purpose of the third cycle is to remind us that even if we think we have obtained perfection (righteousness), there is always room to improve. Nothing ever remains the same; we must continue to grow and be careful not to lose our progress.

Noah was a righteous man who walked with God (Genesis 6:9). When the world was flooded, Noah was safeguarded and God established a covenant with him (Genesis 9:9). Yet, being declared righteous and surviving the flood did not mean his work was over. After being giving the entire world, the first thing Noah did was till the soil so that he could grow wine, get drunk (Genesis 9:20–21), and act like a monkey. In the *Legends of the Jews* there is Midrash about Satan partnering with Noah in his business of planting a vineyard. After agreeing to the partnership, the following occurred:

> *Satan thereupon slaughtered a lamb, and then, in succession, a lion, a pig, and a monkey. The blood of each as it was killed he made to flow under the vine. Thus he conveyed to Noah what the qualities of wine are: before man drinks of it, he is innocent as a lamb; if he drinks of it moderately, he feels as strong as a lion; if he drinks more of it than he can bear, he resembles the pig; and if he drinks to the point of intoxication, then he behaves like a monkey, he dances around, sings, talks obscenely, and knows not what he is doing. This deterred Noah no more than did the example of Adam, whose fall had also been due to wine, for the forbidden fruit had been the grape, with which he had made himself drunk.* (Legends of the Jews 1:4:72–73)

In the Midrash, Noah partakes of the forbidden fruit, and immediately after the world had been purified by water (*Mem*), following the example of Adam, the righteous Noah allowed sin to reenter into the world. In his drunken state, something evil/sinful occurred that caused him to curse Canaan, the son of Ham, which is the son who saw Noah's nakedness (Genesis 9:22). In the Torah, uncovering someone's nakedness is a euphemism for a sexual act. When Reuben mounted his father's bed and uncovered his skirt, it was a euphemism about Reuben raping his stepmother (Genesis 49:4), which occurred when she was passed out drunk (Jubilees 33:3–7, Testament of Reuben 3:11–14). Lot's daughters also used wine to get their father drunk, and then they had sex with him (Genesis 19:30–38). What exactly occurred in Noah's situation is not known. However, the *Legends of the Jews* speculates that Ham did not want Noah to bear any more children and attempted to perform an operation to prevent his father from being able to procreate, which would have contradicted God's instruction for them to be fruitful and multiply (Genesis 9:1).

The value of *Qof* is 100, which is the age that Abraham was when the child of the promise was born to him (Genesis 17:17, 21:5). It is also the age when one ceases being focused on the physical world and is prepared to go beyond it (Pirkei Avot 5:21, Mesliat Yesharim 1:18); the letters *Qof Tsadi* together mean finish, end, or stop. Ten is the number of completion, and *Qof* is the number of completion squared (100%). One hundred is also the number of blessings a person should strive to recite each day (Menachot 43b:15). In addition to righteousness, one should seek *Shalom* (completeness/wholeness), which is the conclusion of the Priestly Blessing (Numbers 6:26).

The value of *Qof* reduces to 1, which refers to the Oneness of God and the first *Sefirah Keter* (Crown)—the destination of those created in his image, as the monkey climbs up the tree. The first of the Ten Commandments is to have no other gods before *HaShem*. The value of the letters that spell *Qof* is 186, which reduces to 15 (*YaH*) and 6 (*Tiferet*). This reminds us of the *Shema* declaring that *HaShem* is One, the only God of Israel, and that they must love him with all their hearts (Deuteronomy 6:4–5). *Tiferet* is the heart (*Lamed Bet*) of the Kabbalah, and it is on the account of the *Lamed Bet Tzadakim* (32 Righteous Persons) that the world is preserved.

The Sefer Yetzirah classifies *Qof* as one of the simple/single letters and associates it with *laughter*, *mirth*, and *happiness* and the Zodiac sign of Pisces. Laughter and mirth can be compared to a person monkeying around (*Legends of the Jews* 1:4:72), like a comedian who "*gets up and acts like a monkey; everything that the comedian does, he mockingly imitates*" (Likutei Moharan 245:2:3).Life is not only about work. One must also enjoy life (Ecclesiastes 9:9) and have joy on Shabbat (Shulhan Arukh 280:1), for it is a gift from God (Ecclesiastes 3:13, 5:19).

On the Hermetic Tree, *Qof* is on the path connecting *Malkut* and *Netzach* and is associated with the Moon card of Tarot. The Moon card is about balancing one's animal instincts/drives (*Nefesh*) with their domesticated/intellectual nature (Neshamah), the mental faculties that differentiate humans from monkeys (*The Guide for the Perplexed*, part 3, 51:2). On the Lurianic Tree, *Qof* is on the path connecting *Binah* and *Chesed*, which represent advancing from the animal (monkey like) instincts displayed within the Garden of Eden (*Binah*) into the covenant with God (*Chesed*).

The numerical Tarot card would be the Sun card, which speaks to God's blessings, unlimited potential, and new birth (Genesis 21:5). On the Cube of the Kabbalah, *Qof* connects *Yesod* and *Netzach*, which can also symbolize birth, since *Netzach* is associated with Venus, and *Yesod* is the location of the marriage of the Sun and Moon. In Hebrew block lettering, the *Qof* is constructed by a *Vav* and a *Kaf*, which would produce the value of the Tetragrammaton (26). In STaM, *Qof* is made with a *Zayin* and *Kaf*, which has a gematria value of 27 (2 + 7 = 9) and another connection to *Yesod*.

The Talisman: This *Kame'ah* includes the first-person name of God (EHeYeH ASheR EHeYeH), the number of completion squared (100%) providing a complete representation of the One. This is the third evolution of the *Alef* and represents humans being created in the image of God. Just as the *Alef* has a *Yod* above and a *Yod* below with a *Vav* as the mirror, the *Vav* serves as a mirror of the *Qof* and *Fei*. The *Sefirah* of *Keter* is also written in Hebrew, being the first emanation at the top of the Kabbalah. The key words, reflection, monkey, and mirth express the attributes of the letter; one should mimic God, master the emanations, and find joy, laughter, happiness, and Shalom while doing so. This talisman/lot can be used as a reminder that one's work is never finished; there is always potential to advance further. While one should be thankful with 100 blessings each day, life must also be enjoyed, and one must have the emotional intelligence to show grace to others, while continuing to tame one's own animal instincts.

THE LETTER *Resh*

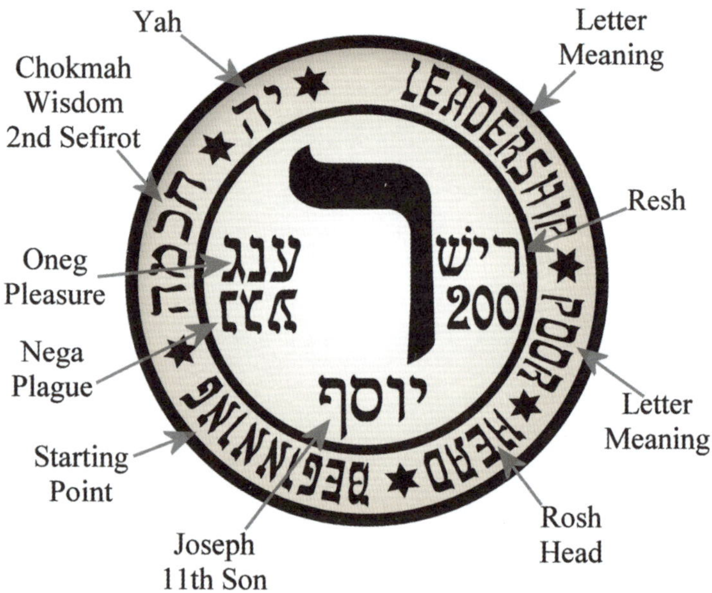

Letter: Resh, Yod, Shin

Transliteration: Resh

English Letter: R

Sound: Receive

Gematria Value: 200

Reduced Value: 2

Etz Chayim Sefirot: Chokmah

Ten Commandments: No idols

Name Value: 200 + 300 + 10 = 510 = 5 + 1 + 0 = 6

Name Meaning: Poor, head, leader, beginning, ruach

Sequential Number: 20 = 2

Sefer Yetzirah Classification: 7 Double

Sefer Yetzirah Attribute: War/peace

Hermetic Tree Path: Yesod-Hod

Hermetic Tarot: Sun

Lurianic Tree Path: Yesod-Tiferet

Kabbalah Cube: South

Numerical Tarot: Judgment

Constructed Gematria: Symbolizes a bowed head, Humble or Shame

Prefix/Suffix: N/A

Mystical Associations: The letter *Resh* is the 20th consecutive letter and has a gematria value of 200. It means *head, beginning,* or *poverty*. The Sefer Yetzirah classifies it as a double letter and associates it with the opposites of *war* and *peace*, the Saturn of the Universe, and the Friday of the Year. The value of *Resh* reduces to 2 and has connections with the *Kaf* and *Bet*. The second *Sefirah* is *Chokmah*, and *Kaf*, *Bet*, and *Chokmah* all have associations with the divine feminine. The value of the letters that spell *Resh* can be reduced to 6 (200 + 300 + 10 = 510 = 5 + 1 + 0 = 6) and represent God giving humans dominion (leadership) over the world (Genesis 1:28).

In this third evolution of the letters, the couple (Adam—male/female) has achieved righteousness (*Tzadi*) and passed through holiness (*Qof*) and should be able to rule with wisdom and justice; however, for those who are given much, much more will be expected (Numbers 15:29–30, Luke 12:48). The reduced value of *ONeG* (Joy) and *NeGA* (Plague) also reduces to 6, since the two words include the same letters, *Ayin*, *Nun*, and *Gimel*, written in a different order. This demonstrates the vast differences in possibilities and perspectives (*Ayin*) that a ruler with great power (*Gimel/Gadol/Giber*) can wield. A ruler's choices can lead/carry (*Gimel*) the person and the world being governed to pleasure (*Oneg/Shekinah*) or plague (*Nega/Lilith*), Miracle (*Nun*) or Failure (*Nun*), Head/Leadership (*Rosh/Resh Alef Shin*) or Poverty (*Resh/Resh Yod Shin*), *Shalom* (Peace/Wholeness/*Oneg*) or War/Evil (*Resh Ayin/Nega*).

After being declared righteous (Genesis 6:9) and being separated (sanctified / made holy) from the sinners (Genesis 6:16–17), Noah was given dominion over the entire earth (Genesis 9:1), as Adam was given previously (Genesis 1:28). King David likewise was righteous (1 Samuel 24:17), was sanctified (made holy) by *HaShem*, received the Holy Spirit (1 Samuel 16:13), and was appointed King over Israel (2 Samuel 2:4). David was a man after God's own heart (1 Samuel 13:14, 2 Samuel 7:2), but following the lust of his own heart (2 Samuel 11:2), David gave in to the *Yetzer HaRa* (Proverbs 7:25–27) and committed adultery, abusing the power that God had entrusted to him (2 Samuel 11:14–15).

The prophet Nathan confronted David with a parable about the rich man taking a lamb from a poor man, and after David was angered over the abuse of power, Nathan revealed that in the story, David represented the rich man (2 Samuel 12:1–6). David's sins were elucidated to him over the next several verses (2 Samuel 12:7–12), and David was ashamed. David sought pleasure but obtained plague. Like Adam and Noah, he was tempted by the serpent (Or HaChaim 49:11:3).

The letter *Resh* represents a person with their head bent down in shame and poverty. However, the letter also represents leadership and can be viewed as God (or anyone in power) watching over his creation (kingdom). The difference between *Oneg* and *Nega* (Pleasure and Plague) rests only in how one arranges the letters; it is what we do with our talents that define our characters (Matthew 25:14–30). The lives of humans can change drastically as "*the Lord makes poor and makes rich, he brings low, and he exalts*" (1 Samuel 2:7) during one's lifetime.

Of the Ten Commandments, the second is not to bow to idols (Exodus 20:5). In Exodus, this commandment comes before the need to keep the Sabbath day holy (Exodus 20:8–11), but in Leviticus, keeping the Sabbath comes before the commandment against idolatry (Leviticus 19:3–4). The *Sefer Yetzirah* associates *Resh* with peace, and *Shalom* (wholeness) is a key aspect of Shabbat, as is the *Mitzvah Oneg Shabbat*, which requires the Sabbath to be enjoyed; it is a *taste* (*Tzadi*) of the *Olam HaBa* (World to Come /Heaven). The *Sefer Yetzirah* also associates the letter with the Friday of the Year. Friday evening is the start of the Sabbath.

When spelled with a *Yod*, *Resh* means *Poverty* and could represent the Hand of God giving someone dominion; however, having power does not guarantee that it will be used appropriately. Adam was trusted with the garden, Noah with the world, and David with a kingdom, but each of them struggled to maintain the balance between war and peace (*Oneg* or *Nega*). Saturn devoured his own children to prevent them from taking away his authority.

If the *Yod* is reduced to an *Alef*, then *Resh Alef Shin* spells *Rosh* (Head, Start, or Beginning). The *Alef* represents humanity as a reflection of God and serves as an example of the type of leader one should strive to be—one after God's own heart (*Tiferet*). *Rosh* is the beginning (a new start), and when combined with *Bet* (*Chokmah*/Wisdom), it spells "*In the Beginning*," which is the first word in the Torah. *Rosh Hashanah* is the Jewish New Year, and *Rosh Hodesh* is the new moon at the beginning of each new month, considered a holiday for women (Megillah 22b:3).

The *Zohar* describes a special chamber in *Keter* (Crown) referred to as *Arich Anpin* (macroprosopus, the extended visage / countenance / long face), which is associated with the Divine Will prior to the creation of the *Sefirot*. The chamber, called *Elohim* (Judges), is filled with the light of the souls of the righteous (Daniel 12:3). It is this aspect of judgment and divine will that is referenced when humanity is said to be created in the image of God. This understanding aligns with Rabbeinu Bachya Ben Asher's interpretation of the mystical aspect of *B'reishit*, where God first created Wisdom, followed by Elohim (this chamber of judgment and divine will), then the heavens (Angels) and the earth (Material Creation). This, according to the *Zohar*, "*is the secret of the words: In the beginning Elohim created*" (Zohar 1:15a:4).

The *Zohar* describes this chamber as having the "*Holy Name Eheyeh engraved upon the sides of Arich Anpin. The name Elohim is engraved on the crown. And this is the secret of Asher, which is a concealed chamber, and is the beginning of the revelation of the secret of the Beginning. The word Asher consists of the same letters as Rosh (Eng. 'head') but in reverse order, as the letter Resh which is the first letter in Rosh is the last letter in Asher. This shows that it is the Rosh that came out of resheet (Eng. 'beginning'), which is Arich Anpin. Therefore, it emerged from the aspect of the head*" (Zohar 1:15a:5).

Humans were endowed with the faculty of judgment, and the world was entrusted to them (Genesis 1:28). The letter *Resh* symbolizes the beginning, leadership, authority, and dominion. Such power can be used to establish peace and justice, or else in the pursuit of war and greed.

The lesson of this letter is to be a good steward with the blessings God has given you, to make the most of whatever state you are in, and to rule your own life with wisdom. *Asher* is part of the name of God given to Moses at the Burning Bush and is used to refer to God in every Talmudic Blessing: "*Blessed are you, Adonai our God, Sovereign of the Universe, ASHeR/who . . .*" The letters in the word *Asher* rearranged spell *Rosh*, which reminds us to use the authority given to us by the Hand of God as a reflection of the divine will. The chamber with the secret of *Asher* is the head (*Rosh*) and represents ideal judgment (*Elohim*) and the Primordial Air of the Mother Letter *Alef*, where the *Yod* above reflects the *Yod* below.

On the Hermetic Tree, *Resh* is on the path connecting *Yesod* and *Hod*, representing the Glory (*Hod*) of the King and Queen after engaging in the

Chymical Wedding (*Yesod*) and being led by the *Ruach* (1 Samuel 16:13). The Major Arcana Tarot card is the Sun, which is also representative of God giving dominion over the earth to his children. On the Kabbalah Cube of Space, *Resh* represents the south, which is associated with the direction the divine feminine comes to Solomon from in the *Aurora Consurgens* (1250).

On the Lurianic Tree of Life, *Resh* is on the path connecting *Yesod* and *Tiferet*, the heart and the sexual organs. This placement emphasizes the need to balance justice and mercy, as *Tiferet* does, particularly in the context of *Oneg Shabbat* (joining with the Shabbat Bride) and the union with the Shabbat Bride. It highlights the importance of controlling one's passions to avoid falling into the *Yetzer HaRa* (the evil inclination) and *Nega* (plague). The numerical Tarot card associated with *Resh* is Judgment, which is fitting for this letter. In the Rider-Waite deck, the Judgment card represents divine judgment and also signifies the reward for those who succeed in the Chymical Wedding, where two become one and multiply, producing a new creation and rectified world of peace and wholeness.

The Talisman: On the *Kame'ah*, the divine name YaH is written, which represents the union of the divine male and female. Its gematria value is 15, which reduces to 6 and represents the world having been created in 6 days and humans being given dominion over the earth. It also has connections with the reduced value of the letters that spell *Resh*, as well as the letters in the words for Pleasure (*Oneg*) and Plague/Affliction (*Nega*), representing this continued struggle to find peace (*Shalom*) during the war between good and evil (*Yetzer HaTov* and *Yetzer HaRa*) taking place within each individual. The value of the letter is 200, which reduces to 2 and has connections to *Kaf* (20) and *Bet* (2), as well as the *Sefirah* of *Chokmah*. *Rosh Hodesh* is a woman's holiday associated with the new moon. Joseph was Jacob's 11th son (1 + 1 = 2), and he experienced both poverty (as a prisoner and slave) and being a ruler. As a *segulah*, this charm can serve as a reminder that once a person has made it to the top, they should not let their guard down. The leader must continue in righteousness and holiness, and one's decisions should be made with justice, peace, and wisdom in mind. The purpose of life is to learn discernment and appropriate judgment. By the time one's spiritual develop reaches the letter *Resh*, they should have already mastered these traits, so they can now serve as an administrator of justice.

THE LETTER *Shin*

Letter: Shin, Yod, Nun

Transliteration: Shin

English Letter: Sh/S

Sound: Shine/sin

Gematria Value: 300

Reduced Value: 3

Etz Chayim Sefirot: Binah

Ten Commandments: Do not misuse the name

Name Value: 360 (300 + 50 + 10 = 360, and 3 + 6 + 0 = 9)

Name Meaning: Tooth/fire

Sequential Number: 21 = 3

Sefer Yetzirah Classification: 3 Mothers

Sefer Yetzirah Attribute: Fire

Hermetic Tree Path: Malkut-Hod

Hermetic Tarot: Judgment

Lurianic Tree Path: Binah-Chokmah

Kabbalah Cube: Fire-heavens

Numerical Tarot: World

Constructed Gematria: 21 = 3 (3 Zayin), 18 = 9 (3 Vav), 19 = 2 (1 Zayin, 2 Vav), or 64 = 10 (2 Zayin, 1 Nun)

Prefix/Suffix: That, which, who, there

Mystical Associations: The letter *Shin/Sin* is the 21st consecutive letter and has a gematria value of 300. It means *tooth* or *fire*, and the Sefer Yetzirah classifies it as one of the three Mother Letters and associates it with primordial fire, the creation of the Heavens, the season of summer, and the head of the body. The Three Pillars of the *Shin* represent the Three Pillars of the Kabbalah, or the three Pillars that support the world (Torah, Prayer, and Righteousness). Like the *Resh*, *Shin* is associated with the head, but unlike the *Resh*, which can also hang its head in shame and fall over (experience poverty), the *Shin* has a stable base and equally balances each of the Three Pillars.

The *Mitzvot* to bind the commandments on one's hands and foreheads (Deuteronomy 6:8) is fulfilled by binding *Tefillin* on one's arm and head. The head *Tefillin* (phylacteries) is a small black cube with four compartments each containing a kosher scroll written by the hand of a *Sofer* (Scribe) in STaM. The left and right sides of the *Tefillin* each contain a *Shin*; the one on the right side (of the wearer) is a three-branched *Shin*, representing the three Patriarchs (Abraham, Isaac, and Jacob). The left side has a *Shin* with four branches, representing the four Matriarchs (Sarah, Rebecca, Leah, and Rachel). Together, there are seven branches, representing the *Menorah* of the Tabernacle, which rested immediately outside the Holiest of Holies (which would represent the mind of the *Tefillin* wearer).

The letter *Shin* is also on *Mezuzot* (doorposts) and represents the divine name *Shaddai*, which stems from the word *breasts* and speaks to the mothering and nurturing nature of God. It is the first letter in the words *Shabbat* (Sabbath), *Shalom* (Peace), *Shekinah* (Divine Presence), and *Shemayim* (Heaven/Sky). On the Dreidel, *Shin* represents the word "*there*," and when the dreidel lands on

Shin, the person *shares* their contribution, representing the need to support and sacrifice oneself for others (Leviticus 19:10, John 15:13). When performing the Priestly Blessing, the High Priest forms the letter *Shin* with his hand, which the Jewish actor Leonard Nimoy popularized as the Vulcan salute on the television show *Star Trek*, along with the saying "*Live long and prosper*," which he also borrowed from the Tanukh (Deuteronomy 5:33).

As for the constructed gematria of the *Shin*, it is written in multiple ways. The simplest would be to assume it is 3 *Vav*, which would equal 18 and share the gematria of *Chai* (life). Sometimes it appears more like 3 *Zayin*, which would equal 21 (its consecutive letter in the *Alef-bet*) and would reduce to 3 and connect the Shekinah with *Gimel*. It can also appear as 1 *Zayin* and 2 *Vav*, which would equal 19 (1 + 9 = 10 = 1), or 2 *Zayin* and a bent *Nun* 64 (6 + 4 = 10 = 1) in order to represent completion. Which of these is correct? Like PaRDeS, each of them can be correct simultaneously.

The value of 300 reduces to 3 and associates *Shin* with *Gimel or* the Three Pillars. The third *Sefirot* is *Binah*, but the *Shin* represents all Three Pillars, and if the letters in *Shin* are rearranged, they can spell *Shai* (Two), connecting it with *Chokmah* (Wisdom). The gematria of the other constructions (1 *Zayin* and 2 *Vav*, 2 *Zayin* and 1 *Nun*, or 3 *Vav*) can link it both to *Keter* (1) and *Yesod* (9). All these connections can be equally relevant. The *Shin/Sin* can also make two sounds, depending on whether the dot above the letter is at the right of the *Shin* or the left of the *Sin*.

Shin can represent the divine *Fire* (*Alef Shin*), representing the union of the divine masculine and feminine—similar to *YaH*, but with the *Alef* abbreviating *Eheieh* or *Adonai* and the *Shin* either *Shekinah* or *Shaddai*. As a prefix, *Shin* can represent *who* or *there* and has a similar meaning to the word *Asher* (used to refer to God in Talmudic blessings and the male counterpart of *Asherah*); this fire of the divine is mixed with the other letters in YaH, adding passion to their human counterparts (Man / *Alef Yod Shin*, and Woman / *Alef Shin Hei*). In the Bible, God is portrayed as a Pillar of Fire (Exodus 13:21, Wisdom 18:3, Hebrews 12:29). The word *Shin* means *Tooth* and represents transformation. In order to extract nutrients out of food, the food must be chewed up first; this suggests the *Baptism of Fire*—the start of the purification process that might be experienced when someone first engages in the Chymical Wedding. The benefits of Wisdom are described by Sirach as follows:

Shin can represent the divine *fire* (*Alef Shin*), symbolizing the union of the divine masculine and feminine; similar to *YaH*, but with the *Alef* abbreviating *Eheieh* or *Adonai* and the *Shin* either *Shekinah* or *Shaddai*. As a prefix, *Shin* can represent *who* or *there* and has a similar meaning to the word *Asher* (used to refer to God in Talmudic blessings). God is portrayed as a Pillar of Fire (Exodus 13:21, Wisdom 18:3, Hebrews 12:29). The word *Shin* means *tooth* and represents transformation. In order to extract nutrients out of food, the food must be chewed up; this represents the *Baptism of Fire*, and the start of the purification process that might be experienced when someone first engages in the Chymical Wedding. The benefits of Wisdom are described by Sirach as follows:

> *Wisdom will exalt her children and help those who seek her. Whoever loves her loves life, and those who seek her will be filled with joy. Whoever holds her fast will obtain glory, and the Lord will bless those she enters. Those who serve her are servants of the Holy One, and the Lord loves those who love her. Those who obey her will judge the nations, and will dwell securely. The one who has faith will obtain her. At first she will guide them through difficult paths of fear and discipline, until she gains their trust. Then she will come to them, gladden them, and will reveal her secrets to them.* (Sirach 4:11–18)

On the Hermetic Tree, *Shin* is on the path connecting *Malkut* and *Hod*, representing the Shekinah leading the initiate out of the world and toward glory/eternity. The Major Arcana Tarot card is Judgment, which in the Rider-Waite deck shows those who engaged in the Chymical Wedding being rewarded with eternal life (Daniel 12:2). On the Kabbalah Cube, *Shin* represents the *Primordial Fire* and is throughout the inside of the cube. On the Lurianic Tree, *Shin* connects *Binah* and *Chokmah*, both of which are related to the divine feminine. According to the numerical order of the Tarot, the 21st card is the World card, which in the Rider-Waite deck shows the Shekinah at its center (representing the Pillar of Unity) and holding the Pillars of Severity and Mercy in her hands as wands; she is in the Heavens, as the Woman Wisdom (*Ruach Elohim*) was after she was created in *Chokmah* and was hovering over the waters (Genesis 1:2) of *Binah* (Proverbs 8:21).

The Talisman: This *goralot* contains the divine name *YHVH Elohim*, which refers to the Creation aspect of God found in Genesis and the Sefer Yetzirah. *Binah* is also written on the outside ring in Hebrew and represents the beginning of the material universe. The gematria value of *Shin* is 300, which reduces to 3. Fire, tooth, and transformation are written around the outer ring and are key attributes associated with the letter. This *Kame'ah* can be used as a reminder of stability and perfect balance that one seeks to obtain. It represents perfect balance of the male and female, the Patriarchs and Matriarchs, the *Menorah*, the *Mezuzah*,

Tefillin, and the Pillars of Study (Torah), Speech (Prayer), and Action (Righteousness), upon which the world is maintained. It is the consuming Pillar of Fire and the transformational power of teeth/fire, and it represents a crown on the head. The symbolism is simple, but powerful.

THE LETTER *Tav*

Letter: Tav, Vav

Transliteration: Tav

English Letter: T/Th/S

Sound: Truth, the

Gematria Value: 400

Reduced Value: 4

Etz Chayim Sefirot: Chesed

Ten Commandments: Remember/Keep the Sabbath

Name Value: 406 (400 + 6 = 406 = 4 + 0 + 6 = 10 = 1+ 0 =1)

Name Meaning: Mark, sign, omen, seal

Sequential Number: 22 (22 = 2 + 2 = 4)

Sefer Yetzirah Classification: 7 Double

Sefer Yetzirah Attribute: Beauty, Ugliness

Hermetic Tree Path: Malkut-Yesod

Hermetic Tarot: World

Lurianic Tree Path: Malkut-Yesod

Kabbalah Cube: Center—foundation stone

Numerical Tarot: 0 Fool

Constructed Gematria: Resh 200 Vav 6 (206 = 8), Dalet 4 Nun 50 (54 = 9)

Prefix/Suffix: Prefix, third-person singular female (She will), second-person future (You will), third-person plural female future (They will); suffix, VT feminine plural, suffix T or AT constructive (of), verb conjugation suffix M/F, second-person singular (You did)

Mystical Associations: The letter *Tav* is the 22nd consecutive letter in the Hebrew *Alef-bet* and has a gematria value of 400. It is the final letter of the *Alef-bet* and represents completion. It reduces to 4 and symbolizes the Tetragrammaton (four-letter name), being the doorway (*Dalet*) to the World to Come (*Olam HaBa*). It is the third cycle of numbers and is connected with the *Dalet* (4) and *Mem* (40), and the calculated values of all previous numbers return to the source (231 + 22 = 253 = 10 = 1). *Tav* is the final letter in the first word of the Bible (BeRAShYT / In the Beginning) and represents the End of the Beginning.

The *Sefer Yetzirah* classifies *Tav* as a double letter and associates it with the opposites beauty/grace and ugliness. The word used for beauty/grace in the *Sefer Yetzirah* is *Chet Nun* (*Chet* 8 + *Nun* 50 = 58, and 5 + 8 = 13, and 1 + 3 = 4), which like the letter *Chet* (*Chet, Yod, Tav*) reduces to 13 and 4 (*Chet* 8 + *Yod* 10 + *Tav* 400 = 418, and 4 + 1 + 8 = 13, and 1 + 3 = 4). The *Chet* represents the couple being united in *love* (AHAVAH/*Alef* 1 + *Hei* 5 + *Bet* 2 + *Hei* 5 = 13, and 1 +3 = 4) beneath the *Chuppah* and the protection of the *Shekinah*. Like *B'reishit*, *Chet* ends with a *Tav*. The fourth *Sefirah* is *Chesed*, which represents

Grace, Loving kindness, and the Covenant with God, providing a Door (*Dalet* 4) into the kingdom.

Tav is a double letter because it can make two sounds. The hard sound is like the "T" in the word *Truth*, and the soft sound can make either the sound "TH" or "S"—depending on cultural pronunciations; in addition to the duality of *Grace* and *Ugliness* (Mercy and Judgment), the *Sefer Yetzirah* associates the letter *Tav* with Jupiter in the Universe, the Sabbath of the Year, and the *Mouth* of the body. Jupiter was the king of the gods in Roman mythology and would be the opposite of the Jewish view of *HaShem*. Where *HaShem* established a covenant of grace with Israel, Rome brought ugliness, oppression, and slaughter. Rome (Revelation 17:9) is the fourth beast spoken of by Daniel (Matthew 24:15)—the final enemy the scattered sheep will face prior to the restoration of the kingdom (Daniel 7:23–27).

As the final *Mouth* of the body, *Tav* represents the gathering of those who were *scattered* (*Pei/Fei*) (Ezekiel 34:12, Jeremiah 31:10, John 11:52, Matthew 25:32). *Tav* is also associated with the Sabbath, providing the righteous (*Tzadikim*) with a taste (*Tzadi*) of the Eternal Sabbath (the world to come). *Tav*, as the final letter, *marks* (*Tav Vav*) the beginning/entrance/doorway (*Dalet*) to the Eternal Shabbat. Of the Ten Commandments, the fourth is to Remember/Keep the Sabbath. *Shabbat* is a word that begins with the *Shin* (Peace/Resting on the Sabbath) and ends with a *Tav* (the beginning of the Eternal Shabbat).

The letter means *seal*, *mark*, *omen*, or *sign*, and the Talmud states, "*The letter Tav is the last letter in the Seal of the Holy One. . . . The Seal of the Holy One is Truth [EMeT], which ends with the letter Tav. . . . The letter Tav teaches that these are the people who observed the entire Torah from Alef through Tav*" (Shabbat 55a:12). EMeT (truth) contains the first, middle, and last letters of the *Alef-bet* and represents God (*Alef*) being the First and the Last (Isaiah 41:4, Revelation 22:3), the purification and revealing of mysteries (*Mem*), and the completion of the beginning (*Tav*). The righteous are the ones who obey the commandments/tradition (Torah) from *Alef* to *Tav* (*Alef Tav* also represents the direct object of the definite article). When determining the position of the letters in the *Alef-bet*, the *Zohar* says that each letter presented itself to God to request the first position. The interaction with *Tav* is as follows:

> *When the Creator thought to create the world, all the letters of the alphabet came to Him in reverse order from last to first. The letter Tav entered first and said, "Master of the world! It is good, and also seemly of you, to create the world with me, with my properties. For I am the seal on your ring, called Truth, that ends with the letter Tav. And that is why you are called Truth, and why it would*

befit the King to begin the universe with the letter Tav, and to create the world by her, by her properties." The Creator answered: "You are beautiful and sincere, but do not merit the world that I conceived to be created by your properties. You are destined to serve as a mark on the foreheads of the faithful, who have kept the Law of the Torah from Alef to Tav. When you appear, they shall die." (Zohar 1:2b:3)

Instead of being the first of the physical world, *Tav* is the end of the beginning (BeRAShYT), and the symbol of the World to Come (*Olam HaBa*). *Tav* is beauty and ugliness, because it represents the final Judgment, which is a mixture of grace and justice. In the book of Ezekiel, the *Tav* is used similar to the Blood of the Passover to identify those who would be spared from God's wrath (Ezekiel 9:3–6). The *Tav* was used as the *sign* and *mark* of those who were saved (Shabbat 55a:5). The Talmud states, "*The Holy One, Blessed by he, said to the angel Gabriel: Go and inscribe a Tav of ink on the foreheads of the righteous as a sign so that the angels of destruction will not have dominion over them. And inscribe a Tav of blood on the foreheads of the wicked as a sign so that the angels of destruction will have dominion over them*" (Shabbat 55a:6).

The Rabbis explained that in relation to the righteous, "*Tav is the first letter of the word tihye, you shall live, indicating that the righteous shall live*," while "*Tav is also the first letter of the word tamut, you shall die, indicating that the wicked shall die*" (Shabbat 55a:11). The *Tefillin* also represents the word of God (Torah) being bound to the foreheads of God's servants. In the Revelation of the Apostle John, it is the name of God that serves as the Seal of God on the foreheads of the righteous (Revelation 7:3, 9:4, 14:1, 22:4).

The *Tav* is the 22nd consecutive letter in the Hebrew *Alef-bet*, and the 22nd of the 613 *Mitzvot* in the order of Rambam is to learn the Torah (Deuteronomy 6:7). The *Zohar* and the Talmud also link this to being the seal/sign/symbol of the righteous—those who keep the Torah from *Alef* to *Tav*. The letter *Tav* is constructed with three lines, representing the Three Pillars of study (Torah), speech (Prayer), and deeds (Righteousness). It is the first letter in the word *Teshuvah* (Repentance / Return to God), and its shape resembles the letter *Chet* (where the marriage covenant begins). The constructed gematria of the letter can vary, since the block letters and STaM have variations and combine different letters in order to form a *Tav*. The letter *Tav* resembles a *Hei* (which has a *Yod* supporting a *Dalet*), but in the *Tav*, the *Yod* is mirrored and appears to be exiting of the door (*Dalet*), to signify a departure from the physical world. The letters *Dalet Yod* spell *Dei* (Enough, Sufficient).

In STaM the letter on the right looks like a *Dalet*, but in block lettering it resembles a *Resh*—the mind and one's actions are the doorway into the next world. The letter on the left can resemble a *Yod*, a *Vav*, or a bent *Nun*. If the letters *Dalet* and *Nun* are combined, it spells Dan, the Tribe of Judgment, which was also the last and final Tribe in Israel's travels (Numbers 2:31). If the letters *Resh* and *Nun* are combined, they spell *Rahn* (Joy/Gladness). *Resh* 200 *Vav* 6 would reduce to (206 = 8), pointing to Eternity/Glorification (*Hod*). *Dalet* 4 *Nun* 50 would reduce to 54 (54 = 9), the results of the union (*Yesod*) under the *Chuppah* (*Chet*).

The gematria value of *Tav* is 400, which reduces to 4. In order to bury Sarah, Abraham bought the cave of *Machpelah* (Genesis 23:9) for 400 shekels of silver (Genesis 23:15–16). The cave of *Machpelah* is said to be the burial place of four couples: Abraham and Sarah, Isaac and Rebecca, Jacob and Leah, and Adam and Eve. The cave is mystically said to represent the entrance to the Garden of Eden (Heaven), which is how the association with Adam and Eve is made—death is the doorway (*Dalet*) to the world to come. Four hundred is also the number of young men who escaped the king's judgment (1 Samuel 30:17) by being carried to safety by camels (*Gimel*).

In the book of 2 Esdras, Ezra describes the time of the Messiah as lasting 400 years. He states that "*the Messiah shall be revealed and those who remain shall rejoice for four hundred years. And after these years, the Messiah shall die, and all who draw human breath*" (2 Esdras 7:28–29). The world will then be re-created over seven days (2 Esdras 7:30–31, Revelation 21:5, Genesis 2:2), and after the seven days, the resurrection of the dead will occur (Daniel 12:2, 2 Esdras 7:32–33, Isaiah 26:9, Ezekiel 37:12, Revelation 20:12–13). The final judgment (Joel 2:32, Amos 5:18–19) will be a day of grace and ugliness (Baruch 4:21–23), rejoicing and despair (Isaiah 65:17–19), pleasure (*Oneg*) and plague (*Nega*). The letter *Tav* is an omen/sign of completion and marks the end of the beginning.

On both the Lurianic and Hermetic Tree of Life, *Tav* is on the path connecting *Malkut* and *Yesod*. In the Major Arcana of the Tarot, this path is associated with the World card and represents one leaving the physical world (*Malkut*) and being led to *Olam HaBa* (World to Come). On the Kabbalah Cube, *Tav* is at the center and represents the Temple, the Throne of God, or the Foundation Stone. In the numerical order of the Tarot, the Major Arcana would have gone full circle and returned to the 0 Fool, which can represent the beauty of innocence or the ugliness of folly, depending on how one is judged. As a prefix or suffix, *Tav* is used in multiple ways and can represent the future, past, or plural forms.

The Talisman: The *Kameòt/Goralot* associated with *Tav* contains the divine name *EL* (*Alef Lamed*), which means God or Mighty. The letters *Alef Lamed* can also mean to/toward, which, like *Tav* (400), reduces to 4 (*Lamed* 30 + *Alef* 1 = 3 + 0 + 1 = 4). The fourth *Sefirah* is *Chesed*, and beauty/grace are attributes associated with *Tav* in the Sefer Yetzirah. Also written in Hebrew around the outer ring are the words EMeT (truth), which the Talmud describes as the Seal of God, and the word *T'Chayah* (you will live), which is the meaning of the *Tav* when it is written on the foreheads of the righteous as a mark of salvation. Seal, sign, and omen are the meanings of *Tav*, and completion is its attribute. The word *Shalom* means peace, completion, or wholeness and is associated with Shabbat. *Tav* represents the Sabbath of the world and the Eternal Shabbat of the *Olam HaBa*. Benjamin was Jacob's final son, who brought both happiness and despair; Rachel died giving birth to Benjamin and named him *son of my sorrow* (Genesis 35:18), but Jacob changed his name to *son of my right hand* (Psalm 110:1; Matthew 22:33, 22:44). As a *goral*, this lot can signify completion or the start of something greater, or it can represent judgment, justice, or any of the other attributes of *Tav* that your intuition causes you to feel is truth (EMeT). As a *Kameàh* (talisman/binding) or *Segulah* (charm/remedy), the *Tav* can represent *Teshuvah* (Return to God) and the reward of the righteous. It is a symbol of truth, justice, grace, and completion.

Creating Talismans

The talismans within this set of casting lots contain the mystical attributes of the Hebrew Letters associated with the Kabbalah. Understanding these connections is part of a deep mystical system, which allows its practitioners to contemplate the gematria values of letters, words, or sentences to unveil secret meanings or develop original mystical connections. Divination is a means of exercising one's mental faculties while contemplating abstract symbolism in order to develop innovative solutions to situations or to obtain spiritual revelation. Talismans can be religious adornments that contain prayers and ask for favors from a deity, or they can be psychological symbols that are meaningful to a particular individual. The talismans in this set can be used either for divination or as a *segulah* (good-luck charm), but one's use of talismans and symbolism need not be restricted to what is contained in this book/set.

The most significant, meaningful, and enjoyable aspects of talismans can be found in their construction. Creating your own talismans is what puts the "*Art*" in *Magical Arts* and the "*Craft*" in *Witchcraft*. Talismans will be more psychologically significant to you when you are the one who chooses the symbolism. To encourage the reader to further explore their own spirituality, this chapter will provide a simple means of talisman creation in order to get you started.

In Sofer STaM (*Sefer, Tefillin, Mezuzah*), *Klaf*—parchment made out of the skin of a kosher animal—is used along with a specially mixed ink, quill, and style of Hebrew lettering in order for the product to be considered kosher by certain sects of Judaism. Many traditional *Kame'ot* follow STaM practices and simply use kosher principles to write out the purpose of the *Kame'ah* in plain language (e.g., Protect this house/person) on a piece of *Klaf*, such as in the *Sefer Raziel HaMalakh*, where the *Kame'ah* against Lilith reads, "*Adam and Eve, without Lilith.*"

Kame'ah to protect babies / pregnant mothers against Lilith.
Sefer Raziel HaMalakh, 1701.

There are many talismans and formulas for creating talismans found in Latin grimoires. Some grimoires specify that certain talismans must be made of certain materials and consecrated at a certain time of day or phase of the moon. However, in each of the above examples, the method and materials are the product and opinions of the authors. When designing your own talismans, the symbolism and material you use should be of your choosing, and the time and method of concentration should be based on what seems significant or has

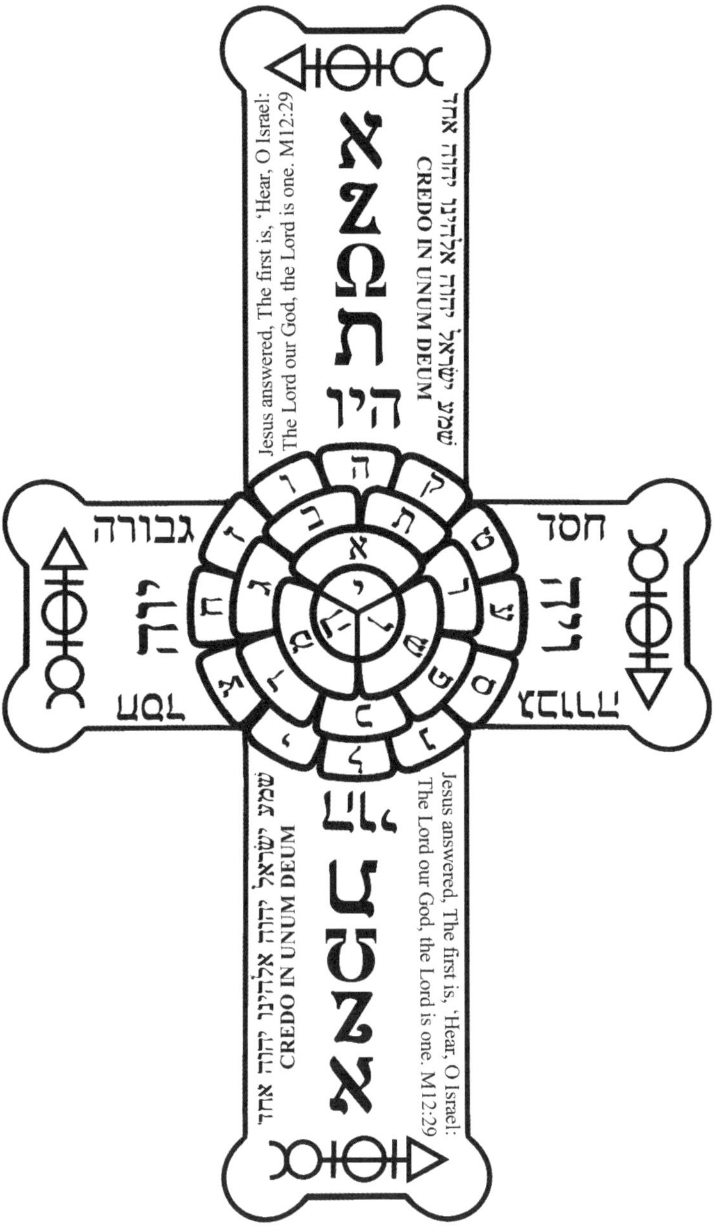

Rose Cross, *Rota Mundi Tarot*

meaning to you. Perhaps studying grimoires and listening to the ideas of others can provide inspiration, but in order to be a magician or creator, the goal is to move past following the instructions of others and to realize and release your own creative expression (self-actualization).

Talismans can be made of any material. They can be burned onto wood, carved into leather or stone, written on paper, or painted on your choice of medium. They can be carved in wood, sculpted out of clay, or cast in metal. Art supply stores sell wood circles, stars, and other shapes that are around 2–3 inches in size and can be easily painted or engraved into a talisman. The choice of materials, colors, and symbolism should be based on what the talisman's creator finds meaningful. The talisman can be any shape, but in this example a simple talisman will be created in a circle, and the symbolism will be based on a keyword or name and a sigil.

In this example, I will use my own name—*Daniel*—to produce the symbolism on the talisman. The name *Daniel* means "*God is my judge*," so to represent judgment, I might use imagery such as the scales of justice. To create a sigil, I will use the image on the back of the *Rota Mundi Tarot* deck. The first step in creating a sigil is to identify the Hebrew letters associated with my name. This can be done by searching for the English version of your name (or keyword) followed by "*in Hebrew*" in a web browser. If the word or name has Hebrew origins (as Daniel does), it will display the Hebrew spelling. If the English word does not originate from Hebrew, the result will be either a Hebrew transliteration (using Hebrew letters to match the sounds of the English word, spelling it phonetically using Hebrew letters) or a Hebrew word that shares the same meaning as the English word.

The name *Daniel* is spelled *Dalet, Nun, Yod, Alef, Lamed*, which gives me a gematria value of four (4 + 50 + 10 + 30 = 94 = 9 + 4 = 13 = 4). I can then select any of the associations to the letters found throughout this book in my symbolism, or I can use the *Sefirot* of *Yesod* (9) and *Chesed* (4) in my symbolism. Since my name has five letters in it, I can use the letter *Hei* in my symbolism—or a shape with five points, such as a pentagram.

Next, I will change the Hebrew letters of my name into a sigil. To do this, I make a dot/point/circle on the corresponding letter rose from the *Rota Mundi Tarot*, then I draw lines from letter to letter to make a small line that goes the opposite way to mark the ending of the word. This system allows anyone who uses the same rose cross pattern to decipher the sigil to reveal what is encoded into the sigil.

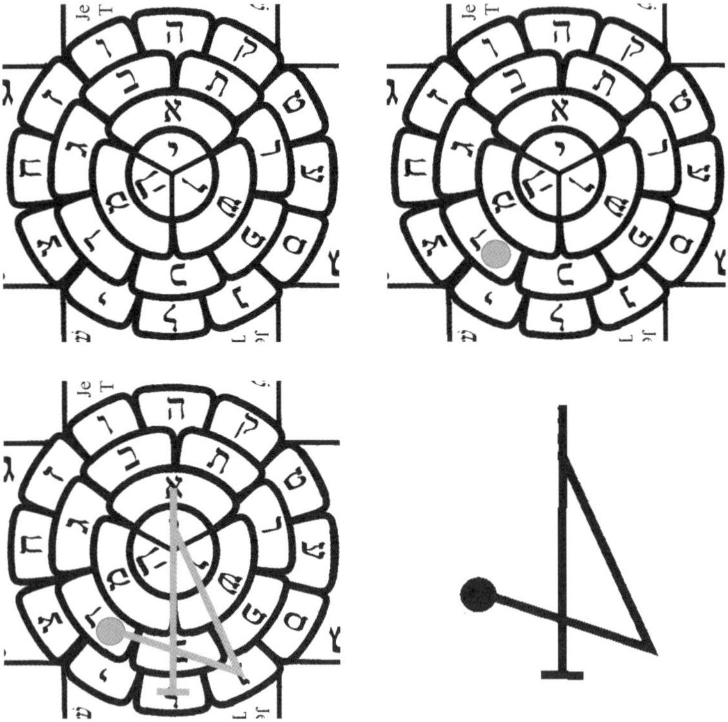

Resulting sigil

After creating this sigil, I added it to the center of my talisman and then incorporated the other elements and attributes of my name into the available spaces on the talisman, according to my artistic preference. In this example, the name "*Daniel*" is written counterclockwise around the outside of the star. At the center of the star is the sigil I created on the basis of the Hebrew letters of my name. The number 4 is placed in the top point of the star, with the other branches including the gematria values that contribute to the number 4. Around the outside of the pentacle, I wrote the meaning of my name, "*God is my Judge*," and the ninth and fourth *Sefirot* and their meanings. The result is a symbolic representation of my name. If I wanted to add more details, I could choose colors that are meaningful, add symbols such as the Scales of Justice, or include the zodiac signs related to my birth month, or anything else I felt was significant.

Blank talisman *(left)*, completed talisman *(right)*

Talismans can be made to represent any symbolism that has meaning to you, or you can write out statements or prayers regarding the desired outcome you would like to manifest. They can be simple reminders of single attributes, or they can be elaborate incantations designed to ward off evil spirits. Magick can be defined as an attempt to influence the physical world through supernatural, ritualistic, or symbolic means.

There are different theories regarding how magick functions. Some believe that angels (Trachtenberg 2004) or spirits respond to your stated intensions and symbolism (or that prayers are answered by God, who may direct angels or spirits to influence the outcome). An example of this might be the Guardian Angel of Esau (Samael) attacking Jacob the night prior to his confrontation with Esau. Alternatively, the symbolism might produce only a psychological response within its designer (or the person it is given to), which can motivate the person to achieve the desired outcome.

Whether it is the result of a psychological response to a subconscious desire or if the spiritual is responding to the physical or vice versa, talismans can produce effective results. Symbolism is the language of the subconscious; the things you focus on, care about, and put your mind to directly affect what you manifest in your life. Whether you are baking a cake or planning an event, the kabbalistic phases of Intention/Conception, Creation/Planning/Design, Formation/Effort/Building, and Action/Manifestation/Achievement all play a role in bringing your intentions into reality.

Bibliography

Abraham, Isaac ben. *Sefer Raziel Ha-Malakh*. Amsterdam: Be-vet M. Mindis Kvitinyo, 1701.

Albo, Joseph. *Sefer HaIkkarim Maamar*. Castille, 1425.

Arama, Isaac Ben Moses. *Akeidat Yitzchak*. Salonica, 1495. Translated by Akeidat Yitzchak. Pressburg, 1849. https://www.sefaria.org/Akeidat_Yitzchak (accessed March 14, 2022).

Attar, Chaim ibn, Rabbi. *Or HaChaim on Genesis*. Morroco Livorno, 1742. https://www.sefaria.org/Or_HaChaim_on_Genesis (accessed March 14, 2022).

Aurora Consurgens. 1250. Translated by Franz Mary-Louise. Inner City Books, 2000.

Briggs Myers, Isabel. *Gifts Differing: Understanding Personality Type*. 2nd ed. CPP, 1995.

Briggs Myers, Isabel, and Mary McCaulley. *Manuel: A Guide to the Development and Use of the Myers–Briggs Type Indicator*. Consulting Psychologists Press, 1985.

Central Conference of American Rabbis. *Mishkan T'Filah for Shabbat*. New York, 2007.

Charles, R. H. *The Apocrypha and Pseudepigrapha of the Old Testament: Book of Jubilees*. Oxford: Clarendon, 1913a.

Charles, R. H. *The Apocrypha and Pseudepigrapha of the Old Testament: Testament of the Patriarchs*. Oxford: Clarendon, 1913b.

Charles, R. H. *The Apocrypha and Pseudepigrapha of the Old Testament: Testament of the Patriarchs, Testament of Benjamin*. Oxford: Clarendon, 1913c.

Charles, R. H. *The Apocrypha and Pseudepigrapha of the Old Testament: Testament of the Solomon*. Oxford: Clarendon, 1913d.

Charles, R. H. The *Apocrypha and Pseudepigrapha of the Old Testament:2 Enoch*. Oxford: Clarendon, 1913e.

Cordovero, Moshe. *Tomer Devorah*. Safed Israel, 1588.

Davidson, William. *"Babylonian Talmud," Bava Batra*. Babylon, 450 CE. www.sefaria.org/Bava_Batra (accessed March 14, 2022).

Davidson, William. *"Babylonian Talmud," Bava Kamma*. Babylon, 450 CE. www.sefaria.org/Bava_Kamma (accessed March 14, 2022).

Davidson, William. *"Babylonian Talmud," Berehot*. Babylon, 450 CE. www.sefaria.org/Bava_Kamma (accessed March 14, 2022).

Davidson, William. *"Babylonian Talmud," Chagigiah*. Babylon, 450 CE. www.sefaria.org/Chagigiah (accessed March 14, 2022).

Davidson, William. *"Babylonian Talmud," Chullin*. Babylon, 450 CE. www.sefaria.org/Chullin (accessed March 14, 2022).

Davidson, William. "*Babylonian Talmud," Megillah*. Babylon, 450 CE. www.sefaria.org/Megillah (accessed March 14, 2022).

Davidson, William. "*Babylonian Talmud," Menachot*. Babylon, 450 CE. www.sefaria.org/Menachot (accessed March 14, 2022).

Davidson, William. "*Babylonian Talmud," Sanhedrin*. Babylon, 450 CE. www.sefaria.org/Sanhedrin (accessed March 14, 2022).

Davidson, William. "*Babylonian Talmud," Shabbat*. Babylon, 450 CE. www.sefaria.org/Shabbat (accessed March 14, 2019).

De Laurence, L. W. (Lauron William). *The Sixth and Seventh Books of Moses*. Chicago: De Laurance, Scott, 1910.

De Leon, Moses. *The Zohar*. 1305. Translated by Maurice Simon. 2nd ed. Soncino, June 1, 1934.

Eliezer, d'Rabbi. *Pirkei DeRabbi Eliezer*. Talmudic Israel/Babylon, 1030. Translated by Rabbi Gerald Friedlander. London, 1916. https://www.sefaria.org/Pirkei_DeRabbi_Eliezer (accessed March 14, 2022).

Feuer, Mike, Rabbi. *Jerusalem Anthology, Bamidbar Rabbah*. Talmudic Israel/Babylon, 1200. https://www.sefaria.org/Bamidbar_Rabbah (accessed March 14, 2022).

Feuer, Mike, Rabbi. *Jerusalem Anthology, Midrash Tehillim*. Narbonne, 1450. Translated by Mike Feuer. Jerusalem Anthology. https://www.sefaria.org/Midrash_Tehillim (accessed March 14, 2019).

Gikatilla Joseph, Rabbi, trans. *Gates of Light (Sha'are Orah)*. 1293. Reprint ed. New Haven, CT: Yale University Press, October 18, 2010.

Ginzberg, Louis, Rabbi. *Legends of the Jews*. Philadelphia: Jewish Publication Society of America, 1909.

Holy Bible, *Good News Translations*. American Bible Society, 1992.

Holy Bible, *King James Version*. 1611. Public domain.

Holy Bible, *Revised Standard Version*. American Bible Society, 1992.

Horovitz, Isaiah, Rabbi. *Sheni Luchot HaBerit*. Palestine, 1611.

Jerusalem Talmud. *Shir HaShirim Rabbah*. Israel/Babylon, 790. Translated by Rabbi Jason Rappoport. 2022. https://www.sefaria.org/Shir_HaShirim_Rabbah (accessed March 14, 2022).

Kalisch, Isidor, Rev. Dr. *Sefer Yetzirah*. New York: L. H. Frank, 1877.

Karo, Joseph. *Shulkhan Arukh*. Safed Israel, 1563.

Keirsey, David. *Please Understand Me II: Temperament Character Intelligence*. Del Mar, CA: Prometheus Nemesis, 2006.

Laurence, Richard, LLD. *The Book of Enoch the Prophet*. London: Kegan Paul, Trench, Paternoster Square, 1883.

Levi, Eliphas. *Clefs Majeures et Clavicules de Salomon*. Paris, 1860.

Lifkin, Aryeh Leib. *The Beginning of Wisdom*. Warsaw, 1887. Translated by Rabbi Amiram Larkel and Michoel Tzvi Wolkenfeld, 2006. https://www.sefaria.org/The_Beginning_of_Wisdom (accessed March 14, 2022).

Luzzatto, Moshe Chaim. *Kalach Pitchei Chokhmah*. Israel, 1746. https://www.sefaria.org/Kalach_Pitchei_Chokhmah (accessed March 14, 2022).

Luzzatto, Moshe Chaim, Rabbi. *Mesliat Yesharim*. Amsterdam, 1738.

Maimonides, Moses (Rambam). *The Guide for the Perplexed*. Fustat, 1190

Mathers, S. L. MacGregor. *The Key of Solomon the King (Clavicula Salomonis)*. London: George Redway, 1889.

Midrash Tanchuma. *Pekudei Siman, Babylonian Talmud*. 800 CE. Translated by Samuel A. Berman, n.d.

Mishnah. *Pirkei Avot*. Talmudic Israel, 230 CE, www.sefaria.org/Pirkei_Avot.5.1?lang=bi (accessed March 14, 2022).

Mishnah. *Pirkei Avot*. Talmudic Israel, 230 CE. Translated by Dr. Joshua Kulp, 1913.

Nachman of Breslov. *Likutei Moharan*. Bratslav, Ukraine, 1808.

Otzar Midrashism. *The Alphabet of ben Sira*. 700 CE. Translated by Judah David Eisenstein. New York, 1915. www.sefaria.org/Otzar_Midrashim%2C_The_Aleph_Bet_of_ben_Sira (accessed October 13, 2021).

Patah, Eliyahu. *Tikkunei Zohar*. Spain, 1400. Translated by Avraham Sutton. https://www.sefaria.org/Tikkunei_Zohar (accessed March 14, 2022).

Portnoy, Marshall, and Josee Wolff. *The Art of Cantillation*. Vol. 2, *A Step-by-Step Guide to Chanting Haftarah and M'gillot*. New York: UAHC Press, 2001.

Reichman, Zev. *Flames of Faith*. Englewood, NJ: Zev Reichman, 2014. https://www.sefaria.org/Flames_of_Faith (accessed March 14, 2022).

Rich, Tracey R. *Judaism 101, 613 Mitzvot*. 1996. www.jewfaq.org/613-commandments (accessed May 4, 2022).

Rivlin, Hillel, Rabbi. *Kol HaTor*. Jerusalem, Israel, 1838.

Solomon, King. *The Testament of Solomon*. 100. Translated by Wissensch Fleck from the codex of the Paris Library, 1837. https://archive.org/stream/jstor-1450398/1450398_djvu.txt(accessed March 14, 2019).

Tanchuma, Rabbi. *Midrash Tanchuma Shemot Siman*. Babylon, 800. Translated by Samuel A. Berman. https://www.sefaria.org/Midrash_Tanchuma (accessed March 14, 2022).

Trachtenberg, Joshua. *Jewish Magic and Superstition: A Study in Folk Religion*. Philadelphia: University of Pennsylvania Press, 2004.

Waite, Arthur Edward. *The Pictorial Key to the Tarot*. New York: Samuel Weiser, 1911.

Yitzhak Saggi Nehor (Isaac the Blind). *Sepher Ha-Bahir*. 1220. Translated by Ary eh Kaplan. Rev. ed. Weiser Books, April 1, 1989.

Yom-Tov Lipmann, Heller, Rabbi. *Derush Chidushei HaLevana*. Vilna, 1649. Translated by Eliyahu Touger, 2017.

Glossary

Adam Kadmon: Primordial Man, often used in the Kabbalah to show how the Tree of the *Sefirot* lines up with the human body.

Adonai: Lord/Master; in scripture and during prayer it is used in place of the Tetragrammaton. In English Bibles, whenever LORD is written in all capital letters, it represents the word Adonai being used in place of the proper name of God.

Arcanum: Mysteries or secrets; the Tarot consists of the minor and major mysteries.

Asenath: The daughter of Dinah and the wife of Joseph.

Asomodeus: A demon and former Nephilim who plots against wedding couples in the Testament of Solomon; he killed each of Sarah's husbands on their wedding nights in the book of Tobit.

Assiah: The fourth world of the Kabbalah, which is related to action or manifestation of an idea or concept within the physical world.

Atziluth: The first and highest world of the Kabbalah, which is associated with conception or emanation. It is the place where an ideal or concept is first conceived.

Aurora Consurgens: An alchemical work that was written by an unknown author around 1250 CE, which linked the Chymical Wedding to a union between the Spirit of Wisdom and the Soul of the alchemist, adding a spiritual component to union of opposites. Aurora Consurgens is Latin for rising dawn, and the term was taken for the Song of Solomon in the Bible.

Ayin HaRa: The Evil Eye, a dirty, scornful, envious, or jealous look that is thought to bring negativity, bad luck, or a curse.

Azazel: A Hebrew word that is translated as "scapegoat" but is also the name of the leader of a group of fallen angels in the book of Enoch that mated with human women and produced Nephilim.

B'tzelem Elohim: "In the Image of God"; the concept that human beings were created in the image of God (the Judges).

Bar/Bat/Bnai Mitzvah: The ceremony to commemorate a boy (Bar), girl (Bat), or child (Bnai) reaching the age of accountability when they become a child of the commandments and responsible for obeying Mitzvot (boys at 13 and girls at 12).

Binah: The third *Sefirah* of the Kabbalah, which means understanding or intuitive intelligence.

Bitachon: Trust in the providence of God and belief that he will cause all things to work for one's good—similar to the concept of *In Shallah* in Islam.

Briah: The second world of the Kabbalah, which is associated with creation. The plan or blueprint based on the original idea is developed.

Cantillation: A system of ritually chanting the *Torah or Haftarah.*

Chesed: The fourth *Sefirah* of the Kabbalah, which means loving kindness.

Chokmah: The second *Sefirah* of the Kabbalah, which means wisdom.

Chuppah: The Jewish wedding canopy, which represents the protection of the Shekinah hovering over the couple.

Chymical Wedding: The union of two elements to form a compound. Spiritually, it represents the union between the soul of the alchemist and the Spirit of Wisdom, marking the beginning of the Great Work.

Derash: A type of biblical interpretation that involves the reading, seeking, or further inquiring in order to find deeper meanings than the literal—finding connections and links to similar concepts.

Diaspora: Jewish communities outside the Land of Israel while they are scattered across the earth. From the Greek "Exile."

Dinah: Jacob's only daughter, who was kidnapped by Shechem. After her brothers rescued her, she gave birth to a daughter named Asenath, who was raised by Potiphar's wife and later married to Joseph.

Divination: Either a practice in which an oracle, device, or tool is used as a means to obtain guidance from the divine, or else symbolism used to extract intuitive information from one's psyche for allegorical interpretation, problem-solving, and predicting possibilities.

Dreidel: A top that is usually made from wood or clay with the letters *Nun*, *Gimel*, *Hei*, and *Shin* written on it. Dreidels are used in a game played around Hanukah, in which players compete for *gelt* (chocolate coins).

Echad: Hebrew for "one."

Esoteric: Intended to be understood only by a small number of people who are part of an inner circle, such as Jesus explaining the meaning of his parables to his disciples in private.

Flaming Sword: A method of examining the order of creation by pathworking down the Tree of the *Sefirot*; the term is used interchangeably with the Lightning Path.

Foundation Stone: The stone from which the world began. It is located within the Dome of the Rock and is the location where the Ark of the Covenant rested in the Holiest of Holies of Solomon's Temple.

Geburah: The fifth *Sefirah* of the Kabbalah, which means strength and embodies the concepts of judgment and justice.

Gematria: A system of numerology within Kabbalah, which is used to calculate the values of letters, words, and verses to uncover mystical significance.

Ger Toshav: A non-Israelite who lives in Israel and is recognized as a resident alien.

Ger Tzadik: Righteous dweller—a true convert to Judaism who obtains the righteousness of an Israelite.

Goral/Goralot: Casting lot, purpose, fate, destiny, or lot in life. Lots can be referred to as *goral*, *pur*, *hevel*, or *holesh*.

Great Work: A concept used in alchemy to refer to the production of the Philosopher's Stone, which is symbolic of the purification and spiritual advancement of the soul of the alchemist.

Haftorah: The Prophets (Nevi'im) sections of the *Tanakh*.

HaMotzi: The blessing over the bread. At the Last Supper, Jesus of Nazareth recited blessing over the bread and wine (Matthew 26:26–27).

HaShem: Hebrew for "the name," used when speaking about the four-letter name of God in common speech. During prayer, the word Adonai is used in place of the Tetragrammaton.

Havdalah: Separation; a short ceremony performed at the end of Shabbat to signify the start of the workweek, and the transition out of the day of rest/holiness.

Hod: The eighth *Sefirah* of the Kabbalah, which means glory or splendor.

Holiest of Holies: The most sacred area within the Tabernacle and Temple of Solomon, where the Ark of the Covenant, which housed the Ten Commandments, was kept.

Kabbalah: A Hebrew word meaning reception or tradition; refers to the mystical aspects of Judaism.

Kame'ah/Kame'ot: Binding, talisman, protective spell. The Shulchan Arukh, in Yoreh De'ah 179:11–13, ruled that it was permitted to whisper spells, heal with talismans, and carry talismans for protection. The Talmud also approved of talismans made by experts.

Kavanah: Intention; heartfelt or sincere effort.

Keter: The first *Sefirah* of the Kabbalah, which means crown and represents both the beginning and the final destination.

Ketubah: A Jewish wedding contract. It is similar to a prenuptial agreement and outlines rights, responsibilities, and obligations.

Ketuvim: The Writings. The other books of scripture within the Tanakh, which are not part of the Torah or Nevi'im.

Kiddush: Sanctification. The blessing over wine or the fruit of the vine (grape juice) that is said each Shabbat and on holidays.

Laylah/Lailah: The Angel of Conception. The word derives from the Hebrew word for night and refers to a female angel who guards the soul of a child within its mother's womb.

Lecha Dodi: "Come My Beloved"—a song written and sung by kabbalists in the 16th century Safed who went outside to greet the Shabbat Bride. The song has been adopted in mainstream Judaism and is sung on Erev Shabbat (Friday evening prayer services) in order to welcome the Shabbat Bride.

Lech-Lecha: "Go forth" was God's commandment for Abraham to leave his father's house and the land of his birth in order to journey to the Promised Land.

Lightning Path: A path down the Kabbalistic Tree of Life from *Keter* to *Malkut*, which is said to represent the path of creation; also referred to as the path of the Flaming Sword.

Lilith: The female counterpart of the fallen angel Samael. Lilith is the serpent that Samael rode on in the Garden of Eden and is associated with a baby-killing demon (the opposite of Laylah, the angel of conception). In folklore, it is said to be a succubus that is responsible for nocturnal emissions, which are used to create demons. In the *Alephabet* of Ben Sira, Lilith is used in an analogy for Adam's first wife, who argues with him over dominance, and in very modern times she has been used as a feminist icon due to her perceived resistance to the patriarchy.

Major Arcana: A section of 22 cards within a Tarot deck that are associated with higher mysteries and the 22 letters of the Hebrew *Alef-bet*.

Malkut: The 10th *Sefirah*, which means "kingdom" and refers to the physical world of action and manifestation.

Merkabah Mysticism: Pre-Kabbalah Jewish mysticism that focused on the Chariot of God found in the book of the Prophet Ezekiel. It is sometimes referred to as the "Work of the Chariot."

Mezuzah: A doorpost and decorative container that holds a handwritten scroll containing the verses of Deuteronomy 6:4–9 and 11:13–21, which instructs those words to be written on the doorpost of one's house.

Midrash: Expansion of biblical stories with allegorical and fictional uses of biblical characters or events in order to teach certain principles or concepts.

Mikvah: A pool or bath of natural water that is used for ritual immersion and purification of people and objects.

Minyan: A group of 10 Jewish persons that is necessary for certain prayers to be recited. A *minya* represents the Jewish community and is based on the amount of righteous people that God told Abraham he would spare Sodom and Gomorrah for.

Mishnah: Study, repetition, the Oral Torah. The Oral Tradition of the Pharisees of the Second Temple period, which was written down at the beginning of the third century CE to prevent the teachings from being lost during the Jewish exile.

Mitzvah/Mitzvot: A precept, commandment, instruction, or religious duty.

Mother Letters: A classification of Hebrew Letters in the *Sefer Yetzirah* associated with the Primordial Elements of Fire, Air, and Water, which it associates with the letters *Shin*, *Alef*, and *Mem*.

Netzach: The seventh *Sefirah* of the Kabbalah, which means victory.

Nevi'im: The Prophets sections of the *Tanakh*.

Olam HaBa: "The World to Come," a re-created world of perfections where the resurrected righteous will live (similar to Heaven).

PaRDeS: The word means "orchard" and is a Hebrew acronym for the words *Peshat* (surface), *Remez* (hints), *Derash* (inquire), and *Sod* (secret). Refers to four differing ways that each verse of scripture can be understood.

Pathworking: The process of contemplating the interconnections between paths and the *Sefirot* in an effort to understand their relationships to each other.

Pentecost: The 50th day, which would be associated with *Shavuot* in Judaism and receiving the Ten Commandments. In Christianity, it is the day with the Apostles received the Holy Spirit.

Phylacteries: *See* **Tefillin**.

Pirkei Avot: Ethical teachings of the fathers. A book of Mishnah and maxims.

Practical Kabbalah: A branch of Jewish Kabbalah that sought to use the teachings for magical purposes.

Priestly Blessing: A blessing prescribed by *HaShem* and recited verbatim, using the language and words he directed.

Promised Land: The land flowing with milk and honey that God promised to give to the descendants of Israel.

Raphael: The Angel of Healing and one of the four archangels.

Raziel: In kabbalistic folklore, Raziel is the angel of secrets who is alleged to have given Adam and Eve the Kabbalah as a means to return to paradise.

Red King: The male counterpart of the Chymical Wedding, which represents the soul of the alchemist and is colored red because Adam is said to have been created out of red clay.

Rosh Hashanah: "Head of the Year" or the Jewish New Year, when God inscribes everyone's fate in the Book of Life and determines who will live or die over the next year. The time between Rosh Hashanah and Yom Kippur is the Days of Awe, which are 10 Days of Repentance. These days give a person an opportunity to return to God (*teshuvah*), because what is written in the Books of Life and Death on Rosh Hashanah is permanently sealed on Yom Kippur.

Rosicrucian: A sect of Christian mystics at the beginning of the seventh century who practiced Kabbalah and alchemy.

Ruach Elohim: Hebrew for Spirit of God.

Ruach Ha-Kodesh: Hebrew for Holy Spirit.

Sabbath/Shabbat: A day set aside as a day of rest, in accordance with the fourth commandment. It begins on Friday night at sundown in fulfillment and ends on Saturday evening.

Samael: A fallen angel that is equated with Satan, who rode on the Serpent in the Garden of Eden. Samael is also said to be Esau's Guardian Angel and is the angel Jacob wrestled with.

Scapegoat: The goat that was selected by lot to carry the sins of Israel off into the desert

Sefer: Scroll or book.

Sefer Bahir: The Book of Illumination/Brightness is an anonymous, pseudepigraphic mystical work attributed to a first-century CE rabbinic sage. The work was first mentioned in the 12th century CE and consists of rabbis discussing mystical topics.

Sefer Raziel HaMalakh: The Book of the Angel Raziel is a 13th-century CE text containing practical Kabbalah and might be considered a Hebrew grimoire. The book claims to be the book provided to Adam by the angel Raziel (the angel of secrets), but it is most likely a compilation of the works of several kabbalists around its time period.

Sefer Yetzirah: The Book of Foundation is a key work of Jewish mysticism stemming from the Merkabkah Mysticism period, and the work formed the basis of Sefirot and inspired the development of the Kabbalah. It provides a mystical interpretation of the biblical account of Genesis. It claims to have been passed down from the patriarch Abraham and was written down sometime between 200 BCE and 200 CE.

Sefer Zohar: The Book of Splendor/Radiance is a 13th-century CE kabbalist work written by Moses de Leon, who claimed to have translated a document he said he had in his possession of a famous first-century CE rabbi, but after Leon's death, it was revealed that no such document existed. Regardless of Sefer HaBahir–like additions, the Zohar provided unique concepts and made a profound contribution to the development of the Kabbalah.

Sefirah/Sefirot: Emanation(s), attribute(s), enumeration(s). It refers to 10 attributes of God. *Sefirot* is the plural form, and *Sefirah* is singular.

Segulah/Segulot: Special treasure, charm, remedy, protection, superstitious practice, doing more than is expected in order to be considered a special treasure in order to fill favor from God.

Shekinah: The indwelling glory of God, which is a feminine word that the Kabbalah associates with the divine feminine.

Shema: A Jewish prayer and creed derived from Deuteronomy 6:4, which states that YHVH is our God and YHVH is one.

Shulkhan Aruch: The Set Table, a code of Jewish legal codes authorized by Joseph Karo in 1563 CE.

Sigil: A seal, signet, or magical symbol that is a pictorial representation of a meaningful word, phrase, spirit, or deity.

Sofer: A Jewish scribe who is trained to copy Torah scrolls and write STaM.

STaM: An acronym for *Sefer Torah*, *Tefillin*, and *Mezuzot*. These sacred texts and objects are written by scribes (*Sofrim*) on *Klaf* (parchment made from the skin of a kosher animal), using a feather quill and specially mixed ink. For a Torah scroll to be considered kosher, it must be handwritten using this specific lettering. Since *Tefillin* and *Mezuzah* are holy objects that contain verses from the Torah, they must also be written in this same lettering to maintain their sanctity.

Tabernacle: A mobile sanctuary and dwelling place of God, which was used when the Hebrew people were traveling in the desert during the time of Moses. It was later replaced by the Temple of Solomon.

Tallit: A prayer shawl, which could be used as a mobile tent for prayer and meditation.

Talmud: The word means "study" and is a collection of Jewish writings composed after the destruction of the Second Temple to prevent the Oral Teachings from being lost while the Jews were in exile.

Tanakh: An acronym: *Tav*, for a collection of Hebrew scripture that includes the Torah (Teachings/Law), *Nevi'im* (Prophets), and *Ketuvim* (Writings). It is the equivalent of the Old Testament found in Protestant Bible.

Tarot: ("Torat," or **"תוראט"** read right to left) is a set of 78 cards with mystical meanings, used as a modern oracle. Eliphas Levi believed the Tarot was a modern replacement of the Urim and Thummim.

Tefillin: Phylacteries are small black leather boxes with leather straps containing passages of scripture, worn in fulfillment of the Mitzvot to bind the commandments on one's hand and between one's eyes. The Tefillin is worn on the head as a three-branched *Shin* on the right side and a four-branched *Shin* on the left.

Teshuvah: Repentance, atonement, and returning to God.

Tetragrammaton: The four-letter proper name of God, consisting of the Hebrew letters *Yod, Hei, Vah, Hei*.

Tiferet: The sixth *Sefirah* of the Kabbalah, which represents beauty, adornment, or majesty.

Tikkun Olam: "Repair of the world." In modern times, it is used to refer to social justice and correcting the injustices of the world. As God's partners in creation, humans have been entrusted with the care and upkeep of the world, *Tikkun Olam* represents the continued effort to care for the world and to fix the things that are broken within it.

Tzadikim: (*Lamed Vav Tzadikim*—36 Righteous Ones / *Tzadikim Nistarim*—Hidden Righteous Ones); a select group of righteous persons by whose piousness God tolerates the existence of the world.

Tzedakah: Charity, philanthropy, and righteous acts/deeds.

Tzitzit: Fringes/tassels worn on the four corners of one's garment, as a reminder to obey the Mitzvot.

Tziyon: Zion can be used to refer to Israel, Jerusalem, or the Jewish people.

White Queen: A concept in alchemy that refers to the universal solvent or the spirit used to extract the essence out of the body.

Yehshua: Hebrew name meaning *Yah* is Salvation; it was translated in the Greek New Testament as "Jesus."

Yesod: The ninth *Sefirah* of the Kabbalah, which means "foundation" and is the location where the marriage of the sun and moon, bride and bridegroom, or *Malkut* and *Tiferet* takes place.

Yetzer HaRa: The Evil Inclination, the desire/temptation to sin.

Yetzer HaTov: The Good Inclination, the choice to do good.

Yetzirah: The third world of the Kabbalah, which is associated with formation. This is where the plan or concept started taking shape, immediately prior to it being put into action.

Yom Kippur: The Day of Atonement; it is a day of fasting, and the day that what God inscribed in the Book of Life on Rosh Hashanah is permanently sealed. In ancient Israel and during Temple times, Lots were casts to select a goat for *HaShem* and a goat to carry away the people's sins to Azazel.

Index

Appendix: The Kabbalah Cube

In order to produce a three-dimensional version of the Kabbalah Cube of Space, either a photocopy of this page (or this page) can be used to create a paper version. The first step would be to cut around the outline of the cube and its folding glue tabs. Fold the cube and each seam and fold the glue tabs. Using tape, paste, or glue, fasten the cube together. Once it is dry, you can use the cube to assist with your meditations or contemplations. Alternately, you can go to a craft store and look for a wooden or foam cube, and Mod Podge or glue the images on the paper to it.

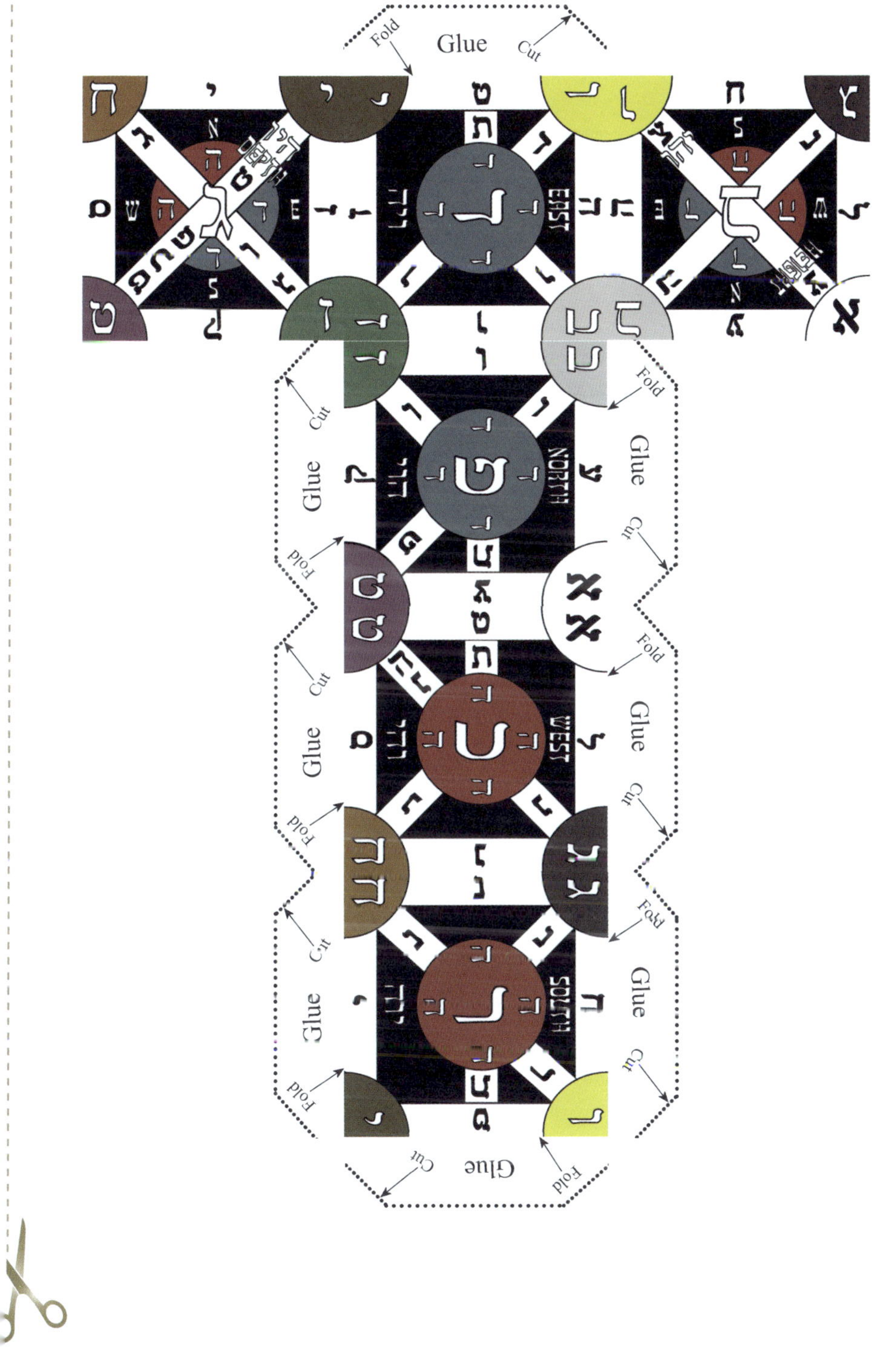
Glue
Fold
Cut
EAST
NORTH
WEST
SOUTH

About the Author

DANIEL E. LOEB is a scholar, occult author, and spiritual mentor who wrote under the pseudonym D. W. Prudence while working in public service and needing to maintain a secret security clearance. He retired after serving 20 years in the US Air Force and continues to work as an author and instructor on topics related to Kabbalah, alchemy, and the Tarot. He graduated from the Hypnosis Training Institute of Central California in 1994 and from the Therapeutic Learning Center School of Massage in 1997. He earned his bachelor's degree in psychology in 2002 and a master's degree in 2008. He has instructed hypnotherapy certification courses internationally; he's worked as a hypnotherapist in private practice and as a Tarot reader. In 2018, he authored the *AlcheMystic Woodcut Tarot: The Secret Wisdom of the Ages*, and in 2021 he authored the *Rota Mundi Tarot: The Rosicrucian Arcanum*. For nine years he's volunteered as a sexual-assault-prevention-and-response victim's advocate, serving 10 years as a deputy sheriff. During the COVID-19 pandemic, he served as a federal law enforcement officer and training instructor and continues to help those in need as a mental health crisis-responder supervisor. Loeb is a Jewish family name of German descent; it means Lion and is a reference to the Tribe of Judah. Kabbalah and Rosicrucianism are in his blood and have been the focus of his studies for many years. His unique life experiences—and his Jewish, Christian, and occult background—have enabled him to interact with diverse cultures and to gain a unique perspective on mysticism and human behavior. He is able to combine the sacred writings of divergent sects into a combined system, showing how all the puzzle pieces fit together. He is a husband and the father of four. His goal is to aid others in understanding the mystical concepts he has a passion for, and to empower his readers in their own spiritual endeavors and mystical pursuits.